S0-ADJ-964

Developmentally Appropriate Practice

Focus on KINDERGARTNERS

Carol Copple, Sue Bredekamp,
Derry Koralek, and Kathy Charner, editors

National Association for the Education of Young Children
Washington, DC

National Association for the
Education of Young Children
1313 L Street NW, Suite 500
Washington, DC 20005-4101
202-232-8777 • 800-424-2460
www.naeyc.org

NAEYC Books

Chief Publishing Officer
Derry Koralek

Editor-in-Chief
Kathy Charner

Director of Creative Services
Edwin C. Malstrom

Managing Editor
Mary Jaffe

Senior Editor
Holly Bohart

Senior Graphic Designer
Malini Dominey

Associate Editor
Elizabeth Wegner

Editorial Assistant
Ryan Smith

Through its publications program, the National Association for the Education of Young Children (NAEYC) provides a forum for discussion of major issues and ideas in the early childhood field, with the hope of provoking thought and promoting professional growth. The views expressed or implied in this book are not necessarily those of the Association or its members.

Photo Credits

Copyright © Ellen B. Senisi: Cover (first, second, and third on left), interior cover (top right and bottom), 3, 27, 37, 40, 43, 44, 49, 128, 147, 152, 154, 157; Peggy Ashbrook: 115, 119; Marilyn Nolt: 23; Martin Cathrae/Wikimedia Commons: 161

Copyright © NAEYC: Cover (right and bottom left), interior cover (top left and third down), 9, 13, 31, 53, 149, 150, 151

Courtesy of the *Young Children* article authors: 115, 122, 125, 132, 135, 137, 139, 141, 142

Contributing editor: *Steve Olle*
Cover design: *Edwin C. Malstrom*

Developmentally Appropriate Practice: Focus on Kindergartners
Copyright © 2014 by the National Association for the Education of Young Children. All rights reserved. Printed in the United States of America.

Library of Congress Control Number: 2013951466
ISBN: 978-1-938113-03-1
NAEYC Item #170

Contents

About the Editors

Carol Copple is a highly respected early childhood education author, educator, and consultant. For 16 years she served as a senior staff member at NAEYC, and her responsibilities included directing the books program. She has taught at Louisiana State University and the New School for Social Research, and she codeveloped and directed a research-based model for preschool education at the Educational Testing Service. With Sue Bredekamp, Carol is coeditor of *Developmentally Appropriate Practice in Early Childhood Programs* (1997; 2009). Among her other books are *Learning to Read and Write: Developmentally Appropriate Practices for Young Children* (NAEYC); *Growing Minds: Building Strong Cognitive Foundations in Early Childhood* (NAEYC); and *Educating the Young Thinker: Classroom Strategies for Cognitive Growth* (Lawrence Erlbaum). She received her doctorate from Cornell University.

Sue Bredekamp is an early childhood education specialist from Washington, DC. She serves as a consultant on developmentally appropriate practice, curriculum, teaching, and professional development for many state and national organizations, including NAEYC, the Council for Professional Recognition, Head Start, and Sesame Workshop. From 1981 to 1998, she was director of accreditation and professional development for NAEYC. Sue is the primary author of the 1987 edition of *Developmentally Appropriate Practice in Early Childhood Programs*, and coeditor (with Carol Copple) of the 1997 and 2009 revisions. She is the author of the introductory textbook *Effective Practices in Early Childhood Education: Building a Foundation, 2nd Edition* (Pearson). Sue was a member of the National Research Council's Committee on Early Childhood Mathematics, and she holds a PhD in curriculum and instruction from the University of Maryland.

Derry Koralek, chief publishing officer of NAEYC, oversees the development of all print and digital publishing, including books, brochures, periodicals, professional development guides, posters, and websites for educators and families. Derry is editor in chief of *Young Children* and *TYC—Teaching Young Children*.

Kathy Charner is editor in chief of NAEYC's Books and Related Resources department, with responsibility for the content, management, publication, and general excellence of the books and brochures published by NAEYC. Before joining NAEYC, Kathy was editor in chief at Gryphon House for more than 20 years.

Acknowledgments

This book—and the NAEYC position statement on developmentally appropriate practice it is based on—reflects the expertise and experience of a great many people working in early childhood education over the years. These individuals have deepened our collective knowledge and understanding of young children through their work with young children and study of early childhood teaching and learning.

In 2006 NAEYC launched a discussion among early childhood professionals to inform the revision of its 1996 position statement. Internet technology made it possible for a wider group of people to participate in the discussion than was ever possible previously. The revision process included a thorough review of current research; open forums at NAEYC conferences; convening of a DAP Working Group to advise on content and to review and revise drafts; input, review, and comment by NAEYC Affiliate Groups and pertinent professional organizations; public invitation to anyone in the field to comment on the draft via NAEYC's website; and finally, consideration and approval by NAEYC's Governing Board.

Space prevents us from acknowledging all of the contributions, but we must mention the following:

The outstanding members of the 2007 DAP Working Group. This delightful, knowledgeable group (Juanita Copley, Carolyn Pope Edwards, Linda Espinosa, Ellen Frede, Mary Louise Hemmeter, Marjorie Kostelnik, and Dorothy Strickland) began their work on the position statement revision in March 2007 and continued to respond to that document and plans for the book as they evolved.

The 2007 group's predecessors, the members of NAEYC's Panel on Revisions to Developmentally Appropriate Practice (1993–1996), who gave tirelessly of their time and wisdom to the conceptualization of the 1996 version of the position statement. And before them, the members of NAEYC's 1985 Commission on Appropriate Education for 4- and 5-Year-Olds, who began the process of codifying the Association's position on quality in early childhood practice that culminated in the first position statements on developmentally appropriate practice in 1985/6.

Members of the NAEYC Governing Board (2006–08) for their useful input and much-appreciated support.

The NAEYC State Affiliates, who were valuable partners in our collective thinking about developmentally appropriate practice. The Affiliate Council highlighted DAP during their face-to-face meetings, and State Affiliates engaged in strategic discussions with their local member communities, forwarding their responses, questions, and suggestions directly to NAEYC. In addition, several State Affiliates hosted regional discussion groups across their states.

Important feedback provided by leaders of the Southern Early Childhood Association (SECA), which shares NAEYC's commitment to developmentally appropriate practice.

Staff and representatives of ZERO TO THREE, for their work on developmentally appropriate practice for infants and toddlers.

The dozens of early childhood leaders, practitioners, and scholars who reacted to our questions about the position statement revision and then to preliminary drafts. Among the many who helped us in this way, we would like to give special thanks to Elena Bodrova, Barbara Bowman, Mon Cochran, Herb Ginsburg, Deborah Leong, Robert Pianta, Sharon Ritchie, Tom Schultz, Barbara Smith, Dorothy Strickland, Ruby Takanishi, Francis Wardle, and Carol Anne Wien for their thoughtful and detailed comments.

Janet Gonzalez-Mena, who contributed substantively to the 2009 book, based on her expertise and wisdom in the areas of infant and toddler care and culture in early care and education.

Gaye Gronlund, project manager for DAP resources and activities for NAEYC.

Of the many supportive colleagues at NAEYC who helped us with the third edition of DAP in so many ways . . .

We especially appreciate the contributions of Linda Halgunseth; Marilou Carey Hyson; Adele Robinson; and the resolute Heather Biggar Tomlinson, whose knowledge and writing skill shine in her chapter, written while parenting a toddler and carrying twins.

The one indispensable person in this effort from start to finish was the incredible Bry Pollack, nominally the then-managing editor for books but our true partner in every aspect of the work. We are also grateful for the sharp skills, hard work, and unflagging dedication of the other members of the books team, Malini Dominey, Melissa Edwards, and Liz Wegner. And to two of our favorite books department alums, freelance editors Lisa Cook and Natalie Cavanagh.

Thanks to Jerlean Daniel, Mark Ginsberg, Marilyn Smith, and Carol Brunson Day for their personal guidance and consistent support over the years and during our work on the third edition.

And finally . . .

Special acknowledgment to Patty Smith Hill, Lois Meek Stolz, and Rose Alschuler for their vision, courage, leadership, and commitment in forming an organization that would one day become NAEYC and for framing as its mission the achievement of developmentally appropriate practice in programs for young children.

Editors' Preface

Young children are born learners. Although individual differences are present at birth, most set out to explore their world with unbridled eagerness and curiosity. Perhaps more than any other time of life, early childhood is a period of never ending possibilities. Similarly, most early childhood educators enthusiastically embrace their work, because every day brings the chance to share in children's excitement of discovery. We enter and stay in the field because we believe that our work can make a significant difference in the lives of children and their families, and so make a profound and lasting contribution to society.

But whether we make that difference in young children's lives is not assured. Children are born learners, but for them to actually learn and develop optimally requires us to provide them with care and education of the highest quality. *Developmentally appropriate practice* is a term that has come to be used within the profession to describe the complex and rewarding work done by excellent early childhood educators.

More than 25 years ago, NAEYC published its first position statements defining and describing developmentally appropriate practice in early childhood programs serving young children. A 1986 statement was expanded and released in book form the next year (see Bredekamp 1986, 1987). The concept of *developmentally appropriate* was certainly not new, having been used by developmental psychologists for more than a century in reference to age-related and individual human variation. NAEYC, however, was motivated by two factors to go on record with more specific guidance for teachers: by the launch of its national program accreditation system, whose standards necessitated clearer interpretation of quality in early childhood practice, and by the growing trend to push down curriculum and teaching methods more appropriate for older children in kindergarten and preschool programs.

A decade later, NAEYC (1996) revisited its position statement on developmentally appropriate practice in response to new knowledge, the changing context, and critiques from within and beyond the profession. Among the major issues reflected in that revised statement and the book containing it (Bredekamp & Copple 1997) were these: the teacher as decision maker; the importance of goals for children being both challenging and achievable; and expanding the basic definition of developmentally appropriate practice to include consideration of social and cultural context. Later, to more clearly communicate the concepts of the 1996 statement, NAEYC published *Basics of Developmentally Appropriate Practice: An Introduction for Teachers of Children 3 to 6* (Copple & Bredekamp 2006).

> We enter and stay in the field because we believe that our work can make a significant difference in the lives of children and their families, and so make a profound and lasting contribution to society.

The current position statement, on which this book is based, was propelled less by critiques from within the field than by the infusion of new knowledge to guide practice and by the rapidly changing context in which early childhood programs operate—including the growing role of public schools and the increasing focus on narrowing the achievement gap. Further, in 2005 NAEYC significantly revised its Early Childhood Program Standards that identify key components of quality programs. To ensure the consistency of NAEYC's most influential sets of guidelines for practice—the Early Childhood Program Standards and the Position Statement on Developmentally Appropriate Practice—revisiting the position statement was timely.

The kindergarten year has a unique place in children's development and learning; it is distinct from both preschool and the primary grades. In recent years much has changed in kindergarten, and there is a great need for informed conversation about what education for this age group should be like. Recognizing these realities, NAEYC published *K Today: Teaching and Learning in the Kindergarten Year* (Gullo 2006b), bringing together perspectives of experts in various learning domains about effective kindergarten teaching and curriculum, and *Basics of Developmentally Appropriate Practice: An Introduction for Teachers of Kindergartners* (Phillips & Scrinzi 2013), showing what developmentally appropriate practice looks like in kindergarten.

This series of books builds on the fundamental principles articulated in 1997 and emphasizes several interrelated themes:

Excellence and equity. Achievement gaps—real and present early in life—persist not because children are lacking in any way but because they lack opportunities to learn. Although the current emphasis on accountability and learning gaps has led to inappropriate practices in some classrooms and raised concerns among early childhood educators, the field has long been commited to improving all children's life chances. A prime example, of course, is Head Start. We know that excellent early childhood education can make a difference, and we simply cannot be content with the inequities in early experience that contribute to school failure and lifelong negative consequences for so many of our nation's children.

Intentionality and effectiveness. Good early childhood teachers are purposeful in the decisions they make about their practices, but they also attend to the consequences of those decisions. The current widespread recognition of the value of early education, as well as the explosion in state funding for prekindergarten programs, derives almost exclusively from its effectiveness in producing positive short- and long-term outcomes for children. Holding ourselves accountable for learning and developmental outcomes (as long as they are the right outcomes) is actually evidence of our increased commitment to all children.

> We simply cannot be content with the inequities in early experience that contribute to school failure and lifelong negative consequences for so many of our nation's children.

Continuity and change. Just as human development through the life span is marked by both continuity and change, so too must be any document that is designed to guide educational practice that reflects knowledge of development. Therefore, the 2009 position statement preserves the enduring values of our field—commitment to the whole child; recognition of the value of play; respect and responsiveness to individual and cultural diversity; and partnerships with families. At the same time, it has responded to the changing and expanding knowledge base about effective practices in addressing these values as well as improving curriculum, teaching, and assessment. Further, the statement challenges our profession to be more precise and clear when advocating for or criticizing practices, from play to structured curriculum.

Joy and learning. In revisiting the position statement in light of new knowledge and the changing context, we were repeatedly reminded of the core value that cuts across all of our work: Certainly an important and legitimate focus of early care and education is helping children toward becoming productive, responsible adults, but we want their childhood years to be full of joy. High-quality early childhood experiences help equip tomorrow's adults, but childhood is and should be its own special time of life. And it is our responsibility to cultivate children's delight in exploring and understanding their world. Early childhood is and should be a time of laughter, love, play, and great fun. While we still believe that fun for fun's sake is an inadequate rationale for planning a program, we also believe strongly that healthy development and learning cannot occur without attention to children's pleasure and interest.

> It is our responsibility to cultivate children's delight in exploring and understanding their world. Early childhood is and should be a time of laughter, love, play, and great fun.

At the same time, we shouldn't forget how much sheer pleasure children obtain from learning something new, mastering a skill after much effort, or solving a challenging problem. Think of the glee a kindergartner feels when she learns to recognize letters of the alphabet, the look of accomplishment when a first-grader reads "a whole book" for the first time, or the "aha" look on a second-grader's face when she finally understands how to add two-digit numbers quickly. Human beings strive for mastery, and we feel both power and pleasure in our own accomplishments.

We conclude with a reminder (though experienced early childhood practitioners will scarcely need it) about why our field values developmentally appropriate practice in the first place. Seeing children joyfully, physically, and intellectually engaged in meaningful learning about their world and everyone and everything in it is the truest measure of our success as early childhood educators.

It is through developmentally appropriate practice that we create a safe, nurturing, and supportive place for young children to experience those unique joys of childhood.

Foreword

Kindergarten is special, and it's something that the two of us couldn't be more passionate about. You see, we are kindergarten teachers through and through. We have dreamt about it, sweated over it, worried about it, advocated for it, and reveled in it throughout our careers. Just like you, we've worked late hours preparing for the next day—meeting with committees, talking with families, and shopping for needed materials. We've pored over our curriculum materials, trying to figure out the best ways to meet the needs of each and every student in our class. We've celebrated small and big steps the children have made, documenting growth in all kinds of ways. We've supported fellow teachers as they, too, worked hard to make a difference in children's lives. Kindergarten is unique. It's powerful. And it's complex! That's why we're both very excited about this resource, *Developmentally Appropriate Practice: Focus on Kindergartners*.

In today's world, there are great expectations about what children need to know and be able to do in order to be successful in a global, interconnected society. Therefore, it's as important as ever to truly understand the children we teach. How do kindergartners learn? How do they develop? What are the best instructional practices for kindergartners? How do I scaffold children's thinking in an effort to guide their learning? How do I structure my day so that it addresses the rigor of the standards in a way that allows children to be successful? How do I provide a meaningful balance between what children need to learn and how I present learning opportunities? These are very important questions. Fortunately, *Developmentally Appropriate Practice: Focus on Kindergartners* brings together research, information, and guidance from leading professionals about how young children grow, develop, and learn. This timely resource will help you answer these key questions.

In this book you will find important and up-to-date information about effective practices in kindergarten. In the first chapter, "What Is Developmentally Appropriate Practice?," readers are reminded of the foundational knowledge provided by NAEYC's framework for working with young children.

In "Teaching in the Kindergarten Year," Cate Heroman and Carol Copple identify ways to create a kindergarten-friendly classroom community with structures that support young children's learning. They also share strategies for instruction and learning contexts that are straightforward, informative, and ready to use tomorrow in your classroom.

In Chapter 3, Heather Biggar Tomlinson dives deeper into the development of the kindergarten child. She examines each area of development (physical, social and emotional, cognitive, language and literacy), explaining the importance of each and providing specific examples and explanations that directly relate to kindergartners. She also addresses the importance of smooth transitions into and out of kindergarten, and offers practical suggestions that you can adapt in your own situation.

Chapter 4, which can be described as the hub of developmentally appropriate practice, unpacks the framework and clearly articulates research-based practices that promote optimal learning and development for kindergartners. You'll find specific examples that promote what exceptional teachers of kindergarten do every day.

The Common Core State Standards (CCSS) are the focus of Chapter 5. Susan Carey Biggam and Marilou Carey Hyson connect the standards with developmentally appropriate practices by identifying essential features of the CCSS and describing how to implement the standards in a way that is appropriate for young children.

The last section of this book provides a sampling of recent and relevant articles from NAEYC's award-winning journal, *Young Children,* that further support the teaching of kindergartners. From integrating science with language and literacy, to involving families in the classroom, to promoting children's cooperation instead of resistance—there's something here for everyone.

As kindergarten teachers, we stand with open arms, greeting each and every student with the hope that we can build upon what they already bring— and propel them as far as they are able to go. As you teach (and learn with) the kindergartners in your class, this resource will help you keep their needs, interests, and strengths in the forefront of your decision making about the environment you provide, the practices you use, and the interactions you have with children. It reminds us that when children are our main focus, our classrooms will reflect current thinking and research-supported practices. We believe that you'll find *Developmentally Appropriate Practice: Focus on Kindergartners* a great addition to your collection of kindergarten resources as you continue to make a difference in the lives of these young children.

—Amy Scrinzi & Eva C. Phillips
Authors of *Basics of Developmentally Appropriate Practice:
An Introduction for Teachers of Kindergartners*

What Is Developmentally Appropriate Practice?

Eva C. Phillips and Amy Scrinzi

Developmentally appropriate practice
means teaching young children in ways that

• Meet children where they are, as individuals and as a group

• Help each child reach challenging and achievable goals that contribute to his or her ongoing development and learning

There's a lot more to it than that, but that's the main idea.

For kindergarten teachers, understanding how young children learn and develop is essential. The more you can know about and tune in to the way the children you teach think and learn, the more effective and satisfying your work with them will be. You will gain a clearer sense of direction to guide your actions, from setting up the classroom environment, to planning curriculum, to assessing children's development and learning.

Meeting Children Where They Are

Teachers today need help creating research- and evidence-based effective kindergarten classrooms. Elsewhere in this book, you'll be reading more about how kindergartners learn. A broad picture of learning and development and what children are like at this age, however, is not all you need in order to teach in a developmentally appropriate way. You won't meet with much success if you consider only what is "typical" of an age group and if you try to teach children in a one-size-fits-all way. Let's step out of the school setting for a moment and visit an everyday scene that illustrates both of these points.

Coach Todd is a winning soccer coach in a league for girls ages 13–15. He has a good sense of what girls this age enjoy, what they're capable of, and what's usually tough for them, and he has experience in what works in coaching them. Bringing this general knowledge with him on the first day of practice, he knows he won't use the advanced techniques he might use with college varsity players, nor will he start out too simply by explaining, "You use your foot to kick the ball." He can make some general plans based on his understanding of what is typical of this age group.

Now, as this season's players take the field for the first time, Coach Todd watches each one closely and also watches how the team plays together. He gets a feel for each player—her strengths and weaknesses, her temperament, how much experience she has. Based on all this, the coach decides where to start the girls' training, and then keeps watching and making adjustments for each individual player and the team as a whole as the season goes along.

A successful coach like Coach Todd knows he has to meet learners where they are, as individuals and as a group. Pitch the instruction too low and you not only waste learners' time but also show disrespect; pitch it too high and they feel incompetent and frustrated. This is a basic fundamental of any teaching.

Effective classroom teachers continually observe children's play, listen to children's conversations, and study their interactions with the physical environment and with other children. These observations provide information about each child's interests, abilities, and developmental progress. On the basis of this individualized information, along with general knowledge about the age group, they plan experiences that enhance children's learning and development. With a classroom of 5-year-olds, for example, meeting learners where they are might look something like this:

> Marcia notices that the kindergartners are engrossed in observing an ant colony outside their classroom. The children ask questions about why the ants travel in single file, what they eat, and how ants build the big hills. Marcia responds by asking the children how they could learn more about ants. This prompts lots more discussion and questions from the children. A little later she finds Josh and Julie on the ground observing the ants with magnifying glasses, and when they return to the classroom she sees José in the science area looking through the books for pictures of ants. Marcia decides to take the children to the library the next day to check out some books on ants and plans to begin a K-W-L chart (**k**now, **w**ant, **l**earn) with the children to see what they already know about ants and what they would like to learn about ants. Because some of the children are dual language learners, Marcia makes a point to provide nonverbal clues to meaning whenever possible, using examples, pictures, objects, gestures, and demonstrations. With careful teacher planning, this study of ants can lead to the development of many of the science, literacy, and mathematical concepts and skills found in the learning standards for kindergarten.

This chapter originally appeared as "The Main Idea" in *Basics of Developmentally Appropriate Practice* (Phillips & Scrinzi 2013).

Eva C. Phillips, EdD, is assistant professor at Winston-Salem State University.

Amy Scrinzi, EdD, is a Race-to-the-Top Early Learning Challenge Grant Project Lead at the North Carolina Department of Public Instruction.

Helping Children Reach Challenging and Achievable Goals

Meeting learners where they are is essential, but no good coach simply leaves his players where they are. Coach Todd's aim is always to help each player improve her soccer skills and understanding as much as she is able, while also making sure she still enjoys the game and wants to continue playing it.

In teaching, these same principles hold. Learners will gain most from materials or experiences that build on what they already know and can do, but also make them stretch a reasonable amount toward what they don't yet know or cannot yet do.

Take the case of choosing books for 5-year-olds. The simple picture books that might be fine for the majority of preschoolers might not be challenging enough for most kindergartners, and lengthy chapter books might be beyond the ability of most 5-year-olds at this point in their literacy development. The kindergarten child is more likely to enjoy and benefit from picture books that offer a range of new vocabulary, more complex sentence structure, more complex plot lines, and novel ways of expressing thoughts and ideas. Because such books introduce children to new ideas and experiences, they will propel the children forward and get them ready for more advanced books. Equally important, they will find the just-within-reach books very satisfying and engrossing.

When such a fit exists—that is, when materials or experiences are challenging but not unreasonably beyond the child's ability—we say those materials or experiences are developmentally appropriate for that learner.

◆　　　◆　　　◆

Here, then, are a few generalizations that can be made about developmentally appropriate teaching:

- Meet learners where they are, taking into account their physical, emotional, social, and cognitive development and characteristics, including home language, culture, family, and interests

- Identify goals for children that are both challenging and achievable—a stretch, but not an impossible leap

- Recognize that what makes something challenging and achievable will vary, depending on the individual learner's development and skills in all areas; his store of experiences, knowledge, and skills; and the cultural context in which the child lives and where the learning opportunity takes place

A cornerstone of developmentally appropriate teaching is *intentionality*. Teaching that meets learners where they are and that helps them to reach challenging and achievable goals does not happen by chance. In everything effective teachers do—from setting up the classroom to assessing children to planning the

Developmentally appropriate practice refers to teaching decisions that vary with and adapt to the age, experience, interests, and abilities of individual children within a given age range.

curriculum—they are intentional. They are purposeful and thoughtful about the actions they take, and they base their actions on the outcomes the school is trying to help children achieve. Even in responding to unexpected opportunities—teachable moments—the intentional teacher is guided by those outcomes.

An intentional teacher plans for and responds to clearly defined learning goals based on state and national learning standards and uses the data from classroom observations, assessments, and information gained from families to thoughtfully plan and implement developmentally appropriate experiences for all children. The intentional kindergarten teacher purposefully chooses teaching strategies that will enable children to achieve the intended goals and continually assesses children's progress, then adjusts strategies to help children reach those goals. She communicates with families about her goals for the children and uses a variety of strategies to create strong relationships with the children's families. With clear-cut goals and plans in mind, intentional teachers are well prepared to tell others—families, administrators, colleagues—about what they are doing. Not only do they know what to do, they also know why they are doing it and can describe that rationale.

Intentional and effective kindergarten teachers strive to balance accountability and standards (*what* children need to learn) with all that is known about *how* kindergartners learn best, while remaining true to what is developmentally appropriate for all children. An intentional kindergarten teacher who understands this balance provides materials and experiences that continue to promote learning and development while supporting kindergartners in developing the skills and concepts encompassed in the goals and standards.

Teaching in the Kindergarten Year

Cate Heroman and Carol Copple

Kindergarten has the potential to be a wonderful year in a child's life. For some children, it is their first experience in "school"; for others, it is the bridge between preschool and "big" school. Kindergarten teachers have a unique opportunity. The decisions they make about their program will convey positive messages about school to the children and their families and will help children lay a solid foundation for future learning—or they will not. In the following vignette, consider how the teacher in this kindergarten classroom supports children's success:

> Walking into the classroom, you see children engaged in different tasks and projects, working purposefully with a variety of materials and cooperating with other children. Individuals and small groups are seated throughout the room, at tables, in centers, and on the rug in the meeting area. The teacher interacts with children individually and in groups, commenting on what she observes and asking occasional questions. As she finds out more about what the children think and know, she is able to build on and help them extend their ideas and language. You see evidence of learning as you watch and listen to children and see the interesting work they do, examples of which are respectfully displayed. Images of the children's culture and community can be seen throughout the room.
>
> The class schedule, posted at children's eye level, includes time for music and movement, outdoor play, snack, and lunch—all important opportunities for children to develop physically and learn healthy habits. Posted by the door is a schedule for family conferences, a place to sign up to volunteer in the classroom, and a copy of the most recent newsletter for families. A parent volunteer is reading with some children on the rug in the meeting area. You can see that families play a pivotal role in supporting their children's development and learning at school. Children's comments let you know that they look forward to coming to school each day.

This is a high-quality program because this teacher is an effective decision maker. At the core of her decision making are three essential domains in which she has substantial knowledge and deep understanding: child development, content and standards, and instructional strategies. She understands child development—who children are and how they learn—and uses this knowledge to ensure reasonable expectations for children. She uses observation and other assessment strategies to learn about children as individuals—their interests, abilities, backgrounds, needs, language, and culture—so that she can individualize the program in ways that allow each child to be successful.

She is also familiar with all areas of the curriculum—that is, the key skills, concepts, and knowledge important for kindergarten children to acquire. In part, what children need to know and be able to do is identified in state standards and in the standards published by professional organizations in the various disciplines. These standards provide her with targets or learning goals so that she knows what she needs to accomplish with the children. In addition to the relevant standards and learning goals, this teacher knows the learning paths that children typically follow to reach these goals.

And finally, in her teaching repertoire she has effective instructional strategies that weave the knowledge base about child development with kindergarten standards and content knowledge in ways that are engaging, meaningful, and relevant to those children.

This chapter introduces curriculum and teaching in the kindergarten year at a general level. It features six dimensions of teaching that serve as a framework for decision making for a high-quality kindergarten program.

Implementing Curriculum in the Kindergarten Year

The *curriculum* consists of the knowledge and skills to be taught in the educational program and the plans for experiences through which learning will take place. The curriculum should reflect standards defining what children should know and be able to do in particular subject areas and grade levels. Kindergarten teachers today often are given a specified curriculum, which has been selected by their school, district, or state.

But kindergarten curricula can vary in numerous ways. They might be locally developed or commercially published; comprehensive (including all subject areas and developmental areas) or focused on a single subject area (such as literacy); highly scripted (telling teachers exactly what to say and do) or flexible (allowing teachers to design or adapt activities and experiences); or complete packages (including all books and materials), curriculum guides (requiring teachers to gather materials), or something between the two.

Fundamental to the teacher's work is having a curriculum that is clear, and then actually using it as a blueprint for classroom decision making. Implementing curriculum effectively means developing well-articulated, standards-based learning goals as well as plans for learning experiences through which these goals will be realized. Teachers also need to account for children's needs, interests, abilities, prior knowledge, and background (Bransford, Brown, & Cocking 2000).

This chapter was first published in *K Today: Teaching and Learning in the Kindergarten Year* (Gullo 2006b).

Cate Heroman is an independent early childhood consultant and an author of curriculum and assessment resources.

Carol Copple, PhD, is coeditor of this book. (See "About the Editors," p. vi.)

To change, develop, or adapt a kindergarten curriculum to help children meet the standards, a teacher's first step is to become familiar with that curriculum. Next, he looks at all of the experiences he provides or might provide during the course of a day through the lens of those standards. He asks himself, "What standards am I addressing? How does the curriculum address the standards? What adaptations do I need to make?" Later, this chapter will discuss ways to integrate standards from multiple subject areas.

Kindergarten teachers apply their core understandings of child development, content standards, and teaching strategies to the myriad decisions they make all day, every day, as they do their work. Effective teachers are thoughtful decision makers. This chapter describes six dimensions of teaching an effective kindergarten program (Bickart, Jablon, & Dodge 1999; Copple & Bredekamp 2009). They cut across all areas of the curriculum to help ensure that curriculum is implemented in ways that foster children's success as learners:

• Knowing kindergartners in general, and the children of the specific classroom in particular

• Building a classroom community in the kindergarten

• Establishing a structure for the kindergarten classroom

• Guiding kindergarten children's learning

• Assessing children's learning in kindergarten

• Building a partnership with kindergarten families

Knowing the Children

Good teaching begins with knowing the learners—what they are like developmentally, individually, and culturally. When teachers know what kindergarten children are like *developmentally*, it means they are familiar with the social and emotional, physical, cognitive, and language characteristics of children at this age. This knowledge enables teachers to have reasonable expectations of what children in a class are likely capable of. To know children *individually* means to recognize that each child comes with unique needs, interests, abilities, language, temperament, prior experiences, and background knowledge. Teachers who know children *culturally* are sensitive to multiple perspectives and consider those perspectives as they make decisions about children's development and learning (Copple & Bredekamp 2009). To know children, effective teachers

• Establish positive, personal relationships with each child

• Learn the developmental characteristics of kindergarten children and consider ways to be responsive in setting up the environment, structuring the day, and guiding and assessing children's learning

• Are flexible in adapting the curriculum to meet the needs of each child and the group as a whole

• Learn about the values, traditions, and expectations for behavior of the cultural groups represented in the classroom

For children of kindergarten age, the most important strategy for teachers is to form relationships with them, because it is through relationships that teachers of young children can guide their learning and behavior.

Building a Classroom Community

People in a *community* share common interests and activities. Children in kindergarten come to the classroom from many different backgrounds and with a wide range of experiences. By creating a community of learners in the classroom, teachers establish common ground among all the children—ways in which the group can function successfully together. In building community, a teacher bases her decisions on the knowledge that young children learn best in the context of social relationships, and that they need to feel accepted, respected, and confident that their individuality is encouraged. Strategies that promote a sense of community include

- Welcoming children into the room by labeling cubbies and hooks with their names

- Using class meetings to encourage group discussions, social problem solving, and sharing of ideas and information

- Bringing each child's home culture and language into the shared culture of the classroom

- Developing classroom guidelines with children

- Planning ways for children to work and play together collaboratively

Creating a community of learners in the classroom has a significant impact on how children work together, how they feel about school, and the relationships that are built with them as individuals and as a group.

Establishing a Structure for the Classroom

Establishing a *structure* includes creating the physical learning environment and organizing the day to be responsive to children's needs and to make the best use of time. The structure of the classroom has a powerful impact on how children learn.

Kindergarten straddles the worlds of preschool and the primary grades. The children are not the same developmentally as first-graders, but they are more "grown up" than preschoolers. Teachers struggle with creating classrooms that are responsive to the developmental needs and potentials of kindergarten children and that support the learning outcomes that prepare children for the curriculum and accountability systems of the upper grades. Kindergarten classrooms look different from preschool or first grade classrooms in their complexity, the levels of responsibility that children assume, their use of symbolic representations, and their reflection of children's growing skills and abilities (Barbour & Seefeldt 1993).

Elements of an Effective Physical Environment

Each kindergarten classroom will be different, first as teachers consider the space, furnishings, and materials available. Later the classroom will be shaped and reshaped as children's new interests and needs emerge. But all classrooms must have certain elements, regardless of their individual resources:

- A space for children to store their work and personal belongings— This space can be cubbies, storage bins, or baskets.

- A place for group meetings—The space should be large enough so children can sit comfortably, either on the floor or on benches, and see one another during conversations.

- A variety of spaces for working—This might mean carefully planned learning centers, a large table, and an open area on the floor. Spaces can be defined with dividers, storage units, and bookshelves. Moveable furnishings allow teachers to create big spaces for larger projects and cozier spaces for a few children to work, as needed.

- Quiet places—Young children need nooks and seating areas where they can get away or work quietly together with a friend or in a small group.

- Places to store materials—Organizing materials logically enables children to find them when needed and return them to their proper place afterward. Creating picture-and-word labels with the children helps them not only care for the classroom environment but also learn print concepts.

- Places to display children's work respectfully—When children's art and other work are displayed attractively, it conveys the message that what they do is important. Display also invites them to reflect on their work and expand their ideas.

Setting Up Learning Centers

Kindergarten children thrive when they can work independently and cooperatively with a small group of peers. They are eager to practice and apply the skills they are learning, engage in conversations, and make choices about what they can do. Using centers to organize and manage the learning environment is a strategy attuned to who kindergarten children are and how they learn. Learning centers offer children a powerful opportunity to develop independence, risk taking, perseverance, initiative, creativity, reasoning, and problem solving—the "learning to learn" skills.

Learning centers, when set up and used effectively, allow children to develop skills in multiple domains. In this vignette, notice the wide range of skills children are practicing and applying.

During center time three children decide they want to create their own board game. They go to various learning centers in the room to find the materials they need, and bring them back to a table. Their teacher observes, strategically posing questions to help them with their planning but careful not to interrupt their progress. They use LEGO pieces for markers, create their own dice by drawing dots on small empty boxes, and design their game board on poster board. They write the words *Go, Stop here, Bonus,* and *You win,* as well as draw shapes and numbers, in the various spaces. When they do not know how to write a word or number, they refer to a chart or word wall in the room or ask a peer or the teacher. They create a rule book. For a timer, the teacher suggests they use a small empty water bottle and sand. Using a drawing program on the computer, they create play money and print it out. The children persist and return to the task for days until it is complete. When the game is ready, they play again and again and teach others how to play.

This example illustrates how a variety of skills and concepts in multiple learning domains were practiced and applied during purposeful play. (See below for more examples of how children practice and use skills and concepts in play.) The three children were allowed to make their own choices. They used the learning centers to locate necessary resources but did not actually work in a particular center. The teacher played an important role in guiding their planning and learning. The activity included skills and concepts in all curriculum areas and enhanced the children's social, emotional, physical, cognitive, and language development. Moreover, problem solving, initiative, persistence, resourcefulness, and creativity had a role.

Learning centers can be used in various ways. During a designated choice time, children might choose their center and what they will do there. Some teachers include a "must do" or a required activity in the centers before opening them up for choice. In planning for learning centers, effective teachers

How a Child Practices and Uses Skills and Concepts in Play

Literacy
- Writes for a purpose
- Uses language to communicate
- Understands print concepts
- Writes letters and words
- Reads simple words

Mathematics
- Uses number concepts
- Develops mathematical language
- Makes predictions
- Creates two- and three-dimensional geometric shapes
- Measures time, money

Science
- Uses recycled materials
- Explores physical properties of materials

Social studies
- Develops rules with others and follows them
- Uses geographic thinking and mapping skills to move marker forward, backward
- Learns about money and its use

The arts
- Draws and creates

Technology
- Uses basic computer skills
- Navigates through software program

- Consider space constraints in determining whether all centers will be used on a given day

- Are creative in thinking about new possibilities for locations of centers (for example, a rarely used teacher's desk might be converted into a learning center, using the drawers for storage, the sides for magnetic boards and flannel boards, and the cozy space underneath as an ideal place for children to work or read alone)

- Rotate or change the materials in the area if children are no longer interested or challenged and as the specific learning focus changes

- Make a popular area larger to accommodate more children, and reduce its size as interest wanes

Most kindergarten classrooms have some basic learning centers that remain throughout the year. The chart on the next page presents a basic list of centers and the types of materials they might include to support children's learning. Not all will be full-fledged centers set off from the rest of the room; some might be "materials hubs" or resource areas, where children go to find a game or set of materials then take these to a work space at a table or on the floor. For example, there might be an art resource area, but art experiences take place throughout the room.

Other learning centers are not so basic and might be set up depending on the available space, materials, and children's interests. Some of these might include centers for cooking, sensory experiences, sand/water play, games, investigating how things work (a "take-apart" center), and project-related activities.

Organizing the Day

The daily schedule provides the framework for what teachers will do each day to help children develop and learn. Planning and organizing the day in a thoughtful, intentional way help teachers achieve their goals for children.

Young children feel secure when they know what happens next. They also gain a sense of time and sequence as they move from event to event. A predictable daily schedule helps kindergartners develop independence, responsibility, and a sense of order. Some of the predictable events likely to be a part of any daily schedule include whole group times, small group times, learning center time, and outdoor play. Routine events such as arrival, departure, nap, transitions between activities, and meals or snacks must also be included in the schedule. When developing a schedule, a teacher often must work around factors outside of her control. Besides beginning and ending times, these factors might include lunch, scheduled time for resource teachers, and special events such as field trips, visiting experts, school-wide events, and unexpected happenings.

Although a daily schedule helps children make sense of their day, it is not intended to be rigidly followed. If children are highly engaged in an activity, extending it for a while is a reasonable decision. Effective teachers also take cues from the children to gauge whether an activity is not working, and

Centers and the Materials They Might Include

Learning Center	Examples of Materials
Books	Books of all genres (predictable, informational, poetry, narrative, wordless, decodable), listening center with books on tape or CDs, storytelling and retelling props (flannel boards, puppets, story clothesline)
Writing	Writing paper, envelopes, blank booklets, journals, pencils, pens, markers, word banks, letter stamps, alphabet cards
Mathematics and games	Collections of objects (buttons, stickers, erasers, bottle caps), number cards, interlocking cubes, parquetry blocks, attribute games, graphing mats, sorting trays, deck of cards, board games, dice
Science/discovery	Plants, class pets, nature objects, collections (shells, rocks, leaves, balls, shiny things), tools for investigating (magnifying glasses, magnets, funnels, lenses), science journals, clipboards
Music and movement	Collection of CDs, digital music on MP3 players, musical instruments, keyboard with headphones, picture songbooks, song cards (color-coded to correspond with colored instruments), props for movement (scarves, flags, streamers)
Art	Materials to paint and draw on (newsprint, butcher paper, finger paint paper, foil), painting and drawing implements (markers, crayons, paints, pens, pencils, charcoal, chalk), materials for molding and sculpting (clay, playdough, tools), cutting and pasting materials (scissors, paste, glue, collage materials) and materials for constructing (foam pieces, wood scraps, wire, pipe cleaners, recyclable materials), art books, photographs, posters
Dramatic play	Props and dress-up clothes, homelike materials reflecting children's culture (kitchen furniture, dolls, phone, message board, empty food containers), open-ended materials (large pieces of fabric, plastic tubing, cardboard boxes), literacy materials (magazines, books, pads of paper, cookbooks, junk mail), mathematics and science materials (calculators, kitchen and bathroom scales, calendars, cash registers, measuring cups and spoons, store coupons)
Blocks	Unit blocks, hollow blocks, props (people figures, vehicles, hats, animal figures), open-ended materials (cardboard tubes, cardboard panels, PVC pipes, vinyl rain gutters), literacy materials (writing tools and paper, signs, books about bridges and buildings)
Technology	Computers, printers, optional technology (webcam, digital camera, scanners, computer microscopes, smartphones, tablets)

they make adjustments accordingly. In some districts and schools, teachers are required to adhere to a schedule specifying the times for each part of the curriculum. Sometimes activities and even what the teachers say are tightly scripted.

When is not the only question teachers must address in organizing the day. They must also do important planning for *what* will happen in the classroom. Effective kindergarten teachers reflect on what they know about the children and make thoughtful decisions about the activities and experiences they will offer to help these children progress. Teachers make plans for meeting the needs of individual children, small groups of children, and the class as a whole. They also consider how they are going to address the numerous learning outcomes in the short time they have with children. An efficient and meaningful way of doing this is through integrating curriculum in projects/studies and units/themes, as discussed later in this chapter.

Guiding Children's Learning

Guiding children's learning takes place all day, every day, across all six dimensions of a teacher's work. While having a well-stocked, thoughtfully organized, and attractive classroom environment enhances the kindergarten program, it is only the beginning. The effective teacher motivates children, builds on their prior knowledge and strengths, and supports their learning using a variety of strategies to increase their skills, knowledge, and understandings.

In order to guide children's learning effectively, kindergarten teachers must be knowledgeable in three specific areas. First, they must understand the content of the various curriculum domains and the learning paths kindergartners typically follow in developing the relevant knowledge, skills, and understanding. Second, kindergarten teachers must know the specific children they teach—what they are like as a group, as well as their individual needs, interests, learning styles, and cultures. And third, teachers must understand which methods work best given the characteristics of kindergarten children and the content to be learned. Knowledge in these three areas provides teachers with a mental roadmap to guide their planning, teacher–child interactions, and assessing.

Teacher–Child Interactions

Teacher–child conversations play an important role in shaping what children learn. It is through these conversations that the teacher *scaffolds* learning. This

Scaffolding in Action

At their morning meeting, Ms. Ankersen tells the children that their hamster, Sparky, has escaped overnight. She asks, "What can we do to find Sparky?"

High level of teacher support	← Scaffolding →		Low level of teacher support
I do…you watch	**I do…you help**	**You do…I help**	**You do…I watch**
In morning meeting, the children and Ms. Ankersen discuss the problem and make plans for how to solve it. As she writes the children's ideas on a chart, she mentions using periods to let people know when to stop reading. She also talks about using capital letters to start a new sentence. She says that names are very special, so Sparky's name will begin with a capital letter, too.	The next day, the children dictate a "Missing Hamster" story to be read by the principal over the intercom during morning messages. Ms. Ankersen reminds the children that the periods and capital letters will help the principal know when one sentence ends and a new one begins. As she records their thoughts, she calls on various children to use the marker to make the period or the capital letter.	For the day's entry into their journals, the children write about the missing hamster. The children are at varying stages in their writing development. Ms. Ankersen makes occasional comments on their use of periods and capital letters and offers suggestions as she talks to them about their entries. To help them in spelling words, she draws their attention to the word walls, their own personal word banks, and other resources.	The children create signs at the writing center to post around the school about the missing hamster, one solution to the problem suggested at the morning meeting. Knowing that their messages will be read by others, they seek to write in a way that will be understood. They refer to the sign on Sparky's cage to make sure their spelling is correct and read their messages to Ms. Ankersen for affirmation.

concept of effective teaching comes from the work of Lev Vygotsky (1978). Just as a carpenter uses a physical scaffold to work on a part of a building that is otherwise out of reach, the teacher provides varying levels of support to help children stretch to learn new concepts, skills, and understandings that are challenging but achievable (Copple & Bredekamp 2006). As children work to master a new skill or acquire a new understanding, the teacher gradually pulls back on the level of support (scaffolding) she offers. The box above describes the varying levels of writing support one teacher offers after the classroom hamster goes missing.

This example incorporates several aspects of effective scaffolding of children's learning: The teacher motivates the children by seizing an opportunity to write for a purpose; she sets the context for learning and offers children multiple ways to learn, practice, and apply skills. She taps into children's prior knowledge; all the children in the class are familiar with Sparky and help take care of him. These children also have participated in dictating stories, morning messages, group meetings, and journal writing as part of their daily activities. She demonstrates her knowledge of these kindergarten children; she knows where various children are in their writing development and the kind of support each is likely to need. She understands the content to be taught; she knows the developmental stages of writing and the conventions of print.

Keeping her learning goals in mind, the teacher is intentional in guiding children's learning about print and in choosing which instructional strategies—conversations, discussions, modeling, or specific feedback—to use at what point. She observes children as they write and helps them reflect on their writing. She offers a safe, supportive environment to take risks.

Today's kindergartners come from a range of backgrounds, have differing needs, and because of age-eligibility differences, range in age from 4¾ to 6 years old or more. Kindergarten teachers are most successful in supporting children's development and learning when they use a range of approaches to address the unique needs of each child in the classroom. No single approach works for all children and all occasions.

Using a Variety of Instructional Strategies

In building a table or repairing a roof, no carpenter tries to do each part of the work with a single tool. Like competent carpenters, good teachers have many tools, or *instructional strategies,* in their tool belts. The best strategy to use at any given moment depends on the learning goal, the specific situation, and the individual child. The teacher chooses the strategy that will be most useful in the particular situation. Often she tries one strategy, sees that it does not work, and tries something else. What is important is to have a variety of strategies ready and to remain flexible and observant. Here are several of the many strategies teachers should have at their disposal to do their jobs well (Copple & Bredekamp 2006):

Encourage. Offer comments or nonverbal actions that promote children's persistence and effort ("That wasn't easy, but you kept trying different things") rather than giving evaluative praise ("Good job").

Give specific feedback. Offer specific rather than general comments on the child's performance ("That's a *d,* Lily, not a *b*—it looks a lot like a *b* but it's turned the other way, see?").

Model. Display for children a skill or desirable way of behaving (whispering when you want the children to lower their own voices; modeling cooperation and problem solving by saying, "You both want to use the computer, so let's think about how you could use it together").

Create or add challenge. Generate a problem or add difficulty to a task so that it is just beyond what children already have mastered (once a child counts up to five items accurately, begin engaging him in counting sets of six to eight).

Give a cue, hint, or other assistance. Help children to work "on the edge" of their current competence (such as initially labeling cubbies with both picture and print labels, with the pictures to be removed later).

Provide information. Directly give children facts ("Birds make nests like this one to live in"), verbal labels ("This is a cylinder"), and other information.

Give directions. Provide specific instructions for children's action or behavior ("Move the mouse to this icon and click on it"; "Pour very slowly so we don't lose any of the liquid").

Teachers can and do use these strategies in any context. For instance, when children are engaging in an open-ended activity such as investigating at the water table, the teacher might choose to model a technique, provide information, or create challenges. Likewise, in a planned small or large group, the teacher might engage the children in open-ended thinking and use any of the instructional strategies in her repertoire.

Using a Variety of Learning Contexts

Each part of the day offers opportunities to guide children's learning. Key learning contexts are whole group, small group, learning centers, and daily routines.

Whole group. Also called large group, group meeting, or circle time, whole group is ideal for class discussions, making plans, and sharing work. At whole group gatherings during the day, opportunities are provided for children to learn and practice a variety of social and academic skills, such as speaking to a group about their experiences, listening to their classmates and responding appropriately with questions or comments, working cooperatively, and using and processing new information.

Small group. In a small group setting, teachers can give children more focused attention than in a whole group. Children also have the opportunity to engage in conversations with peers and solve problems collaboratively. Teachers often use this format for planned, focused experiences in which they might introduce a new skill or concept or reinforce skills and concepts the children have recently encountered. Small group experiences tend to take place during learning center time. Some children work with one adult in a small group while the others work more or less independently with another adult available to them. Small groups vary in size, usually ranging from four to six children, and might be formed based on a common interest or on a need as determined by assessment information.

What is important is to have a variety of strategies ready and to remain flexible and observant.

Learning centers. For each center, the teacher carefully selects materials to support educational goals. The teacher's role is to observe what children are doing and respond when he sees opportunities to extend their exploration, play, and problem solving. The teacher also serves as a resource person to help children locate what they need in order to accomplish tasks. Sometimes he proactively engages children, and might even become a co-player with them to promote richer play and learning.

Daily routines. Other opportunities for learning occur throughout the day during daily routines such as arrival, departure, meals and snacks, and transitions. Children learn skills and concepts at each of these times, as they sing a song focusing on phonemic awareness during a transition, make comparisons of the number of boys and girls present during circle time, or figure out how many crackers will be needed in order for each person to have three. When children practice and apply new skills during such routines, the skills become more meaningful to them.

Individualizing and Differentiating for All Learners

No two kindergartners are alike. Each child has unique needs, temperament, interests, abilities, background knowledge, and life experiences. Based on this understanding, teachers offer children multiple ways of taking in information and making sense of ideas. The three essential understandings for teachers presented earlier in this chapter—child development, content and standards, and instructional strategies—serve as a foundation for a teacher to guide children's learning.

To individualize for children, it is important for teachers to observe what children are doing throughout the day. Then they ask themselves, "What does this mean? How does this relate to my learning goals and content standards? How can I use this experience to help this child progress?" Having considered these questions, a teacher is able to respond in ways that take into account each child's individual needs and help that child progress along the learning path.

Another aspect of meeting individual needs is *differentiated instruction* (Tomlinson & McTighe 2006). This type of instruction offers children multiple paths to the same learning goals. Teachers modify elements such as the materials used, the experiences offered to achieve desired outcomes, the ways in which children represent their ideas, and the physical learning environment. For example, to help children learn the concept of patterning, a teacher first considers how patterning skills develop and what the children as a group already know about patterns. To get a picture of each child's level of understanding, she offers multiple opportunities in different modalities for children to create patterns: using interlocking cubes, sponge painting a patterned border on a picture, repeating a clapping pattern. As the teacher observes children, she scaffolds their learning to enable them to take the next step in that learning. A child who is able to copy various patterns might be next encouraged to extend a pattern created by the teacher. Another child might be challenged with a more complicated pattern or asked to describe the pattern he created. Differentiated learning gives children multiple paths to reach similar goals.

Approaches to Content Teaching and Learning

Teachers use multiple strategies to help children learn, understand, and apply content knowledge. They make informed decisions regarding the most effective teaching method to use for a given learning goal. When teachers are skilled, they will always engage in quite a bit of on-the-spot teaching. Though not planned in advance, this teaching too is intentional. That is, such teaching is guided by the teacher's goals, her familiarity with what children need to know and be able to do, and her knowledge of the learning paths to enable them to achieve these goals. For example, on the playground a child spontaneously hands the teacher a dandelion; the teacher shows how to blow it and talks about how the seeds travel by the wind to faraway places where new dandelions will grow.

Knowing children—including their prior knowledge, abilities, interests, learning styles, and culture—serves as the foundation for all learning to take place. In some instances, it makes the most sense to teach a concept or skill directly. In other cases, higher levels of thinking and engagement can occur during an in-depth study of a topic. During the course of the year in kindergarten, teachers might use one or more of a broad spectrum of approaches (some of which are defined below). Helm and Katz (2011) point out that these approaches vary by the level of child involvement, initiation, participation, and decision making, as well as by the time devoted to the topic, the teacher's role, the timing of field trips, and the use of a variety of resources.

Single-concept or single-skill approach. Some skills and concepts need to be taught directly. For example, the kindergarten teacher writes the morning message on a chart about a field trip to the flower shop and models how to begin each sentence with a capital letter. He invites the children to circle each capital letter used in the message. Later, children will have the opportunity to practice using capital letters as they write in their flower journals, and the teacher will assess their understanding of the concept.

Unit/theme approach. In a unit approach, the teacher identifies key concepts for a topic and introduces the concepts over a designated period of time. The children take part in follow-up activities related to the unit topic. For example, in a unit on flowers, the teacher reviews the science standards and determines that children should learn that flowers are living things; that they are part of a plant; that they need water, air, and sunlight to live and grow; and that plants and animals depend on each other to live. She uses different methods for teaching these concepts, such as informational books, experiments, field trips, and visits from experts.

In addition to the strategies used in planning a unit, the teacher can also examine other skills she must teach and find a way to link them to the topic, creating a theme for the class. These activities might help children develop skills, but not all are planned in order to help children gain a deeper understanding of the topic. For instance, in a thematic unit on flowers, not only will children learn about how flowers live and grow, but they also will engage in flower-related activities to learn skills in other content areas. They might count plastic flowers and place them in pots with numerals written on them. They might add flower words to the word wall and make a flower dictionary. They might practice scissor skills by cutting out construction paper flowers. One topic can open the door to countless new opportunities.

Project-based approach. Project-based learning takes many forms, such as the project approach (Helm & Katz 2011; Katz & Chard 2000), emergent curriculum (Jones & Nimmo 1994), Reggio Emilia's projects (Edwards, Gandini, & Forman 1998), and long-term studies (Bickart, Jablon, & Dodge 1999; Dodge, Colker, & Heroman 2002). It offers children rich opportunities to investigate, make decisions, and become deeply engaged in building content knowledge. The focus of project-based learning is to follow children's interests or potential interests and find answers to their questions. Much thought is devoted to selecting appropriate topics.

For the most part, children study topics that they can investigate first-hand. Before deciding whether a topic is worthy of investing valuable class time in, the teacher might identify big ideas related to the topic in science, social studies, mathematics, and other areas by creating a *concept web*. Once a project begins, children investigate their questions using literacy, mathematics, science, and technology skills to gain a deeper understanding of the topic and to represent and communicate their learning. For example, in a study of flowers children might wonder why birds and insects are attracted to some flowers and not others. They represent their ideas through discussions, drawings, and other art forms. To find out the answer, the children make predictions about which flowers birds and insects like best. They observe the flowers over time and record what they see by creating observational drawings and writing in journals. The teacher offers remarks or open-ended questions: "I wonder what color of flowers butterflies like best. How can we find out?"

The project or study duration is determined by children's engagement and usually is not predetermined. As the project culminates, children can share what they have learned with others outside of their classroom. In the study of flowers, they might set up a flower show with flowers they have grown and share the findings of their investigations with invited guests.

Assessing Children's Learning

Assessment and instruction go hand in hand. Teachers assess continually in order to make careful, intentional decisions about children's learning. In a joint position statement, NAEYC and the National Association of Early Childhood Specialists in State Departments of Education (NAECS/SDE) define assessment as "a systematic procedure for obtaining information from observations, interviews, portfolios, projects, tests, and other sources that can be used to make judgments about children's skills, dispositions, health, or other characteristics" (2003, 27).

In the kindergarten classroom, a major assessment tool is teachers' observing children to learn about them. *Observation* provides information they need to build relationships with individual children and enable those children to be successful learners (McAfee, Leong, & Bodrova 2004). With the information gained from observing, teachers can select materials to match children's style and level of learning; plan activities that respond to children's interests, experiences, and skills; and ask questions that extend children's thinking and learning (Jablon, Dombro, & Dichtelmiller 1999).

What other methods are there?

Building a Partnership With Families

Finally, a crucial dimension of a kindergarten teacher's work is to welcome families into the "school" system. The relationship that the teacher forms with them during the kindergarten year sets the tone for their children's entire school career.

Entering kindergarten is a huge transition for most children. Families talk about going to school, meeting the new teacher, and making new friends. The more a teacher knows the children and their families, the more she will be able to ease their transition into kindergarten and start off the year on a positive note. At the beginning of the school year, teachers can use these strategies to establish positive relationships with families:

- Contact children and families before the school year begins. This helps children feel more at ease on the first day and conveys a positive message to families. Initial contacts might include phone calls, letters to the children, letters to families, home visits, and an informal meet-the-teacher day.

- Gather information such as previous group experiences, number of siblings, parent occupations, and languages in the home. Find out critical health information such as allergies, disabilities, and medication. Ask family members to help supply this information.

- Invite families to share their goals for their children through informal conversations, initial contacts or conferences, and at parent orientation.

- In parent orientation, whether done individually or with all the families together, talk about goals for the year ahead, their approach to teaching, and other plans for the year.

Throughout the year, it is vital for teachers to maintain open lines of communication with families. Families want to know that the teacher knows their children. Moreover, they want to share with that teacher and hear about their children's strengths, likes and dislikes, and social relationships. When a teacher has formed a positive relationship with a family, it's much easier to cooperate in solving problems that might arise.

❖　　　❖　　　❖

The kindergarten teacher is vital to children's school success. Effective teachers use what they know about children's learning and development to create an exciting and dynamic learning experience for each child. They make time to build positive relationships with children and families. They take pleasure in children's successes. They bring passion to the classroom by sharing their interest in learning with them. Rather than being daunted by the myriad expectations for teaching and learning in kindergarten, teachers can use the powerful tool of reflective decision making to steer by as they help children achieve.

An Overview of Development in the Kindergarten Year

Heather Biggar Tomlinson

Experienced kindergarten teachers often reflect that kindergartners, despite wide individual variation, have common attributes such as enthusiasm for learning, an increased ability to integrate information and inhibit impulses, and a captivating interest in interacting with others, all of which makes them ready for a new phase in their education. As originally conceived, kindergarten was a preparatory year of schooling, designed primarily to support children's social and emotional adjustment to group learning.

However, the increased number of children attending preschool and child care programs at younger ages combined with the increased academic demands of the early years of school have greatly transformed the role of kindergarten. More than a preparatory year—about 95 percent of kindergarten-age children in America are enrolled in some type of kindergarten program (NCES 2008)—kindergarten is now generally considered the first year of school.

The age at which children are eligible (or required) to begin kindergarten varies from state to state. Kindergarten primarily serves 5-year-olds, but the age range can span from 4¾ to 7¼ years (Berk 2006a). Sometimes families feel compelled or are encouraged to hold their children out of kindergarten until they are older and can cope with the academic, emotional, and physical demands required of kindergartners, a practice known as "redshirting." About 10 percent of families defer kindergarten entry (NCES 1997), so there are many

In writing this chapter, the author drew extensively from four chapters authored by Stephen Sanders (physical education), Martha Bronson (social and emotional competence), Susan Golbeck (cognitive skills), and Laura Berk (learning and development of the kindergarten child) from the NAEYC book *K Today: Teaching and Learning in the Kindergarten Year* (Gullo 2006b). The full citation for each of those chapters appears in the references.

6-year-olds in kindergarten classrooms (despite the fact that age of entry into kindergarten has not been shown to be a major factor in school performance [NICHD-NCCRN 2007]).

There is a major and well-documented shift in cognition that occurs between ages 5 and 7 (Piaget 1952; Sameroff & McDonough 1994; White 1965, 1970). Before this shift occurs, children are developmentally more like preschoolers than like school-age children; throughout and after the shift, children show increased levels of personal responsibility, self-direction, and logical thinking. The change that occurs has been marked throughout time and across cultures as "achieving the age of reason" (Whiting & Edwards 1988).

The changes associated with this "5 to 7 shift" affect development across physical, social and emotional, cognitive, and language domains. They also affect children's "approaches to learning," another important domain of development that includes children's *enthusiasm* for learning (their interest, joy, and motivation to learn) and their *engagement* in learning (their focused attention, persistence, flexibility, and self-regulation) (Hyson 2008).

Experiences at home and in early childhood programs can either support or undermine children's enthusiasm for and engagement in learning. In this respect, kindergarten is a critical year. At their best, kindergarten experiences nurture positive approaches to learning and prepare children for the more rigorous academic expectations of the primary grades. In these circumstances, teachers can nurture kindergartners' positive approaches to learning by implementing an engaging curriculum and teaching methods that draw children in and challenge them to reflect, try out their ideas, and tackle meaningful problems.

Pressured by expectations for children's performance on a narrow range of skills, teachers may inadvertently discourage kindergartners' interest in learning and fail to provide time to develop qualities such as persistence and flexibility. By carefully reviewing the curriculum and teaching methods with children's approaches to learning in mind, teachers can help ensure that children are neither overwhelmed by nor bored with the curriculum and teaching practices. By stoking children's enthusiasm and engagement, teachers support children to enter the primary grades not only academically prepared but also with positive learning attitudes and effective learning behaviors.

Because of the great individual variation among kindergartners and the wide age range that often exists in a kindergarten classroom, teaching practices must be responsive to developmental, individual, and cultural variation (as is true for every other grade, as well). Although most 5-year-olds are developmentally more like preschoolers than like older children, kindergartens are usually housed institutionally with elementary schools. Teachers have to strike a fine balance in meeting the needs of children's varied capacities and vertically aligning curricula with both preschool and first grade.

In spite of the challenges, and because of the many opportunities for teaching and learning, it's a very exciting period for children and their teachers.

This chapter was first published in *Developmentally Appropriate Practice in Early Childhood Programs Serving Children From Birth Through Age 8* (Copple & Bredekamp 2009).

Heather Biggar Tomlinson, PhD, is an early childhood development consultant for The World Bank.

Physical Development

Kindergartners are fascinated with learning what their bodies can do—how fast they can run, how high they can jump, how skillfully they can move. They are becoming more sophisticated in their movements, more coordinated in their physical endeavors, and increasingly competent in physical skills such as balance and eye–hand coordination. They use movement to express their feelings, manipulate objects, and learn about their world. They delight in physical accomplishment.

Motor skills are the result of a dynamic developmental system: jointly contributing are kindergarten children's longer, leaner bodies; their motivation to attain new goals; their advancing cognition; their improved ability to cooperate with peers; and opportunities for extensive practice (Thelen & Smith 1998). As children participate in small group games with reciprocal roles, they integrate previously acquired motor skills into more complex actions. Kindergartners need teachers to guide them in making choices about physical activity and in acquiring and refining skills. The ideal time for children to develop basic physical skills (e.g., throwing, catching, kicking, skipping, and balancing) is from ages 2–7—during their "fundamental" movement phase (Gallahue 1995, 131–3).

Most 2- and 3-year-olds attempt to throw, catch, or jump, but their movements are relatively crude and uncoordinated. At 4 and 5, most children have matured to an elementary skill stage. They have greater control over their movements, although they still look awkward and their movements are not yet fluid. (Many adults never exit the elementary stage in basic activities such as throwing and catching.) By age 6, many children have the developmental potential to be at a mature stage in most fundamental movement skills. This means that they can integrate all the parts of a particular pattern of movement into a well-coordinated, mechanically correct act appropriate to the demands of the task.

As with all areas of development, no two children are alike. Some kindergartners will come close to or reach the mature level for some skills, while others will need more guidance and practice. In general, girls tend to be more advanced than boys in fine motor skills and in gross motor skills that require precision such as hopping and skipping. Boys tend to do better with skills that require force and power such as running and jumping (Berk 2008).

Although they will delight in movement programs, most kindergartners are not yet ready for the skills and pressures of organized sports such as soccer or gymnastics. Activities designed for youth or adults that are pushed on kindergartners can be both frustrating and unsafe for them. They usually are not able to achieve a consistently high level of competence in a sport until they have had instruction in specific skills (e.g., climbing, throwing a ball, jumping) and opportunities over time and contexts to practice.

Gross Motor Development

In the gross motor area, kindergartners run more quickly and smoothly than when they were younger and can change directions easily. They throw and catch with increasing involvement of their whole body, shifting their weight with the release of the ball and varying the force of their throw in accord with where they want the ball to land. When a ball is thrown to them, kindergartners can anticipate its place of landing by moving forward, backward, and sideways and by "giving" with their body to absorb the force of the ball (Cratty 1986; Roberton 1984).

By the end of the year, kindergarten children should be able to do things such as walking and running using mature form, traveling forward and sideways in a variety of patterns, changing direction quickly in response to a signal, demonstrating clear contrasts between slow and fast movement, rolling sideways without hesitating or stopping, tossing a ball and catching it before it bounces twice, kicking a stationary ball using a smooth continuous running step, and maintaining momentary stillness while bearing weight on various body parts (Gallahue 1995; Sanders 2002).

Fine Motor Development

A child's attention span usually lengthens during kindergarten, and control of the hands and fingers improves, both of which lead to greater enjoyment of and involvement in fine motor activities. Many kindergartners initially struggle with tasks that require detail, patience, steadiness, and fine motor coordination, such as writing, drawing, and cutting with precision. By the end of the year, however, they will have benefited from activities that allow practice in these areas and that better develop hand muscles, such as writing, drawing and painting, working with clay, and constructing with LEGOs. They improve in activities such as sorting small objects; stringing beads; zipping, buttoning, and tying various articles of clothing; using scissors; pouring milk or juice at snack; and setting the table. Children with disabilities improve in fine motor skills with the help of assistive technology such as Velcro shoes and weighted bowls and utensils.

Writing is an especially important area of fine motor development at this age, as children develop an increased desire to communicate through written expression. Most kindergarten children are adept at gripping a crayon or pencil as a result of experimentation during the preschool years. They may have tried different forms of pencil holding, gradually learning the grip and angle that maximizes stability and writing efficiency (Greer & Lockman 1998). By age 5, children use an adult pencil grip when writing and drawing—a milestone that results from the child's own active reorganization of behavior. In their efforts to write, kindergartners gradually improve in their renditions of the letters.

Promoting Physical Development in Kindergarten

Early childhood educators have always placed great importance on children's learning about and with their bodies through play and being outdoors (Brooks 1913). But we now understand that, in the case of physical development, children also need to learn through instruction; they do not develop physical skills through play alone (Manross 1994, 2000). In other words, sending children out to recess and encouraging them to participate in free play does not guarantee that they will develop physical skills and healthy attitudes, competencies, and habits. Teachers (and specialists, where available) working with kindergarten children should teach basic physical skills and then offer play-based opportunities so children can experiment and be creative with the skills they are learning.

National recommendations state that kindergartners need at least 60 minutes (not more than 30 minutes at a time) of moderate to vigorous physical activity on all or most days of the week (NASPE 2004, 2008a; USDHHS & USDA 2005). Today, many children get such exercise only at shool. Scheduling bouts of physical activity interspersed with sedentary activities helps reduce inattentiveness and misbehavior (Mahar et al. 2006; NASPE 2008b).

The role of kindergarten teachers in physical education is to create positive and success-based environments in which children can develop fundamental motor skills through play-based learning activities. The teacher and the school can strive to create an environment that includes the following:

• Inside and outside physical activity areas with adequate space for children to move freely and safely without bumping into each other

• Opportunities for daily, high-quality movement instruction with plenty of time for practice—exclusive of the outdoor play time that should also occur

• Appropriate equipment so that each child benefits from maximum participation

The ideal environment offers children opportunities to develop both fine and gross motor skills. Kindergartners have opportunities to learn and practice fine motor skills in the course of classroom activities such as writing, drawing, doing puzzles, and working with manipulatives. However, learning and practicing gross motor skills requires open space, such as a large room, a gym, or a spacious hallway or outdoor area so that children can throw, kick, strike, run, and skip. There must also be enough equipment so that many children can participate in similar physical education activities at the same time (i.e., every child has a ball to dribble, or every child has a jump rope to practice jumping). If space is a problem, setting up physical education stations (supervised by adults such as student teachers or trained parent volunteers) can allow children to move from place to place to practice a variety of skills.

A physical education center—a semipermanent space similar to a reading or science center—can also provide space for children to practice gross motor skills. Here, small groups of children can practice developing a specific movement skill, deepen their understanding of movement and movement concepts, and use their physical education skills in ways that link to other areas of the curriculum. For example, in a center where children are learning about moving through space, they might plot a route on a map they have created, construct a miniature obstacle course using playdough and props, or measure various lengths of jumps and leaps using rope segments or tape measures.

When introducing motor development activities teachers can foster the growth of children's physical education skills by focusing first on large body movements such as throwing or kicking, and then designing tasks for gradual and sequential learning. For example, tasks such as working on puzzles and perfecting cutting skills help develop better eye–hand coordination, which in turn improves the ability to catch or bounce a ball. Tasks should have a definite purpose, progress logically, and be structured to yield high rates of success.

Breaking down motor skills into small, doable actions—a form of scaffolding—allows everyone to participate, even if participation is partial for some. For instance, if a child cannot grasp a racket to strike a balloon, she might be encouraged to strike the balloon with her hand. Also, it is helpful to provide cues and suggestions that help children refine specific skills. Many children have difficulties understanding verbal instruction (or understanding directions in English) and may do better when they can watch someone practicing the skill they are being asked to do.

Presenting multiple skills and offering appealing choices (e.g., partners, equipment, space, and activities) and challenges help maintain children's interest as they learn. Activities should be open-ended so children can experiment with and explore materials and their abilities. Offering a variety of tasks, materials, and learning centers helps children practice specific skills and learn to use different types and sizes of equipment. Movement and skill activities should involve everyone in the class and should promote inclusion and cooperation rather than exclusion and competition. Teachers who foster a sense of community, emphasizing that everyone can participate and has strengths, will find delighted responsiveness from most children. However, not all children will be performing the same task at the same time or with the same skill level. As with other domains, teachers should individualize or modify a task based on the abilities and interests of each child.

Kindergarten teachers not only can help children develop an immediate foundation in physical skills; they also can instill healthy habits that will affect children's well-being for a lifetime.

Social and Emotional Development

Social and emotional competence matters a great deal in school and in life. Skill in basic areas of social and emotional competence has pervasive and long-lasting consequences, such as success in school, avoiding criminal behaviors, and social and psychological adjustment throughout the life span (e.g., McClelland, Acock, & Morrison 2006; Raver 2002; Schultz et al. 2001). As kin-

dergartners, children are expected to regulate their emotions and behavior appropriately under most circumstances. They are expected to be able to delay, defer, and accept substitutions for their preferred goals without becoming aggressive or overly frustrated. They are also expected to cope well with challenges in the environment or to new events (Sroufe 1995).

Social Development

The ability to form and sustain relationships with others, both with adults and children, is central to a child's social development—not to mention his happiness. Kindergarten children are intensely interested in interacting with their peers, and for the most part they do well in engaging cooperatively, getting along, and forming friendships. Social skills relate not only to the obvious correlates such as peer acceptance but also to broader well-being, such as success in school (McClelland, Acock, & Morrison 2006) and future adjustment (Kupersmidt & Coie 1990).

Some kindergarten children do struggle in the social arena, though; they may be overly shy, aggressive, or generally unable to regulate their emotions and behavior in prosocial ways. Kindergartners who are rejected by their peers are likely to have long-term problems, including difficulties in friendships later in childhood and even adulthood and academic difficulties in school (Achenback & Edelbrock 1991; Cowen et al. 1973).

Prosocial behavior. Prosocial behavior includes cooperating, resolving conflicts with peers in peaceful, positive ways, following classroom rules and adult requests, and other helpful actions (Shonkoff & Phillips 2000). Teachers of young children have always valued these skills in creating a classroom environment where all children can thrive. Recently there has been a surge of interest in fostering prosocial skills in order to cope with the growing number of serious behavior problems sometimes seen in schools, including kindergarten classrooms (Gartrell 2004).

Kindergartners are better able than younger children to apply an internal control that uses rules, strategies, and plans to guide behavior. They begin to internalize standards and monitor their own actions and tend to seek permission to transition to another activity (Schunk 1994; Wood 2007). A sense of conscience continues to build, and children may feel guilty when they violate standards, wanting instead to be "good." Older kindergartners are more able to act responsibly and to hold themselves accountable for their behavior, but they can be unpredictable, behaving well at home and poorly at school or vice versa, being oppositional at times, and wanting to test limits more frequently (Whiting & Edwards 1988; Wood 2007). Adults may see a regression to temper tantrums, complaining, and acting out later in the year, making the consistency of rules and consequences even more important than it was earlier in the year.

Kindergartners overall are more able to interact cooperatively than younger children; they like to be helpful and follow rules. They can use negotiation and reciprocity to some degree to settle disputes, although they still benefit from adult modeling and guidance in applying these skills. They do best with following rules and showing cooperative behaviors in environments with clear and simple expectations and consistent rules and consequences.

In addition to being more skilled at dealing with potential conflicts by sharing and taking turns, kindergarten children can, given guidance and opportunity, use proactive strategies to organize, direct, and sustain interactions with others (Bodrova & Leong 2008; Bronson 1994). These include making initial suggestions about what to do (*Let's pretend the baby has to go to the hospital*), continuing suggestions about how to proceed (*Now let's say the baby is all better and we take her home*), assigning roles or resources to the participants (*You take the thermometer, and I'll use the stethoscope*), and laying out the rules or constraints of a proposed activity (*The doctor has to say it's okay for the baby to go home*). These proactive strategies allow children to have more complex interactions with fewer conflicts.

Children who exhibit positive behaviors such as cooperation and conflict-resolution skills tend to show better overall social skills and have more friends (Howes 1988; Katz & McClellan 1997). They also are more likely to be well adjusted, good at coping, and able to manage their emotions and behavior in ways appropriate to the situation (Eisenberg & Mussen 1989).

Sociability. As in other periods of early childhood development, a child's secure, warm attachment with an adult or adults in kindergarten is the foundation for constructive development and learning across all domains. Relationships with parents or other family adults are most important, but teacher–child relationships are also very powerful and can be a buffer in times of stress. Kindergartners, even more than children of other ages, especially seek and tune in to teachers' approval and want to be viewed as being good (Wood 2007).

Kindergartners learn best when they feel valued, needed, and loved by the teacher, are confident the teacher will meet their basic needs promptly, and can count on the teacher to interact with them in intimate, playful, and personal ways (Hyson 2004). When the teacher and the classroom atmosphere reflect these qualities, children are able to devote the necessary energy to the developmental and learning tasks at hand.

Research shows that in early childhood classrooms in which teachers provide high-quality emotional and instructional support along with helpful feedback and a structured, predictable environment, children develop better social skills than children in other classrooms (Rimm-Kaufman et al. 2005; Wilson,

Pianta, & Stuhlman 2007). Furthermore, children who have warm and supportive teachers demonstrate greater prosocial behavior, empathy, self-regulation, and social competence (Eisenberg & Fabes 1998). Having a positive relationship with the teacher in kindergarten is correlated with school success during that year, and it predicts future school achievement as well (Hamre & Pianta 2001; Pianta et al. 2008).

As children's interest in friendship-building intensifies throughout the kindergarten year, their communication skills and understanding of others' thoughts and feelings improve, and thus, their skills in interacting with other children improve. Cooperative play—in which children orient toward a common goal, such as building a block structure or acting out a make-believe theme—increases during their preschool years. Likewise, kindergarten children also engage in solitary and in parallel play—in which a child plays near other children with similar materials but does not interact (Howes & Matheson 1992). Teachers may wonder whether a child who often plays alone is developing normally. Most kindergartners who tend to play by themselves enjoy it, and their solitary activities are positive and constructive (e.g., painting, looking at books, working puzzles, building with blocks). Such children are usually well adjusted, and when they do play with peers, they show good social skills (Coplan et al. 2004).

A few children, however, may retreat into solitary activities when they would rather be playing with classmates but have been rejected by them. Some are temperamentally introverted children whose social fearfulness causes them to withdraw (Rubin, Burgess, & Hastings 2002). Others are immature, impulsive children who find it difficult to regulate their anger and aggression. Ongoing observations will inform the teacher as to whether there is cause for concern about a child's sociability and a need for intervention.

The ability to make and keep friends increases the joy and pleasure in life and has important correlates, both contemporary and long-term. For example, having close friendships tends to foster positive attitudes toward school and correlates with better academic performance, perhaps because these rewarding relationships energize cooperation and initiative in the classroom (Ladd, Birch, & Buhs 1999; Ladd, Buhs, & Seid 2000). Young children with gratifying friendships are also more likely to become psychologically healthy and competent adolescents and young adults (Bagwell et al. 2001; Bukowski 2001).

Like older children, kindergartners seek compatibility in their friendships, often choosing friends who are similar not just in gender but also in age, socioeconomic status, ethnicity, personality (sociability, helpfulness, aggression), and school performance (Hartup 1996). However, children who attend ethnically diverse schools and live in integrated neighborhoods often form friendships with peers of other ethnicities (Quillian & Campbell 2003).

One of the most noticeable features of kindergartners' sociability is their preference for play with peers of their same sex, which strengthens over early childhood; by age 6, children play with same-sex peers 11 times more than they play with other-sex peers (Maccoby & Jacklin 1987; Martin & Fabes 2001). Children tend to choose play partners whose interests and behaviors are compatible with their own. Social pressure also plays a role; children pick up a wealth of gender stereotypes in early childhood (*Trucks are for boys*; *Only girls can be nurses*), which certainly contributes to gender segregation.

For most kindergartners, friendships involve at least a degree of sensitivity, caring, emotional expressiveness, sharing, cooperation, and joy—qualities that promote emotional understanding, empathy, sympathy, and positive social behavior (Hartup 1996; Vaughn et al. 2001). However, sometimes friendships are argumentative and aggressive, which interferes with children's adjustment. Kindergartners with conflict-ridden peer relationships are less likely than others to have lasting friendships and more likely to dislike school and to achieve poorly (Dodge et al. 2003; McClelland, Acock, & Morrison 2006). Shy or self-centered children also are likely to have few or no friends (Ladd 1999). Teachers' efforts to help less socially adept children develop and maintain friendships will do much to bring joy, confidence, and success into their lives.

Self-concept. The development of self-concept, which becomes better established in kindergarten, occurs within the context of children's maturing awareness of the social environment. Kindergartners develop their emerging self-concept in part by comparing themselves with peers, usually comparing against one classmate at a time. When asked to describe themselves, kindergartners typically focus on observable characteristics: their name, physical appearance, possessions, and everyday behaviors (Harter 1996). They also mention typical emotions and attitudes, such as "I'm happy when we get to run outside" or "I don't like to be with kids I don't know"—statements that suggest a budding grasp of their own unique personality (Eder & Mangelsdorf 1997).

Kindergartners readily internalize adult evaluations. Positive messages from adults about their growing knowledge, skills, and prosocial behaviors, as well as respect, warmth, and positive guidance, enhance children's self-concept. On the other hand, repeatedly negative messages contribute to early signs of self-criticism, anxiety about failing, and weakened motivation that can seriously interfere with learning and academic progress (Burhans & Dweck 1995).

In kind, children cannot yet sort out the precise causes of their successes and failures, instead developing a global self-image. They tend to view all good things as going together: A person who tries hard is also a smart person who is going to succeed. As a result, most kindergartners are "learning optimists," who rate their own ability very highly, underestimate the difficulty of tasks, and are willing to exert effort when presented with new challenges (Harter 2003). These attitudes contribute greatly to kindergartners' initiative during a period in which they must master many new skills.

Emotional Development

Kindergartners grow in the complexity of their emotional experiences, their ability to interpret the emotional cues of others, and their awareness that each person has an inner life of beliefs, opinions, and interpretations of reality different from their own (Bronson 2006; Wellman, Cross, & Watson 2001). As a result, and with modeling and guidance, children come to interact in increasingly intentional, sympathetic, skilled, and positive ways with others. A variety of factors contributes to these expanded skills, including the development

of the frontal lobes of the cerebral cortex, cognitive and language development, a solidifying self-concept, conversations with adults and peers about mental states, make-believe play, and the patient guidance and reasonable expectations of adults.

Research in school settings shows that when prekindergarten, kindergarten, and primary grade children have warm, caring relationships with the teacher, these relationships foster their development and learning (Pianta, Hamre, & Stuhlman 2003). However, research finds that some teachers, especially those in poor-quality child care settings, are emotionally insensitive and detached (Cost, Quality & Child Outcomes Study Team 1995). The tendency to deny or ignore children's emotional development most hurts those with special vulnerabilities, such as children with special needs and those growing up in poverty (Peth-Pierce 2000; Raver & Knitzer 2002). Vulnerable children who lack a foundation of emotional security also are at risk for eliciting further criticism and harshness because they show inappropriate behavior that is hard for teachers and peers to respond to in positive ways; this cycle decreases such children's chances of social and academic success (Hyson 2004).

For most children, however, age 5 is generally a time of happiness. "Life is good," a kindergartner might say (Wood 2007). The kindergarten teacher can enhance that happiness and help the child grow emotionally when he develops a bond with the child, designs activities to meet emotional needs, encourages open expression of feelings, helps develop positive feelings such as joy and satisfaction, and is aware of the child's unique emotional responses to various tasks and situations (Hyson 2004).

Emotional understanding and empathy. When adults exhibit warmth, encourage children's emotional expressiveness, and show sensitive concern for their feelings (modeling sympathy), children are more likely to react in a concerned way to the distress of others (Koestner, Franz, & Weinberger 1990; Strayer & Roberts 2004). Likewise, teachers who convey the importance of kindness and intervene when a child displays inappropriate emotion (such as taking pleasure in another's misfortune) help that child respond to others' distress with sympathy (Eisenberg 2003).

Given an emotionally secure foundation, kindergarten-age children gain a considerable understanding of emotion. Children at ages 5 to 6 are developing a greater understanding of others' minds and emotions (Denham & Kochanoff 2002; Perner, Lang, & Kloo 2002) and can correctly judge the causes of emotions in many cases (*She's mad because she thought it was her turn*). They also can predict the consequences of many emotions with reasonable accuracy (an angry child might hit someone; a happy child is more likely to share). Furthermore, kindergartners show advancing skills in thinking of ways to relieve others' negative feelings, such as giving a hug to comfort someone or sharing a favorite toy when someone is sick.

These skills in understanding and empathizing, in turn, greatly help children get along with others. It is related to kindergartners' kind, friendly, and considerate behavior; willingness to make amends after harming another; and peer acceptance (Dunn, Brown, & Maguire 1995; Eisenberg & Fabes 1998; Fabes et al. 2001).

About 3 percent of kindergartners, mostly boys, are highly aggressive. These children, who strike out at others with verbal and physical hostility, are limited in their ability to take another's perspective and are less empathic and sympathetic than other children. They need teachers to intervene by helping them to reinterpret others' behaviors in more positive ways (e.g., that being hit by a ball was an accident, not an attack) and to learn new coping strategies in the face of negative emotions (Pettit 2004; Tremblay 2000).

Self-regulation of emotions. Self-regulation is an internal ability to intentionally control our emotions and behavior as the situation demands. It involves children either making themselves not do something, such as not blurt out an answer, or making themselves do something even when the desire is not there, such as stop playing and clean up the puzzle pieces (Bodrova & Leong 2008). Self-regulation pertains to three aspects of development: emotions (discussed here), thoughts—in particular, attention (discussed in "Cognitive Development" below)—and behaviors (discussed in both sections). Compared with younger children, kindergartners are typically more able to regulate the ways they express emotions as they interact with other people (Eisenberg, Fabes, & Losoya 1997).

During preschool, given the right modeling of self-regulation, as well as patience, warmth, and guidance from adults, children, with effort, do improve in their ability to self-regulate their behaviors. Yet they do not all improve to the same degree, and children enter kindergarten with varying levels of self-regulation skills. Some are quite good at delaying gratification and thinking about the consequences of their actions, while others struggle. Teachers rate "difficulty following directions" as their number one concern about children because they say that more than half of the children they teach have difficulty in this area of self-regulation (Rimm-Kaufman, Pianta, & Cox 2001).

Being able to adjust one's emotional state to a comfortable level of intensity is an important skill for engaging productively in tasks, interacting in positive ways with others, and succeeding in school (Howse et al. 2003). As experienced kindergarten teachers will attest, this skill is important for success with peers and academics. With age and experience, children become more able to control their impulses, which allows them to become more accepted and liked by other children (Eisenberg & Fabes 1992). Social competence is, in turn, associated with an ability to manage how one acts and to show few problem behaviors (Caspi 1998). Furthermore, children who develop these skills in the early years get on a positive trajectory, and they tend to have better peer acceptance and the ability to regulate their emotions as adults (Sroufe, Carlson, & Shulman 1993).

Children with highly emotionally volatile temperaments have greater difficulty regulating their feelings; they require extra adult support in developing self-regulation skills (Kochanska & Knaack 2003). Hyson (2004) delineates five major benefits of gains in emotion regulation: children (1) reach the goals they desire, (2) feel better having more control, (3) experience mastery and competence, (4) become part of the culture and are accepted more readily, and (5) become more socially competent and able to direct attention to others.

Promoting Social and Emotional Development in Kindergarten

Kindergarten teachers can support children's social and emotional development in myriad ways, three of which are discussed below. The common denominator in enhancing development and learning in these areas is having a warm, positive relationship with the teacher and family members.

Prosocial behavior and attitudes. Relationships are the context that supports children's internalization of the rules and values in their world. This internalization reveals itself as kindergartners show more and more prosocial behaviors—cooperating, resolving conflicts peacefully, following classroom rules, and other positive actions. Teachers strengthen children's prosocial tendencies when they model prosocial behaviors; call attention to prosocial statements made by children; give explicit instructions about helping, sharing, and like behaviors; and reward these behaviors when they occur (Eisenberg & Mussen 1989). Effective teachers monitor children's interactions in the classroom, knowing that both negative and positive behaviors occur and that other children imitate the bad as well as the good. Some indirect methods of monitoring peer interaction include "stage setting" (providing time, space, materials, and arrangements of materials for positive and appropriate interactions) and "coaching" (suggesting positive social interaction and problem-solving strategies as needed in the context of ongoing interactions between children) (Hoffman 1983).

In addition to creating a warm, responsive emotional climate, teachers can foster prosocial attitudes by interpreting social situations in ways that show sympathy and caring. For example, when a teacher responds to an accident by saying, "Oh, Jacob's juice spilled; let's help him clean it up," children learn to be sympathetic and helpful to others. Modeling caring behaviors accompanied by a general prosocial lesson (*We must help people who are hurt*) promotes these attitudes in children.

Kindergarten children are beginning to understand the feelings of others, and they are more likely to develop prosocial dispositions when their teacher connects behaviors with their consequences (*He is sad because you wouldn't let him play the game with you*) and rules with reasons (*We don't push others on the*

steps because somebody might fall). Teachers can also encourage cooperative interactions by suggesting sharing, taking turns, or other ways of negotiating disputes. Encouraging children to take responsibility for tasks that serve the classroom community also helps to promote prosocial attitudes. When teachers expect children to contribute to the common good, children internalize these expectations.

Social interaction skills. Children learn how to interact with others from their early close relationships. When a teacher is caring and responsive to children's interests and feelings, she creates an atmosphere that fosters social development. Children are more likely to cooperate with and model a teacher with whom they have a positive relationship (Birch & Ladd 1998; Hyson 2004; Pianta & Stuhlman 2004). When children can rely on the teacher to care about them as individuals, validate their interests and feelings, and support their efforts to regulate themselves, they are more likely to develop trust, feel secure, and be ready to interact confidently with the social and physical environment.

Teachers must be careful to show a positive attitude toward *all* children—kindergartners notice when an adult likes or dislikes particular children. Because adults' attitudes and interaction styles influence children's own attitudes and behaviors, it is important that teachers act as positive role models—for example, showing interest in and kindness toward others and having respect for others' ideas, points of view, and emotions.

Because interactions with peers are critical for social learning, teachers must make sure to provide children ample time and opportunities for those interactions, such as space, materials, and encouragement for dramatic play, cooperative work, and problem-solving activities, conversations, and group discussions. They should also help children who need assistance to find play partners and should teach children proactive strategies for entering and participating in social activities. Part of the teacher's role is to monitor children's social activities and provide positive ways of solving problems, settling disputes, and keeping interactions fair and inclusive, without interfering unnecessarily (Katz & McClellan 1997). Teachers also model and teach the use of language to communicate ideas and emotions, negotiate differences, and treat others respectfully.

Self-regulation skills (emotional and behavioral control). The development of emotional and behavioral control—self-regulation—is a skill that should be taught to all children, not just those who demonstrate behavioral problems (Vieillevoye & Nader-Grosbois 2008). A teacher provides the foundation of support for children's control over emotions and behavior by creating a safe, warm, and supportive atmosphere that enables them to feel secure and capable of emotional control. She helps children maintain self-control by providing language that children can internalize and use for self-guidance, by helping them understand the relationship between their goals and the behavior strategies they use to reach those goals, and by allowing opportunities and supports for sustained dramatic play, which enhances their self-regulation skills (Bodrova & Leong 2008; Yang 2000). Teachers help children learn and rehearse strategies for negotiating social problems before they occur.

When a kindergartner's control fails, the teacher should focus on problem solving with the child (and, in some cases, the other children who were involved in the incident) and on helping him consider what else he could have done. The incident becomes a learning opportunity, and the child gains experience in making choices and using strategies that will help him the next time he needs his self-control. This is more effective for the child than just curbing behaviors for which he might get caught and punished.

Guidelines and rules for children's behavior should be simple and consistent and should include rationales so children can understand that rules are designed to help and protect them and all members of the classroom community. Kindergarten children are mature enough to participate in discussions about classroom problems, and they can help generate ideas about possible solutions and rules. Such discussions help children understand why guidelines are necessary and give them a sense of control and responsibility. Having opportunities to set and monitor their own rules contributes to young children's increasing capacity for regulating themselves rather than having to be regulated by adults (Bodrova & Leong 2008).

Teachers also should discuss emotions with children. When children learn to talk about what they and others are feeling, possible causes for the feelings, and what might be done about them (*How do you think he felt when you wouldn't let him be in the game? How could you make him feel better?*), children become able to separate emotions from action, reflect on their actions, and exercise more self-control.

The ways in which adults organize the environment also affect children's ability to exercise control. Children are more likely to learn self-regulation and be effective problem solvers if they are given a considerable amount of choice and control over their own activities (Ryan & Deci 2000). It is important to minimize sources of frustration, overstimulation, and stress in the environment that might be more than children can handle. Teachers also can provide visual and tangible reminders about self-regulation; for example, providing a coin for children to toss to settle an argument or decide who gets the next turn on the computer (Bodrova & Leong 2008).

Play, particularly complex dramatic or make-believe play, is a crucial vehicle for allowing children to develop and practice self-regulation skills. Such play allows children to gain understanding of their emotions, as well as the feelings of others, as they act out situations that induce strong emotions and resolve those feelings. It also provides practice in remaining within a prescribed role and play scenario and in establishing, negotiating, and following their own rules—and thus it promotes self-regulation skills more powerfully than adult-directed play.

This is not to say that play should be without adult guidance and support. In fact, children often require adult modeling and scaffolding to help them learn to engage in the sustained, complex play that is most beneficial to their development. However, once opportunity and guidance have been provided, teachers should remove themselves, as children tend to show more complex and beneficial social play in the absence of adults (Kontos & Keyes 1999; Leong & Bodrova 2005).

Dramatic play experiences are especially advantageous for impulsive children, who are behind their peers in self-regulatory development (Elias & Berk 2002). To foster self-regulation skills, teachers should make sure children have ample opportunity, materials, and encouragement to engage in play, such as make-believe play and play with made-up rules (Bodrova & Leong 2008; Elias & Berk 2002; Yang 2000).

Cognitive Development

Compared with younger children, kindergartners show more flexibility in their thinking, greater ability to conceptualize categories, advances in reasoning and problem solving, and gains in knowledge of the world, ability to pay attention, and use of memory. In short, kindergartners' thinking is reorganizing, gradually becoming more systematic, accurate, and complex. This transition—from preschool thought to the style of thinking more typical of middle childhood—is the "5 to 7 shift" mentioned in the beginning of the chapter (Flavell, Miller, & Miller 2001; Newcombe 2005; Sameroff & McDonough 1994). It stems from a congruence of major changes in the brain and greater societal expectations and opportunities.

Brain Development and a Key Shift in Thinking Abilities

New research in cognitive neuroscience shows that, given healthy environments, a child's neurological system develops dramatically during the early childhood years (Halfon, Shulman, & Hochstein 2001). The first five to seven years of life are a sensitive period for brain development; the brain is especially responsive to stimulation, which prompts a massive wiring of neurons and sculpting of brain regions. The brain is more malleable than it will be later, making kindergarten an optimum time for learning and effective intervention with all children.

When children have appropriately stimulating surroundings, including interaction with responsive caretakers, rapid brain growth occurs during this time; from preschool to kindergarten, the brain grows steadily, increasing from 70 percent to 90 percent of its eventual adult weight (Thatcher et al. 1996). In addition to gains in size, the brain undergoes much reshaping and refining. There is a thickening of the coating of the nerve cells in the brain's cerebral cortex and "pruning" of neural networks that are not being used, allowing active portions of the brain to become more powerful. Such changes enable the child to better meet the particular demands of the environment. Profound changes also occur in the frontal lobes of the cerebral cortex, areas devoted to regulating thought and action.

At about age 5, children have nearly twice as many connections between neurons (synapses) as adults in some brain areas, including the frontal lobes. This overabundance of communication channels supports the brain's "plasticity," or high capacity for learning. It helps ensure that the child will be able to acquire basic human abilities even if some brain areas happen to be damaged. As the child interacts with others and the environment and learning occurs, the synaptic connections of the neurons become increasingly elaborate and committed to specific functions (Huttenlocher 2002; Nelson 2002).

The frontal lobes are important because they govern the inhibition of impulse, orderly memory, and the integration of information—capacities that facilitate reasoning and problem solving, as well as emotional self-regulation. All these skills improve considerably in the kindergarten child.

The interaction of these brain developments and stimulating, supportive environments leads to children's thought patterns becoming more systematic and organized. This is evident in the

way children explore new situations, acquire concepts, respond to directions, play games, approach problems, and carry out everyday activities. By the end of kindergarten, children are more aware of patterns and regularities. They also begin to redefine confusing problems and combine concepts they previously used only alone. Kindergartners begin to recognize event sequences in many ways—as they appear in stories, in the physical world, in biological cycles within the physical world, in daily routines within the classroom, and in larger societal routines.

Kindergartners also demonstrate an emerging awareness of part/whole relationships. This development becomes more evident in the next few years as children's attention to stories and the complex connections between plot lines and characters' emotions as motivating factors grows. This awareness of part/whole relations is also evident in mathematics and science, as in spontaneous comments such as "I see five fish—two blue ones and three yellow ones."

During kindergarten, children's thinking typically becomes less rigidly fixed and egocentric; it better accounts for multiple perspectives, is more flexible, and is beginning to be able to transform ideas and representations (Dunn 1988; Halford & Andrews 2006; Harris 2006). In the physical domain, children can now grasp that the same object or set of objects can look very different depending on the observer's vantage point. In the social domain, children are better able to make inferences about what another person knows or feels. For example, if a child sees someone try to trick someone else, the child might infer that the child being tricked is unaware of what is happening.

In a variety of situations, children begin to see multiple sides of an issue. Unlike preschoolers, who assume that other people see things as they do, 5-year-olds begin to recognize that their own perspective on a situation may differ from someone else's—although this is an emerging ability that should not be expected on a regular basis. They may struggle to predict precisely what it is that someone else sees, but they are not surprised that another's view is different from their own. For example, a child may turn a book around so a friend can see it better. She begins to (but again, will not consistently) recognize that what her father would like as a gift is not what she would like. This awareness reflects an emerging ability to consider more information at one time.

An increase in flexible thinking is evident in other ways, as well. Children can mentally rearrange or transform information—they are less bound by the first thing they see or hear. For example, a kindergartner can figure out a couple of ways to combine blocks to create a structure of a particular shape. Or sometimes children can temporarily put aside their own feelings and be sensitive to the needs of another, especially if that person is a friend or loved one—and if there is no conflict with the child's own needs and desires.

This flexibility of thinking is apparent in geometric, spatial, and mathematical thinking. Children begin to apply visual spatial strategies and mental images to solve problems in the everyday world. Children understand that they can divide things, such as a cookie, so that everyone can have some—one thing becomes many. And they understand that a tangram with ten separate pieces can be returned to its original appearance by putting the pieces together again—many things become one. This idea of applying visual spatial strategies applies to stable objects, such as puzzles and their parts, and to things that move through space. With a bit of exploring, for example, children may be able to predict the expected pathway of a cone-shaped object rolling down an incline. They might discover that shadows are influenced by the orientation of the light source.

A child's skill in using these mental transformations will expand and improve throughout the course of middle childhood, but significant changes begin to appear in kindergarten. Children continue to learn best with hands-on exploration of materials and with repetition.

In comparison with preschoolers, 5- and 6-year-olds are more likely to look for conceptual categories rather than just simple associations. For example, they understand that when they are looking for cereal in the grocery store, they probably will not find it in the dairy aisle. They also have a greater ability to think about their own thinking—that is, to engage in metacognition. To demonstrate, as anyone who has shared a secret with a kindergartner knows, the child is able to recognize (with excitement!) that he knows something that someone else does not know (*Let's surprise Ms. Plum by bringing muffins and juice for her birthday on Friday*). They can reflect on how they know something (*How do you know the plant will wilt if we don't water it all week?*), make connections with other things they've learned (*What does this remind you of that we examined last week?*), and predict and plan for the future (*What instructions should we give Mr. Sweenie to take good care of our pet rabbits during winter break?*).

A description of kindergartners' cognitive development and learning must include at least a brief account of their progress in two domains emphasized in the kindergarten curriculum—mathematics (discussed in this section) and literacy (discussed in "Language and Literacy Development," p. 43).

For each grade the National Council of Teachers of Mathematics has defined key learning goals (termed "curriculum focal points") based on children's abilities and mathematics educators' judgment about what children at that grade—in this case, kindergartners—need to learn to have a strong foundation for continued progress in math (NCTM 2006).

Research in math and literacy has contributed to our knowledge of what children of this age group are capable of learning and doing in these domains. To some extent, typical accomplishments in the kindergarten year reflect the expectations and instructions prevalent in many US schools; they also reflect kindergartners' cognitive and perceptual abilities and their eagerness to learn to read and write and make sense of their world in spatial and numerical ways. Unfortunately, the potential for great gains in academic areas during the kindergarten year are not equally realized by all children. Children from families with low incomes and diverse cultural, linguistic, and racial backgrounds are at particular risk for not advancing in academic areas; as many as one-third of children entering kindergarten are already behind their peers (CCNY 1998). The failure to achieve affects children from middle-class families as well (Zill & West 2001)—when education programs are not high quality, when families are not supported and involved, and when teachers are not well prepared and supported. The achievement gap that may evolve or widen in the kindergarten year distressingly leads to an ever-widening long-term gap in achievement (CCNY 1998).

As described in the following sections, children's advancing reasoning and problem solving, demonstrated in the various curricular areas, is supported by gains in knowledge of the world, attention, and memory.

Reasoning and Representational Thinking

Both brain development and experience contribute to give older children a larger memory span, and thus they are better able to hold in mind and consider, at times, two or more dimensions of an object or event at once (Case 1998; Cowan et al. 1999). Kindergartners' advances in reasoning are initially fragile, and they may revert to earlier and more simplistic ways of thinking, including considering only one dimension at a time (AAAS 2008). Consequently, the kindergarten child's thinking sometimes seems limited and inflexible, and at other times quite advanced.

This move toward more complex thinking shows up in many ways. In everyday activities such as drawing pictures, for example, a 4- or 5-year-old often depicts people and objects separately, ignoring their spatial arrangement. Older kindergartners may be able to coordinate these two aspects so the drawing depicts both the features of objects and the objects' spatial relationship to one another. In creating stories, a similar progression takes place. Younger children focus on only a single character's actions and emotions;

older children can combine two characters' actions and emotions in a single plot (Case & Okamoto 1996).

Because of variations in their experiences, interests, and goals, children display better-developed thinking on some tasks than on others (Sternberg 2002). In this respect, culture is profoundly influential. For example, a child who comes from a cultural group in which children are expected to be quiet and learn through observing adults would have difficulty demonstrating her competence in a classroom where she is expected to speak up and address the adult in reciprocal conversation. But she might well have impressive competence in areas where she has ample experience, such as sorting and counting household items, caring for younger siblings, or collaborating with an adult in preparing a family meal. What is valued as "intelligent" behavior varies considerably from one cultural group to another (Sternberg & Grikorenko 2004).

Self-Regulation and Attention

Self-regulation skills, as previously mentioned, have both emotional and cognitive aspects. One of the most important aspects of self-regulation in the cognitive domain relates to a child's ability to focus attention. The ability to not give in to distraction, to listen to what others are saying, and to focus on a given task for a productive length of time is crucial for success in school (for all ages, not just kindergarten). Self-regulation in kindergarten has been shown to correlate with achievement in math and reading, independent of a child's general level of intelligence (Blair & Razza 2007).

Kindergartners in well-structured and well-supported classrooms can often work for 15 to 20 minutes at a time on a quiet, seated activity (Wood 2007). Their improved ability to focus and manage their attention contributes to transformations in their reasoning. Development of the frontal lobes of the cerebral cortex leads to greater cognitive inhibition—an improved ability, while engaged in a task, to prevent the mind from being distracted and straying to alternative thoughts (Bush, Luu, & Posner 2000). The capacity for cognitive inhibition, which already increases throughout the preschool years, improves dramatically beginning at about age 5 or 6 (Dempster 1993; Harnishfeger 1995; Sameroff & McDonough 1994). This increased ability enables children to focus more intently on the types of tasks they will encounter often in school. Still, kindergartners tend to have a limited attention span compared with older children or adults—unless they are pursuing self-chosen activities that are highly motivating to them. With the support of adults, kindergartners are also increasingly capable of planning; they can think out a short, orderly sequence of actions ahead of time and allocate their attention accordingly (Hudson, Sosa, & Shapiro 1997).

Memory

The combination of brain growth and improved use of memory strategies eventually improve children's ability to recall information. However, kindergartners are not yet good at deliberate use of memory strategies unless teachers help them. When asked to recall items such as a list of toys or groceries, children might rehearse on one occasion but not on another, and even when they do rehearse, their recall rarely improves. At this age, applying a memory strategy initially requires so much effort and attention that children have little attention left for the memory task itself (Schneider 2002). Nonetheless, teachers can help children improve memory skills by prompting the use of strategies such as rehearsing information, organizing it into categories, or simply alerting children to the need to remember something.

Although they show limited memory for unrelated or nonmeaningful information, kindergartners show good memory for information that is meaningful to them (Ely 2005). For example, at about ages 4½ to 5, children can give chronologically organized, detailed, and evaluative accounts of personal experiences, as this kindergartner illustrates: "We went to the lake. Then we fished and waited. I caught a big catfish! Dad cooked it. It was so good we ate it all up!" Increased memory capacity—when combined with teacher-guided opportunities to practice personal storytelling and other skills—is a manifestation of growing cognitive skills.

Promoting Cognitive Development in Kindergarten

To enable all children to thrive academically and to reduce the achievement gap, schools and teachers should implement high-quality curricula and teaching strategies, engage and empower families, and embed teaching and learning in caring, nurturing relationships (CCNY 1998). One study of ethnically diverse families with low incomes showed that increases in family involvement in school predicted improvements in children's literacy and mathematics skills (Dearing, Kreider, & Weiss 2008). It is important for teachers to offer inviting, well-organized classrooms and to establish warm and trusting relationships with children to create the conditions that foster children's thinking abilities. Emotional security frees children to devote energy to the cognitive tasks they encounter in the classroom. Organization of instruction allows for taking advantage of teachable moments in planned and systematic ways (Clements 2001).

Children continue to build on their early knowledge areas, and teachers who are sensitive to what children already know and think can help them refine and add to that base. Often these expanded ideas can be linked to specific curriculum content. For example, learning in science can be linked to children's own ideas about the physical world (Gelman & Brenneman 2004). If a child explains that we sleep "because it's nighttime," the teacher can build on that belief to explore the biological needs and rhythms of humans and other living organisms. Teachers also can help children connect concepts. Children can relate number concepts to geometry, for instance, by counting the sides of shapes or measuring the length of a rug, which strengthens their understanding of mathematics as a coherent *system* (Sarama & Clements 2006). The key for teachers is to understand the concepts themselves and also to understand how each child makes sense of the world and what interests him.

One way to support cognitive development is by asking children thought-provoking questions (*How do you get to the cafeteria from here?* or *How could we remember how many we have?*) and making comments (*I wonder how many big blocks it would take to cover the rug* or *Our plant didn't grow as much this week as before; I wonder if we did something differently*) that encourage children to think and reflect. Questions might focus on descriptions of events and changes in the physical and social world or on thought processes themselves, since kindergartners now have some capacity for metacognition. These questions encourage "thinking about thinking," directing children's attention to awareness of how they know something and how they might remember or solve a problem.

Teachers also promote cognitive development when they encourage children to record and document their knowledge by using various representational methods, such as words and gestures, writing, and drawing and by making diagrams, graphs, and models. Children are most highly motivated when sharing a message that is important to them. In such instances, children are likely to notice when their message is not getting across and perhaps grasp that it needs to be modified, though they are not yet skilled in knowing how to change the message to communicate more effectively. An important focus in the kindergarten year is enhancing children's understanding of the many ways that we use representations to communicate and share knowledge. A teacher might invite children to describe through words or actions something seen on a field trip to the zoo, create a page for a memory album, and build a model of the zoo (Golbeck 2006).

As with children of all ages, kindergartners learn from their interactions not only with adults but also with peers. Children frequently test their ideas with peers and learn a lot from the reactions they receive. Sometimes the child's peers understand her and respond positively to her ideas; sometimes they do not. Teachers greatly promote kindergartners' cognitive development by recognizing the value of peer interactions for kindergartners' cognitive growth and by designing learning environments and planning experiences that encourage children to interact and collaborate.

Finally, children need to be able to make choices. Choices empower children to be active thinkers who challenge themselves. Teachers who offer children choices do not give up control, nor are they passive. Rather, they look for ways to be active participants in children's learning processes while ensuring that the children are also active and engaged. Overall, the kindergarten year requires teachers to provide a nuanced balance for optimal cognitive development. On the one hand, there should be plenty of play, child choice, and verbal interaction; on the other, there should be adult-guided activities that are engaging to children and adaptable to their varying readiness. Kindergartners learn best under conditions in which adults guide and support their active efforts, with a gradual and measured introduction of more formal lessons.

It is also worth noting that most kindergarten-age brain growth occurs in the course of everyday experiences as adults offer young children age-appropriate play materials and stimulating, enjoyable daily routines and social interaction: a shared meal, a picture book to discuss, a song to sing, or an outing at the park or another type of field trip. The resulting growth readies the brain for later, more advanced brain development, such as that necessary for reading comprehension, solving mathematical problems, or investigating scientific hypotheses (Huttenlocher 2002; Shonkoff & Phillips 2000). Hurrying a young child into mastering skills that depend on extensive training—such as advanced reading and comprehension, musical performance, or sports—runs the risk of overwhelming the brain's neural circuits and reducing its sensitivity to the experiences needed for healthy brain development (Bruer 1999).

Language and Literacy Development

From infancy on, most children learn from the adults around them that listening and talking are enjoyable activities that often help them in getting what they need. Early on, they learn how to use language to communicate what they want or need and how to take turns in conversation. By kindergarten age, they have learned extraordinary amounts. Not only do they listen to conversation (and music) for pleasure, but they also listen and speak (and sing) with attention. They know the sounds of their home language and can identify sounds in their environment.

Kindergartners become increasingly knowledgeable about the features of language. For example, they have a good sense of the concept of *word*. When an adult reading a story stops to ask, "What was the last word I said?" children almost always answer correctly (Karmiloff-Smith et al. 1996). They know sentence structure and use correct grammatical structures most of the time in increasingly complex ways (Seefeldt 2005). They show awareness of the need for "style shifting" in language use; for example, they use different language in the classroom than on the playground (Strickland 2006).

Most children of this age can maintain a topic of discussion over many speaker turns with both peers and adults (Tager-Flusberg 2005). In addition to being capable of such conversations, many kindergartners will also speak up in small groups and before the whole class. They ask and answer questions and like to both explain and have things explained to them. Further, their communication becomes more precise; for example, they are better able to describe one object among a group of similar objects in a way that distinguishes it.

Kindergartners know the meanings of a substantial and growing number of words. In the early grades, children learn about 20 new words each day (Anglin 1993). Of course, these gains depend on being in language-rich environments where children are exposed to a reasonably wide range of words; where they hear and participate in rich conversations; and where books, stories, and other forms of written expression are valued and enjoyed. A 6-year-old's vocabulary

is typically about 10,000 words (Bloom 1998)—again, if he is exposed to a language-rich environment. Because of large socioeconomic differences in language used in the home, some children begin kindergarten with far more limited knowledge of language and word meanings (Hart & Risley 1995; Snow, Burns, & Griffin 1998), and the gap continues to widen over time.

Oral language is the foundation for literacy learning, which also begins in infancy and not in kindergarten, as is commonly thought; language and literacy develop in tandem (Strickland 2006). Two things make a big difference in children's progress in these two areas: knowledge about the world and knowledge about print and books (RAND 2002). In particular, children advance in language and literacy areas with shared adult–child reading experiences in which adults (parents and teachers) explore the idea and uses of print, have conversations with children about a book's content and meaning, and convey the value of books for the pleasure, information, and empowerment they bring.

Also essential for becoming a skilled reader is a solid base of knowledge and conceptual development. Not only for the sake of improving reading comprehension but for wider curricular purposes as well, teachers work to expand children's content and vocabulary knowledge by providing interesting objects, nonfiction and fiction books, and encounters with the broader world (e.g., field trips and virtual field trips that are now possible through technology). Meaningful projects and investigations enable children to expand and use their knowledge, as well as gain research skills from searching books, asking adult

Focus on Kindergartners

experts, or using the Internet. Teachers focus children's attention by asking questions that encourage children to observe carefully, make comparisons, or review their past experiences.

One ability strongly linked to mastering reading is phonological awareness (Whitehurst 1999); that is, noticing the sounds of spoken language—speech sounds and rhythms, rhyme and other sound similarities, and, at the highest level, phonemes, the smallest units of speech that make a difference in communication (hence the term *phonemic awareness*). Phonemic awareness does not occur automatically for most children, but they acquire it when teachers purposefully support it and provide the assistance that each child needs (which varies considerably from one individual to another). Phonics, which is not the same as phonological or phonemic awareness, is a system of teaching how letters and combinations of letters correspond to sounds of spoken language and is typically introduced in kindergarten or first grade. At around age 5, children start making great strides in phonological awareness (this continues until about age 8)—an awareness also reflected in kindergartners' increasing sensitivity to incorrect pronunciation (Foy & Mann 2003).

By the time they enter kindergarten, children who have had quality literacy experiences in the preschool years have acquired some basic knowledge about print. For example, they are likely to understand that print performs a variety of functions, recognize print in the environment, distinguish separate words, and realize that English print is read left to right and top to bottom. They know letters by name and have begun to connect some letters with sounds. They are ready to go farther in mastering the alphabetic principle (i.e., the systematic relationship between letters and sounds).

Continuing in a print-rich and conversation-rich environment, kindergartners often make great strides in their reading skills over the course of the year. They become more comfortable and interactive with books and read-aloud times and often enjoy partner reading, where more able readers pair up with beginning readers (as long as both play an active role) (Wood 2007). They tend to do best in phonics groups that include others at similar skill levels, however.

They also like it when adults read aloud to them, and they benefit from hearing predictable books—books with few words, a good deal of repetition, and pictures that reinforce the story. These types of books help them practice decoding words. Kindergartners have generally learned that books have titles, authors, and illustrators and that pictures can convey ideas but cannot be read (Strickland & Schickedanz 2004). They begin to develop the concept of *story structure* and even come up with their own theme stories with classmates—favorite themes include families, pets, babies, school, seasons or holidays, and of course, themselves (Seefeldt 2005; Wood 2007). Books aside, kindergartners have fun with their newfound abilities to understand some signs, posters, labels, and charts.

As reading comprehension and fine motor skills progress, kindergartners also move forward in writing skills. Engaging children in writing helps them learn about print and the written words that they will increasingly learn to read and spell. Further, when children write—even at a very basic level—they begin thinking of themselves as writers, and this idea is a powerful catalyst to their advancing in literacy and self-expression. As young children experiment with writing, teachers have many opportunities to convey basic information about print. Kindergarten children recognize and can produce recognizable letters and words, usually writing first in uppercase letters. They often tell stories through the use of drawings, incorporating print into the drawing or painting to express their ideas.

They might begin the writing process by using a beginning consonant letter to stand for a word in their stories, such as to label a drawing (e.g., "F" for *family*) or to string together to compose a sentence (e.g., "HIMH" for *here is my house*). They are likely to use developmental or emergent word spellings as well, showing attempts to associate sounds with letters; for example, writing "kak" for *cake* or "bfl" for *butterfly*. More and more, they are eager to learn to spell words correctly and often ask teachers and peers how to spell words as they write. Kindergartners progress to more conventional spelling with experience (Seefeldt 2005). They usually write with irregular spacing between their letters and words.

Overall, there are two paramount goals for kindergarten teachers in promoting children's literacy in effective and appropriate ways. The first is to inculcate a solid familiarity with the structure and uses of print, basic phonemic awareness, and ability to recognize and write most letters of the alphabet. The second is to instill interest in and reliance on print, since children's future learning depends in large part on their ability to get knowledge from books and other print sources (Burns, Griffin, & Snow 1999).

Dual Language Learners

In 2011, nearly 21 percent of US residents reported speaking a language other than English at home (US Census Bureau 2013). Spanish accounts for almost 62 percent of the non-English languages, but more than 460 languages are spoken by dual language learners nationwide. The dramatic rise in ethnic and linguistic diversity in the United States means more and more children in kindergarten and other early childhood programs speak a language other than English as their first language. Because many consider kindergarten the beginning of "real school," the language issue tends to become more critical at kindergarten age for families of dual language learners and their teachers.

Young children are adept at learning more than one language, but the process of learning two (or more) languages simultaneously may look different and occur at different rates than for children learning only one language. Many children learning a second language exhibit a silent period, in which they stop speaking almost altogether in order to focus intently on listening to the new language they are working to acquire. Children (and adults) using more than one language sometimes use words and phrases of both languages in an intermingled way. Neither the silent period nor mingling languages for a time is an indication of confusion or a problem, but rather typically indicates active learning and navigation, often savvy navigation, between the two or more languages.

Compared with those learning only in English, children with limited proficiency in English are more likely to experience long-term academic success when they receive systematic, deliberate exposure to English combined with

ongoing opportunities to learn important concepts in their home language (Thomas & Collier 2002). If English replaces the home language and children do not have an opportunity to continue to learn in the language they know, their future linguistic, conceptual, and academic development in English is at risk (Espinosa 2008).

A national longitudinal study found that dual language learners who attend English-only mainstream programs beginning in kindergarten show large decreases in reading and math achievement by grade 5 and are more at risk for dropping out of school when compared with their peers who participated in language support programs such as bilingual education (Thomas & Collier 2002).

Promoting Language and Literacy Development in Kindergarten

Children's language development is profoundly affected by early conversational and literacy experiences, and kindergartners vary greatly in such experiences (Hart & Risley 2003). For example, children's exposure to hearing books read aloud to them—an important predictor of children's language development—varies depending on the quantity of books in the home, the literacy level of adults in the family and their interest in reading, access to a children's library, and so forth. Before starting kindergarten, a child from an average middle-class family has been read to for a total of 1,000 hours, whereas a child from an average family living in poverty has been read to for only 25 hours (Neuman 2003). As a result, kindergartners from families with chronically low incomes often arrive at the kindergarten door with a disadvantage based on their different experiences. As an illustration, their vocabularies are, on average, one-fourth the size of their middle-class peers' (Lee & Burkam 2002).

In light of the wide variation in language, conversation, and literacy experiences with which children enter kindergarten, it is important to note that language-rich (and literacy-rich) kindergarten environments are crucial for narrowing gaps and reducing children's chances of academic failure. There is a great deal teachers can do to foster language skills, which includes listening and speaking, using vocabulary to build comprehension, and cultivating awareness of the sounds of language.

First, a word on teaching children whose home language is not English. There is a great need for more bilingual teachers who can promote both English and children's home languages. However, in many contemporary classrooms teachers do not speak the language(s) used by children in their classrooms—and often these are numerous (Ray, Bowman, & Robbins 2006). This mismatch could be less than ideal in supporting children's language development, but it doesn't have to be. The critical issue is the teacher's attitude and effort toward promoting dual-language development.

When the atmosphere in the classroom and the school is one of valuing each child's home language, children tend to be less inhibited and can thrive in their language development and learning (Strickland 2002). Teachers support the language development of dual language learners when they take the time to show appreciation for the child's home language by, for example, correctly pronouncing the child's name, learning at least a few words in the home language, celebrating the unique contributions of the child's culture, and playing music in the child's home language.

Teachers can also add to the richness of their own curriculum by (1) introducing nursery rhymes, songs, or vocabulary in the child's languages to the entire class, (2) enlisting the resources and members of the community, and (3) engaging the parents of dual language learners and incorporating their talents, skills, and interests into the curriculum (Espinosa 2007).

Demonstrating respect for the language, as well as for cultural traditions, values, and preferred interaction styles, sends a clear message to children that using words or phrases in more than one language is welcomed. It also sends a message to families: not only are their culture and language valued, but building language skills and vocabulary in more than one language benefits—and does not harm—children's development and engenders later academic success (Espinosa 2007, 2008).

Teachers might promote language development for dual language learners through the use of pictures and props, physical demonstration (either pretend or actual) of actions and requests, and pairing words heard in stories with words written on a chalkboard. Explicitly teaching reading comprehension will help children as they learn science, mathematics, social studies, and other subject matter areas. Teachers should be sure to help with comprehension by summarizing what was heard; using brief, simple explanations of new vocabulary words; modeling how to think out loud (*This sounds confusing to me. Let's read it again*); and asking questions to see how much children have understood and learned (Colorín Colorado 2007).

For all kindergarten children, principles of developmentally appropriate practice are especially salient in the area of language development. For example, teachers need to plan for and provide a balance between adult-guided and child-guided experiences in the kindergarten day. Opportunities to learn and practice listening and speaking skills should occur in a variety of formats. At whole group time, for instance, the teacher asks several children who have worked on a project together to tell the others about a problem they encountered and how they solved it. A collaborative small group investigation of worms promotes children's language as well as their science knowledge and reasoning. As an individual activity, the teacher makes available a variety of audiobooks for children to listen to when they wish.

It is important for teachers to combine language learning with other curricular areas, such as mathematics, science, and physical development. Language gains will influence comprehension of these other areas, and knowledge of other areas will enhance vocabulary and communication skills.

And last, teaching language development and learning should occur through a scaffolded approach, in which teachers model good listening and communication skills, peers work together and teach each other, and the schedule allows for times of guided, independent practice.

Strickland (2006) suggests various strategies and activities teachers might use to promote language and literacy learning. Reading aloud and then setting aside time for children to respond to what they have heard and fostering

extended conversations about the story or related personal experiences encourage listening and speaking skills as well as comprehension. Explaining new vocabulary words introduced by the book is a good way to enhance that comprehension as well as build vocabulary.

Enhancement of language skills and vocabulary knowledge also occurs when teachers provide materials and opportunity for children to engage in dramatic play. Having various thematic topics for class discussion and study (e.g., transportation, how things grow) can help organize children's thoughts and vocabulary, as well. Phonemic awareness skills can be fostered by listening for and making rhymes, listening to similarities in the beginning sounds of words, and counting the number of syllables in a word. A literacy learning center in the classroom should not only have plenty of books but also include audiobooks to be listened to with headphones.

The creative, effective ways to scaffold reading and writing experiences for kindergartners are limitless for intentional teachers. Reading to children, facilitating discussion about book content, and providing opportunities for children to respond to what they have heard is a foundation for enhancing kindergartners' love of reading and literature. Repeated readings of favorites allow for deepened understanding of the events in the story as well as the vocabulary and concepts conveyed. Teachers can compose charts or lists stemming from a book or topic of study, with the children helping by dictating their ideas. And teachers can use the opportunity to comment on conventions of written language, such as capital letters and punctuation. They can foster letter recognition, phonemic awareness, and understanding of sound/letter correspondence by focusing on children's names, naming letters in books that teach the alphabet, making rhymes, and identifying beginning sounds of words. Having children dictate or write stories and illustrate them is a rich activity that gives children the sense of being writers.

Regardless of the specific activity or strategy, good teachers will be promoting language skills throughout the kindergarten day. It is best to differentiate instruction—that is, to allow children at different levels to gain new knowledge and skills within the same lesson or activity. Moving from the easy to the difficult and the known to the unknown through a range of experiences and opportunities ensures that all children will make progress in their language skills, regardless of where they start (Strickland 2006).

Easing the Transition Into and Out of Kindergarten

For many children, two of their most dramatic transitions occur around kindergarten—first participation in a group program and, at the end of kindergarten, entry into the primary grades. In addition, many kindergartners also transition within the school day to an after-school program or an out-of-home caregiver. When all adults caring for a child—teachers, family members, care providers—work together to create positive, communicative relationships, transitions can be smooth for the child (and adults) instead of stressful.

The two major points of transition—entering kindergarten and leaving kindergarten—are discussed below.

Transitioning Into Kindergarten

About 56 percent of 3- and 4-year-old children in the United States are enrolled in a preschool program of some kind, whether a private setting, a community-based organization, Head Start, or a public school prekindergarten class (NCES 2008). This means that almost as many children—44 percent—enter kindergarten without having a preschool experience to prepare them in some way to participate and learn in the kindergarten group setting.

The transition experience for all participants—the child, the family, and the teacher—will differ depending not only on the child's individual characteristics and cultural experiences but also on his or her experience or lack of experience in a preschool setting. For adults and children alike, change is stressful. But for young children who have limited experience and few well-developed coping strategies, change can be very upsetting. Adult relationships (between teachers and families and among teachers) will make all the difference in how children experience the transition.

The home–school connection. When children enter kindergarten, they essentially become citizens of two cultures—home and school. They must learn to navigate the new etiquette, rules, and conditions of the classroom, which are different from those at home, regardless of ethnicity or cultural background (Lam & Pollard 2006). As active, participatory learners, they learn to make sense of and adapt to the new environment in creative and dynamic ways, some children more quickly and easily than others. The amount of stress and the time required to make a successful adjustment can be lessened significantly when teachers and administrators plan and work together with parents to make adjusting as easy as possible for the child.

Communication is critical, including about cultural issues such as the interplay between the values and expectations at home and those of the school. Today, as most teachers know, cultural variety is the American norm. Children develop and learn within a cultural context, using that context to understand the world, what behavior is appropriate, and how to show what they know and can do.

Children can most easily show their accomplishments in environments with which they are comfortable and familiar. They experience easier transitions and feel more successful when the skills, abilities, and understandings they construct in their family and community are congruent with the expecta-

tions of the classroom. Likewise, families will feel better prepared and more able to support their child if they know what is expected—within the context of and in relation to what happens at home—and that their own traditions and expectations are valued (Rhodes, Enz, & LaCount 2006).

If children's developmental accomplishments, which are culturally bound events, go unrecognized, their adjustment to school may be very difficult. For example, a child may be very competent and effective at communicating in the home language but not yet proficient in English, and the teacher may fail to recognize the child's language competence. On the other hand, confidence and self-esteem can blossom when the teacher recognizes the child's competence and looks for evidence of it in the classroom—in either language.

When children enter school, their self-esteem comes to include perceptions of their families by teachers and others at school. Having the sense that teachers respect and value their family strengthens a child's sense of self-esteem and competence. Fully knowing children and responding to their individuality are possible only if parents are active partners in the education process. This informed responsiveness happens when teachers and parents communicate frequently and respectfully and parents feel welcome in the school at all times. If children's culture and background are rejected—or worse, treated as a deficit or somehow less worthy than the primary culture of the classroom—children's healthy development and capacity to learn face a serious threat.

Even when cultural cues are very similar between the home and school environment, there are myriad differences between the culture of a classroom environment—the rules, values, and expectations of that group setting—and that of a home—the rules, values, and expectations unique to each family. Families usually feel as anxious as their children do about school transitions, and children sense their stress. If parents feel less anxious, then their children are likely to face the change with more confidence and enthusiasm.

Transitions tend to be more successful when teachers and families develop respectful, reciprocal relationships founded on good communication, and then they can work together to help children negotiate the changes. Teachers might reach out to each family through visits, phone calls, or emails, as well as with resources such as brochures and newsletters in each family's home language that help families know what to expect (Duda & Minick 2006). In these two-way relationships, teachers tell parents about plans, expectations, and observations, and they seek out parents' concerns, hopes, and goals for their children. Good teacher–family relationships have endless benefits for children, one of which is making the transition into school easier.

The program-to-program (preschool-to-kindergarten) connection. Differences in program content, teaching strategies, and expectations of children between preschool and kindergarten settings are not only normal but desirable. Programs *should* vary depending on the age of children and the needs and interests of individual children and families. Nevertheless, when the kindergarten program is developmentally appropriate, children's transitions from preschool (and later to a developmentally appropriate first grade) will be smoother and more successful.

The preschool and kindergarten settings may differ starkly with respect to the length of the day, class size, and the instructional style or room setup. The greater the disparity in developmental expectations and teaching practices between preschool and kindergarten, the more potential stress there is for the child making the transition. When kindergarten is a lot more like second or third grade, with desks and workbooks, than it is like preschool, with blocks and dramatic play props, the change is so sharp that many children have difficulty adapting. When such a stark contrast exists, it is not the case that the preschool teacher should introduce inappropriate academic instruction to help her group of children "get ready" for kindergarten, but rather that all teachers involved should work to better align the programs (Pianta & Kraft-Sayre 2003).

This is not solely a teacher responsibility, however; administrators at both the preschool and kindergarten levels have a responsibility to align programs and to ensure they support teachers in implementing developmentally appropriate curricula. Directors and principals should support teachers in designing environments that allow children to choose some activities, in having materials and space available to allow for healthy growth across all domains of development and learning, and in using practices that benefit young children, such as positive guidance, appropriate individual and group instruction, and good daily transition practices.

At the teacher level, classroom-to-classroom connections are very important. Too often there is an expectation that responsibility for a smooth transition into kindergarten lies with preschool or Head Start teachers—that they should make sure children are "ready to learn" when they enter kindergarten. It is equally the responsibility of the kindergarten teacher to communicate with those teachers and administrators to smooth the way.

For example, kindergarten teachers might invite local Head Start teachers, children, and parents to visit their classrooms to observe, meet the teacher and current students, and ask questions. If children are coming from too many programs to realistically arrange such visits, the kindergarten teacher could develop a letter for the preschool teachers, outlining kindergarten activities, the structure of a typical day, how routines are handled, favorite songs or books, and perhaps include classroom and playground photos.

Such cooperation is advantageous, not only for the child but also for the kindergarten teacher, because children are better prepared and less fearful. Also, teachers have a chance to learn from each other, enhance their classrooms, broaden professional contacts, and feel good about meeting the developmental needs of the children in their care. Transitions will be easiest when there is good communication between preschool and kindergarten administrators and between kindergarten and preschool teachers.

More teacher-initiated activities to ease the transition into kindergarten can be adapted from the activities discussed below.

Transitioning Out of Kindergarten

Many kindergartners move on to a first grade where expectations are radically different from what they have experienced—so different that the transition

Focus on Kindergartners

is sometimes called "hitting the wall." In the face of such a drastic shift, children who previously loved going to school may quickly lose their enthusiasm for school and learning. They may become anxious and intimidated. Such a turn of events is distressing and problematic because the adjustment from kindergarten to first grade can have long-lasting effects on school success (Entwisle & Alexander 1998) as well as happiness, so a good transition is important. Kindergarten teachers can play an important role in helping children better adjust.

Downer, Driscoll, and Pianta (2006) explain the value of taking a "developmental/ecological" approach to the transition, as compared with a skills-only approach. In a skills-only approach, teachers focus only on the child's current abilities and skills, such as the number of letters she can write at the end of kindergarten. In this view, the major considerations in determining the child's readiness are age and certain skills—to the exclusion of program quality, instructional practices, or the teacher–child relationship.

In contrast, the developmental/ecological approach considers all the interconnected factors that influence development and learning, including the family, school, peers, and community in which the child lives. It acknowledges that young children learn in uneven and episodic ways; a kindergartner may know or be able to do something one day and not the next, or may be able to do it at school but not at home or vice versa. It considers not only the child's readiness to move on to first grade but also the school's readiness to work with each new child who enters its classrooms, regardless of the child's skills or background. Schools that take a developmental/ecological approach understand that communication and information sharing are instrumental in supporting children and families in making the transition to first grade.

Communication and information sharing can take many forms and should occur between teachers and families and also among teachers (or among administrators). Downer, Driscoll, and Pianta (2006) provide many ideas for easing the transition. For example, kindergarten teachers can prepare parents and other family members by hosting family nights, arranging meetings about what to expect in the coming school year, providing transition packets or handouts, and organizing back-to-school nights at both the beginning and end of kindergarten as an orientation about expectations. Teachers should initiate communication with families and should be responsive when families contact them.

Kindergarten teachers can establish connections with first grade teachers by observing the first grade classroom to learn about the curriculum and routines, discussing and agreeing on a common assessment tool, and meeting together to share information about individual children. This knowledge allows teachers to better prepare children for the new environment.

Positive, honest comments that get children excited about the new opportunities and challenges that await them in primary school are appropriate and helpful. Children need time to talk about their feelings, and they need sensitive adults to listen and help prepare them for the exciting and positive changes that are a natural part of growing up (Hyson 2004).

The kindergarten teachers might also, time and resources permitting, arrange a group visit to a first grade classroom, have children practice first grade behaviors or routines, invite first-graders to read to the kindergarten children, arrange a joint summer activity, and encourage their children to ask questions about what they've seen or heard. They also can reassure children that they will stay in touch by sending letters or making visits in the next year, which will greatly hearten these kindergartners, who likely have become warmly attached to their teachers.

With all that kindergarten (and other) teachers have to do, these ideas are not meant to add to an already full plate. Rather, they are meant to increase simplicity from the continuity that should emerge and to allow for deeper relationship building with the children, which will strengthen and make easier every aspect of implementing the curriculum, from emotional to academic domains.

Using these strategies, with a particular focus on communication, should lessen the negative impact of transition and perhaps even make transition points times of joy and celebration.

Examples of K–1 Transition Practices

Activity	How	When
Family–School Connections		
Contact families during the first few days of kindergarten and first grade	Telephone calls, emails, visits	First week of kindergarten and first grade
Maintain periodic contact with the family	Telephone calls, emails, notes, newsletters, blogs, visits	Ongoing
Encourage family participation in home learning activities	Materials and/or instructions sent home	Ongoing, particularly during the summer between grades
Encourage family participation in the classroom and at school events	Telephone calls, emails, notes, newsletters, blogs, visits	Ongoing, particularly at the start of the school year
Conduct regular family meetings at school	Lunches, family nights	Ongoing and at regular intervals
Conduct family meetings about transition issues	Family nights, workshops	During kindergarten spring, summer, and first grade fall
Coordinate information sharing about individual children between the families and teachers	Conferences	During kindergarten spring or summer
Create newsletters and resource materials	Transition packets, tips, handouts	Ongoing
Conduct parent orientation after the beginning of kindergarten and first grade	Back-to-school nights	First two weeks of kindergarten and first grade
Child–School Connections		
Establish a connection between the kindergarten child and the first grade teacher	Visits to the first grade classroom by the child or visits by first grade teacher to the kindergarten classroom	During kindergarten spring
Create a connection between the child and the first grade using special school functions	School fairs, assemblies, playground parties	During kindergarten spring and summer

Activity	How	When
Have children practice first grade rituals in kindergarten	Practice behaviors, sing songs, read stories	During kindergarten spring
Incorporate kindergarten activities into the first grade year	Read a favorite book, introduce similar activities	During first grade fall
Encourage kindergarten teachers to stay in contact with former students	Letters, school visits	During first grade fall
Peer Connections		
Establish peer connections within the kindergarten class	Purposeful classroom assignments	During the summers before kindergarten and first grade
Establish peer connections outside of school	Play dates	Ongoing, particularly during the summer
Establish connections with peers who will be in first grade	Activities with other kindergartens	Ongoing, particularly during kindergarten spring and summer
Establish kindergarten peer connections with first grade peers	School visits, summer school	During kindergarten spring and summer
Classroom–Classroom Connections		
Share curriculum activities and classroom routines between kindergarten and first grade	Teachers observe each others' classrooms and hold regular meetings	Ongoing
Agree on a common assessment tool to describe individual children and their families	Meet to decide what information will be helpful to both teachers	Ongoing

Note: This table is intended to serve as a flexible menu from which teachers can pick and choose transition activities that fit their situation. In fact, teachers are encouraged to be creative and add their own ideas to this list as they build a developmentally and ecologically responsive transition plan.

Source: Downer, Driscoll & Pianta (2006, 156–7)

Developmentally Appropriate Examples to Consider

4

The framework of developmentally

appropriate practice derives from what the early childhood field knows from research and experience about

how children develop and learn. Major points from this knowledge base are highlighted in the position statement and summarized in the overview in Chapter 3. As no learning tool clarifies understanding better than examples, the chart that follows presents many examples of practices to consider.

The chart addresses developmentally appropriate practice in five areas important in the teacher's role: creating a caring community of learners, teaching to enhance development and learning, planning curriculum to achieve important goals, assessing children's development and learning, and establishing reciprocal relationships with families. The set of examples offered here is not exhaustive, and the goal is not to describe best practice comprehensively. We have tried to capture major aspects of practice that one sees in excellent kindergarten classrooms and, by contrast, in those kindergartens that in some respects have not achieved a high level of quality. Neither is the aim to issue a prescriptive formula to be rigidly followed. Instead, the examples are meant to encourage readers to reflect on their practice. Establishing a habit of thoughtful reflection is essential in working with young children because of their varying family backgrounds, preferences, and needs.

In the chart's left column, under the heading "Developmentally Appropriate," are examples of practices consistent with available research and that most in the field agree promote young children's optimal learning and development. The examples in the "In Contrast" column are intended to aid reflection by helping readers see clearly the kinds of things that well-intentioned adults

This chapter was first published in *Developmentally Appropriate Practice in Early Childhood Programs Serving Children From Birth Through Age 8* (Copple & Bredekamp 2009).

might do but that are not likely to serve children well. Many of the "In Contrast" examples are very prevalent in early childhood settings. A few of those practices are dangerous or would cause children lasting damage. Others are unlikely to harm children significantly but also are less likely to promote their optimal development. Sometimes context affects whether a practice should be used or adapted.

Where they appear, the comments sections expand on the practice examples presented in the chart cells above them. Some of the comments speak to cultural factors to consider when determining what practices to use. Other comments elaborate on a practice that is briefly described in a column, and some indicate the research finding on which it is based.

Finally, most of the examples are phrased as descriptions of what teachers do or fail to do. For the "In Contrast" examples, however, that wording is not meant to imply that deficient or questionable practices are necessarily teachers' fault. Most teachers are working hard and doing their best—but are often constrained by very challenging circumstances, including large class size, limited resources, and administrative requirements. The hope of this chapter is to help them in their efforts.

Developmentally appropriate	In contrast

Creating a Caring Community of Learners

Fostering Positive Relationships

Developmentally appropriate	In contrast
Teachers are warm, caring, and responsive. They are encouraging to children and respectful to their families. They come to know children well and make reaching out to families a priority.	○ Teachers do not see the importance of forming relationships with children and families. Or large class sizes make it very difficult for teachers to know children and families well. ○ Teachers devote time and attention to those children who present challenging behaviors, while others are overlooked. Some children are repeatedly singled out for discipline. Others receive little attention because they are quiet or speak limited English.
Teachers model positive interaction with others and encourage prosocial behavior. All children in the class are provided opportunities to get to know and work with each other, and friendships are encouraged. Teachers actively involve children in conflict resolution.	○ Classrooms are managed rigidly with little opportunity for interaction. Children who need assistance forming friendships are not given teacher support. Teasing and rejection in the classroom go unchecked, and procedures are not in place to deal with bullying. ○ Teachers rely heavily on a directive approach to classroom conflicts rather than helping children learn conflict resolution skills. Adults typically react after the fact but do not give thought to preventive measures that would reduce conflict.

Creating a Caring Community of Learners (cont.)

Fostering Positive Relationships (cont.)

Teachers include all children in the social aspects of the classroom. For example, children with special needs and children with limited social skills are provided with resources and encouragement. Teachers act to promote a sense of positive self-identity for all children in the classroom.

○ Children who need assistance interacting with others lack support, resulting in social isolation. Interaction with children who have special needs is largely left to specialists.

Teachers design all classroom activities to allow for the full participation of all children, including those who are not fluent in English.

○ Dual language learners cannot understand or take part in some classroom activities because teachers fail to make modifications or provide assistance to make their full participation possible.

Comments on fostering positive relationships:

—Supporting social and emotional growth is one of the most important aspects of the kindergarten year, yet it is sometimes overshadowed by curricular goals and the need to maintain order in the classroom. The capacity to form and sustain positive social relationships is crucial for social development and overall success in school (Bronson 2006). Children who are neglected or rejected by peers are negatively affected academically as well as socially and emotionally.

—When teachers form warm and caring relationships with children, they in turn help to foster greater prosocial behavior. And when children are able to form positive relationships with peers, their overall attitudes toward school and learning improve.

Building Classroom Community

Teachers act to create a cohesive community of learners by establishing common ground in the classroom. Children have opportunities to act as leaders and helpers with specific tasks; all children are given a chance to participate and are drawn into class activities in a variety of ways. Class meetings are used to solve and prevent problems and provide a forum for discussion.

○ The classroom environment and tone are rigid, and the organization (or disorganization) of the classroom limits children's interaction with one another. Children are required to stay in their seats throughout much of the day.

A variety of opportunities for peer interaction are offered throughout the day and throughout the week. Children work with partners as well as in small and whole group situations. Teachers encourage peer-to-peer scaffolding and assistance when possible.

○ Teachers rely heavily on whole group settings, with children remaining at their places. There is little opportunity for peer interaction.

○ Teachers do not encourage children to work problems out independently or with peers.

Creating a Caring Community of Learners (cont.)

Building Classroom Community (cont.)

Teachers respect the diversity of the classroom community, providing activities and initiating discussions that explore the cultures and languages represented in both the class and the larger society. The class explores similarities and differences among people in ways that engender respect and appreciation without singling out individual children. The environment promotes all children's positive self-identity, including cultural identity.

○ Diversity in the classroom is ignored, as is cultural variety in the larger society. Teachers do not make an effort to avoid presenting stereotypes in the classroom and do not adequately intervene when teasing or rejection occur. No thought is given to fostering positive self-identity.

○ Diversity is addressed but in ways that single out individual children in the classroom as representative of entire cultures or groups. This leads children to see themselves as outsiders to the class as a whole.

Teachers promote children's sense of community involvement beyond their classroom—in the school or center as a whole, the neighborhood, or town/city. For example, children make a sign to alert the other classes in the building about an upcoming event, collect clothing for a local shelter, take walks in the neighborhood, and note what shops and services are available to the local community.

○ No effort is made to build a sense of the group as a community or to link classroom matters to those of the larger community and society.

Comments on building classroom community:

—A climate of respect for all members of the classroom community is crucial for children's well-being in kindergarten. In such an environment, all children feel accepted and have a sense of belonging. Conversely, when children insult or reject others, not only are they devaluing those they reject, they also are not learning the important prosocial skills they need to function and succeed in school and in society.

—Providing opportunities for collaboration and learning from one another strengthens a sense of the classroom as community when children see their impact on the group as a whole. And when activities reflect the diversity of the homes, neighborhoods, and daily lives of the class, all children increase their awareness and appreciation of differing cultures and abilities. Children learn to recognize that they can enjoy and work with others from many backgrounds.

Teaching to Enhance Development and Learning

Environment and Schedule

Developmentally appropriate	In contrast
Teachers carefully plan the physical layout of the classroom, providing several discrete areas in the room where children can interact with peers and materials. If children have desks, they are grouped together to form small tables or circles.	○ Teachers give insufficient thought to the physical environment of the classroom. Desks often are set up in rows, limiting children's interaction with peers.
Teachers and assistants provide a safe environment and attentive supervision.	○ Supervision is lax. Health care personnel are not stationed at the school at all times.
	○ Teachers are overly cautious in the classroom, restricting children's activities. Teachers and aides often help children with tasks they could do or could learn to do on their own instead of challenging children to learn new skills.
Teachers foster a learning environment that encourages exploration, initiative, positive peer interaction, and cognitive growth. They choose materials that comfortably challenge children's skills. The classroom includes spaces for children to keep their work and personal belongings; a place for group meetings; a variety of spaces for working, such as learning centers and tables of different sizes; a comfortable library area and other quiet places for independent work or conversation with friends; places to store materials; and displays of children's work.	○ The environment is disorderly, with little structure or predictability. Consequently, children's behavior is frantic or disengaged. The noise level is stressful for children and adults, making it hard to focus or have a conversation.
	○ The arrangement of the environment severely limits children's opportunities to pursue engaging learning experiences. For example, children generally have to ask teachers for materials rather than finding materials readily accessible.
	○ The environment, materials, and experiences reflect only a single culture or in other respects provide too little variety, interest, or choice for children (e.g., all games are at one level of difficulty).
The daily schedule includes periods of activity and movement and also quiet and restful times. Half-day kindergarten includes a morning snack, and full-day kindergarten includes a morning and afternoon snack as well as lunch.	○ Children are bustled from one activity to the next with little downtime and frequently become overtired, overstimulated, and distracted. Snack time is overlooked or rushed, and/or snacks have limited nutritional value.

Developmentally appropriate	In contrast

Teaching to Enhance Development and Learning (cont.)

Environment and Schedule (cont.)

Teachers allocate extended periods of time in learning centers (60 minutes or more in full-day and at least 45 minutes in half-day kindergarten) so that children are able to get deeply involved in an activity at a complex level. The classroom includes a dramatic play area to which all children have frequent access. Children have ample time and opportunity to investigate what sparks their curiosity. Schedules are set but not rigid—if children are highly engaged in an activity, the teacher may choose to extend it.

○ Frequent transitions and excessive emphasis on rituals such as "doing the calendar" every day or lining up to go outside take up too much time, often interrupting children's engagement in learning activities. This prevents children from gaining maximum benefit from sustained investigations, construction, dramatic play, or other such activities. The schedule is rigidly followed with activities tightly scripted.

Comments on environment and schedule:

—An important way to help kindergartners feel secure is to focus on smooth transitions between learning experiences. These times can be challenging for young children, who may either be eager to rush on to the next activity or be engrossed in what they are doing and reluctant to start a new task.

—Requiring kindergartners to sit still for extended periods of time is usually counterproductive. One useful strategy to help children retain their energy and focus is to break up an extended block of time into several different learning experiences and formats. For example, a language arts block could begin with a brief large group instruction and discussion of new concepts, time for children to work in small groups or individually, as the teacher observes and offers individual help as needed, and finish with a whole group teacher read-aloud.

Teaching Methods

Teachers provide a variety of engaging learning experiences and hands-on materials. Materials include books, writing materials, math-related games and manipulatives, natural objects and tools for science investigations, CDs and musical instruments, art materials, props for dramatic play, and blocks (and computers, if budgets allow).

Materials are chosen for how well they support the overall curriculum and goals of the classroom.

○ Learning materials are primarily workbooks, worksheets, flashcards, and other materials that do not engage children's interest, promote their self-regulation, or involve them in problem solving and other higher-order thinking skills.

○ The same materials are available week after week. Children have few new choices and little variety in materials and activities.

○ Teachers choose materials based on entertainment value and popular culture fads, such as stickers from a new movie. Candy and other sweets are often used as incentives.

Teaching to Enhance Development and Learning (cont.)

Teaching Methods (cont.)

Teachers use a variety of learning contexts throughout the day and throughout the week in order to guide children's learning. These include a whole group setting, small groups, learning centers, and daily routines.

○ Teachers overuse one or two learning formats in the course of the day and make little or no use of others. For example, teachers give children very little time in interest areas or fail to use the small group format when it would be the most effective approach.

○ Group work tends to be didactic, with teachers being largely unresponsive to children's ideas and contributions.

Teachers use a variety of instructional strategies to suit particular learning goals, specific situations, and the needs of individual children. These strategies can include encouraging children; offering specific feedback; modeling skills or positive behavior; creating or adding challenge; giving a cue, hint, or other assistance; telling information directly; and giving directions. Such approaches are used within any learning context and during child-guided activities.

○ Teachers have a hands-off approach during much of the day. Beyond setting up the materials, teachers' involvement in center time is limited to observation; teachers step in only to mediate conflicts that arise. Interactions with children during less structured times are very basic, such as giving directions.

○ Teachers make excessive use of direct instruction methods (e.g., giving directions, presenting information), which are useful for some purposes but not effective as the predominant strategy in teaching young children. Children spend long periods of time on seatwork that does not extend their learning.

In addition to teacher-guided lessons and activities, there is time allotted each day for child-guided experiences, including play. These may be during center time or other parts of the day. Teachers support children's deep engagement in these experiences by adequately scheduling time, providing interesting materials, and thoughtfully intervening and assisting as needed (e.g., helping an introverted child gain access to a group).

○ Teachers are too passive in the classroom, planning too few adult-guided learning experiences and rarely taking action, even when children's behaviors are aimless or disruptive. When children are engaged in play and interest centers, teachers contribute little or nothing to their play and learning. Teachers use play as a reward for acceptable behavior or for children who finish their "work."

○ Too little time (or none at all) is allotted for child-guided activities, and teachers do not recognize how important it is for children to guide some of their own activities. They frequently interrupt and undermine children's immersion in and management of their own activities.

Teaching to Enhance Development and Learning (cont.)

Teaching Methods (cont.)

Teachers frequently engage children in planning or in reflecting on their experiences, discussing a past experience, and working to represent it (e.g., drawing, writing and dictating, making charts). Such opportunities let the teacher discover what children are thinking and encourage children to deepen and refine their own concepts and understanding. Teachers frequently document children's answers to monitor comprehension and learning across the year.

○ Feeling pressured to cover the standard curriculum and believing that returning to the same topic or experience is a waste of time, teachers present a topic or experience only once and fail to provide opportunities for revisiting and reexamining experiences, which would make fuller, more refined understanding possible.

Teachers provide many opportunities for children to learn to collaborate with others and work through ideas and solutions as well as develop social skills, such as cooperating, helping, negotiating, and talking with other people to solve social problems. Children work collaboratively to answer questions, such as those encountered in studying mathematics or science.

○ Children have few opportunities for meaningful social interaction with other children, especially in half-day kindergarten programs where teachers feel pressed for time.

○ Though teachers may recognize the social dimension of children's interactions, they do not see this dimension as integral to children's cognitive development and learning. Thus, teachers rarely make use of children's interactions and relationships in addressing learning goals.

Comments on teaching methods:

—Children learn best when they are deeply engaged. Both when they themselves primarily shape the activity (as in play) and in thoughtfully planned activities guided by adults (as in a large group read-aloud or a small group science activity), children are often highly engaged and learning.

—For a discussion of the purposes behind each classroom format (small group, large group, etc.), see the position statement on developmentally appropriate practice (www.naeyc.org/positionstatements/dap).

Communication and Language Use

Teachers talk often and warmly with every child—getting to know children, building positive relationships with them, and gathering information about them.

○ Teachers' speech is mostly one way, much more often *telling* children things than conversing with or listening to them.

○ Teachers usually speak to children as a group. For the most part, teachers address individual children only to admonish or discipline them.

Teaching to Enhance Development and Learning (cont.)

Communication and Language Use (cont.)

Developmentally appropriate	In contrast
When talking with children, teachers take into account children's capabilities as listeners, recognizing that there is a wide range of individual variation in kindergartners' verbal skills and ability to focus attention. Teachers communicate information in small units, tie new information to what children already know, check for understanding, and invite questions or comments to engage their interest.	○ Teachers talk at length or read aloud for long periods; they expect attentiveness during these times, but children often become restless or tune out. ○ Teachers put a high priority on children being silent unless addressed; they ignore or correct children for talking or for not waiting to be called on. ○ Teachers talk down to children or answer for children who are sometimes slow to respond (e.g., dual language learners).
When children are talking, teachers take into account their capabilities as speakers, giving children time to express themselves and responding attentively to their speech. Teachers share with children the role of setting the topic and purpose of talk.	○ Adult agendas dominate classroom conversations. Teachers often view children's talk as interruptions of the adults' talk or work. ○ Teachers don't respect children as speakers (e.g., asking questions without really expecting children to answer).
Teachers encourage children's efforts to communicate. They make it a priority to involve dual language learners in meaningful interactions at whatever level the children are able. Teachers allow children time to think about how they want to respond to a question or comment (*wait time*).	○ Teachers are so focused on the shortcomings of kindergartners' language skills that they neglect or miss the messages children are attempting to communicate. ○ Teachers insist on children's speaking only in English or only with proper grammar, correcting them every time they diverge from standard English usage.
Teachers engage individual children and groups in real conversations about their experiences and projects as well as current events. Teachers encourage children to describe their work products or explain their thinking, and teachers express interest in children's opinions, observations, and feelings.	○ Teachers interrupt children and dominate conversations instead of taking conversational turns. ○ Teachers don't talk in-depth with children, often underestimating children's complexity of thought because they can't yet communicate it fully.

Developmentally Appropriate Examples to Consider

Teaching to Enhance Development and Learning (cont.)

Communication and Language Use (cont.)

Teachers use wide-ranging vocabulary in their talk to and with children, including words that are unfamiliar to them. When teachers use words unfamiliar to a child, they give sufficient information for the child to grasp the meaning. With a dual language learner, teachers provide *nonverbal* cues to enable the child to learn what the new words mean (e.g., using gestures, pointing to objects or pictured items).

○ Teachers talk down to children both in terms of content and oversimplified speech, using relatively limited vocabulary in their conversational exchanges.

○ Teachers use a fairly rich vocabulary, but when they use words unfamiliar to children, teachers do not give sufficient information for children to grasp the meaning.

Teachers talk with *all* children, making it a priority to talk often with dual language learners and those with delayed language development or limited vocabulary.

○ Teachers don't make extra effort to talk with children who are quiet or hesitant, have communication difficulties, or are dual language learners.

○ Teachers pay so much attention to dual language learners (and draw their peers' attention to them, as well) that those children feel unusual or outside the community of learners.

Comments on communication and language use:

—By their interest in and responsiveness to what children say, teachers help initiate children to the back-and-forth sharing of conversation, and they enhance the complexity of children's language and the size of their vocabulary.

—For teachers to draw special attention to dual language learners may be problematic if those children are from cultural groups in which getting singled out for attention, even positive attention, is not desirable.

Motivation and Positive Approaches to Learning

Recognizing children's natural curiosity and desire to make sense of their world and gain new skills, teachers consistently plan learning experiences that children find highly interesting and engaging and that contribute to their development and learning.

○ Most classroom experiences either are uninteresting and unchallenging or are so difficult and frustrating that they undermine children's intrinsic motivation to learn. Teachers do not use what they know about the children to inform curriculum in order to better reflect their interests.

○ Seeking to motivate children, teachers rely heavily on external rewards (stickers, privileges, etc.) or chastise children for their mistakes or shortcomings.

Teaching to Enhance Development and Learning (cont.)

Motivation and Positive Approaches to Learning (cont.)

Teachers use verbal encouragement in ways that are genuine and related to what the child is doing. They acknowledge the child's effort and work with specific comments (*You've been working very hard on your drawing*, or *I see from your chart that you ate peanut butter and jelly three times for lunch last week*).

○ Teachers make such frequent use of non-specific praise (*Good job!* or *What a nice block tower*) that it becomes meaningless either to provide useful feedback or to motivate the child. Children may also become focused on pleasing the teacher rather than on the learning experience itself.

○ Teachers' feedback consists mostly of negative comments and correction of errors.

Comments on motivation and positive approaches to learning:

—Genuine, positive feedback promotes children's intrinsic motivation. However, many kindergarten classrooms focus heavily on a system of tangible rewards, giving out small prizes and treats for good behavior or for mastering skills. There are some cases where using a reward system for a limited time may help children (e.g., with certain special needs or challenging behaviors). For most children, though, such a system focuses their attention on the rewards rather than on the learning experience itself and thus is a shortsighted strategy that undermines internal motivation.

Guidance

Teachers model and encourage calm, patient behavior and facilitate children's development of self-regulation by supporting them in thinking ahead, planning their activities, and considering strategies to solve social problems.

○ Teachers are uncontrolled in their own behavior (e.g., showing irritation, stress, impulsive responses) with children and with other adults.

○ Not knowing what kindergarten children are capable of, teachers do not involve children in thinking through and solving problems and learning to regulate their own behavior, emotions, and thinking.

Teachers offer opportunities for positive interactions through a range of teacher-supported, child-guided experiences (e.g., dramatic play, exploring books, manipulatives). Teachers focus on helping children to become self-regulated. They monitor children's interactions, and when children present challenging behavior, adults help them to resolve conflicts by teaching them communication, emotional regulation, and social skills.

○ Children flit from one activity to another, simply reacting in the moment rather than being planful or reflective. Or activities are highly teacher-directed, so children remain too adult-regulated and don't develop self-regulation skills.

Teaching to Enhance Development and Learning (cont.)

Guidance (cont.)

Developmentally appropriate	In contrast
Teachers set clear limits regarding unacceptable behaviors and enforce these limits with explanations in a climate of mutual respect and caring. Teachers attend to children consistently, not principally when they are engaging in problematic behaviors. Class meetings and group discussions are often used to talk about and set rules together.	○ Teachers do not set clear limits and do not hold children accountable to standards of acceptable behavior. The environment is chaotic. Teachers do not help children learn classroom rules or let them participate in setting rules, so children have difficulty incorporating the rules as their own. ○ Teachers spend a great deal of time punishing unacceptable behavior, refereeing disagreements, and repeatedly putting the same children in time-out or disciplining them in other ways unrelated to their actions. These strategies attempt to control children rather than promote children's self-regulation, conflict resolution skills, and social problem solving.
When a child consistently displays challenging behaviors, teachers identify events, activities, interactions, and other contextual factors that occur with the behavior and may provoke it. Then, to help the child progress toward more acceptable behavior, teachers (in collaboration with families) make modifications in the activities and environment and give the child adult and peer support.	○ Teachers and school administrators push to get children with challenging behaviors excluded from regular kindergarten classrooms and placed in special programs. ○ Children with special needs or behavioral problems are isolated or reprimanded for failure to meet group expectations, rather than having teachers provide them with learning experiences that are at a reasonable level of difficulty.

Comments on guidance:

—The age range of kindergarten children within a single classroom can be wide, from as young as age 4 to as old as age 7. Children's levels of self-control and self-regulation can be similarly varied. In addition, children's experience of being part of a social group will vary considerably, depending on their prior care and preschool education, if any. Teachers may find that some children are able to assimilate prosocial behavior modeled by adults easily, while others may need more systematic, positive behavior support.

—It will help most children improve their self-regulation skills if teachers form caring relationships with them, organize the environment to promote positive interactions, and model and support prosocial behavior. However, kindergarten is often the first setting in which children who have special needs related to aggressiveness or who show other serious challenging behaviors may be identified. Because early interactions set the course for those later in school, it is important that teachers implement an individualized behavior support plan with the child's family and school specialists, if necessary, for the benefit of the child.

—For more on self-regulation in the kindergarten year, see Chapter 3.

Planning Curriculum to Achieve Important Goals

Curriculum Essentials

Comprehensive Scope; Important Goals

The curriculum addresses key goals in all areas of development (physical, social, emotional, cognitive) and in the domains of physical education and health, language and literacy, mathematics, science, social studies, and creative arts.

○ Curriculum goals are narrowly focused on a few learning domains (e.g., literacy and math) without recognition that all areas of a child's development and learning are interrelated and important.

In each area, the curriculum is consistent with high-quality, achievable, and challenging early learning standards, such as those adopted at the state level. Curriculum is informed by recommendations from the relevant professional organization.

○ Curriculum content lacks intellectual integrity and is trivial and unworthy of children's attention.

The curriculum is designed to help children explore and acquire the key concepts ("big ideas") and the tools of inquiry for each discipline in ways that are effective for kindergarten children (e.g., language experiences exploring sound/letter relationships, hands-on science activities).

○ The curriculum is developed by extending expectations for first grade downward, rather than by reflecting what kindergarten children are capable of—thus, expectations may be too high. Alternatively, expectations are set too low or are otherwise not a good fit with the children.

Coherence and Integration

Teachers are knowledgeable about the sequence and pace that development and learning typically follow as children build understandings and skills in each content area. For example, teachers' understanding of the progression of concepts and skills involved in joining sets (addition) enables them to introduce the concepts to children in a coherent way and to scaffold children's progress from each idea and ability to the next.

○ Because the standards on which the curriculum is based include too many topics or learning objectives, learning experiences touch on topics only superficially, and children are unable to gain real understanding of any single topic.

○ Teachers fail to recognize the sequences of learning in the discipline areas and how these apply to children in this age range.

Planning Curriculum to Achieve Important Goals (cont.)

Coherence and Integration (cont.)

Teachers integrate ideas and content from multiple domains and disciplines through themes, projects, play opportunities, and other learning experiences so that children are able to develop an understanding of concepts and make connections across disciplines. For example, in discussing a certain kind of pattern in math, teachers draw children's attention to the same pattern in songs.

○ Children's learning is seen as occurring in separate content areas, and times are set aside to teach each subject without integration. Teachers fail to connect curriculum topics in ways that are meaningful to children. As a result, learning is often fragmented, and children are less likely to generalize ideas and apply them across content areas.

○ Teachers use a "holiday curriculum" or choose other themes based only on their initial appeal to children (even when the topics do not provide opportunities for learning important content and skills).

Effective Implementation

The curriculum, which exists in written form, provides teachers with a useful and flexible framework for planning learning experiences and materials and for seeing how those experiences can fit together to accomplish the school's stated goals.

○ If there is a prescribed curriculum (published or adopted by a district or school), teachers do not have the flexibility or the capability to make adaptations in the curriculum to optimize its interest and effectiveness with the particular children in the group.

Teachers refer to and use the curriculum framework as they plan what they will do with children, so classroom experiences are coherent. Teachers plan and implement experiences to help children achieve important developmental and learning goals.

○ Teachers do not consider the curriculum framework in their planning. Children's learning experiences do not follow a logical sequence. Curriculum goals are unclear or unknown.

In planning and implementing learning experiences, teachers draw on their knowledge of the content, awareness of what is likely to interest children of that age, and understanding of the cultural and social contexts of children's lives. Teachers value children's input and let it shape curriculum as appropriate (e.g., letting children suggest topics for project work).

○ Teachers rigidly follow a prescribed curriculum plan without attention to individual children's interests and needs or the specific and changing context (e.g., studying weather change because it is in the October curriculum, even though a national election is about to occur). Teachers stick with their previously planned topics regardless of circumstances or events (e.g., a child's uncle is performing in a local concert). No effort is made to let children's interests inform classroom activities.

Planning Curriculum to Achieve Important Goals (cont.)

Effective Implementation (cont.)

Teachers plan curriculum that is responsive to and respectful of the specific contexts of children's experiences. Culturally diverse and nonsexist activities and materials are provided to help children develop positive self-identity, relate new concepts to their own life experiences, and respect differences and similarities. For example, books and pictures include people of different races, ages, and abilities and of both genders in various roles.

○ Children's cultural and linguistic backgrounds and other individual differences are ignored or treated as deficits to be overcome. Insufficient resources are allocated to help children who are dual language learners.

○ Multicultural curriculum reflects a "tourist approach" in which artifacts, food, or other aspects of different cultures are presented without meaningful connections to the children's own experiences. Teachers point out a culture's traditions in ways that convey these are exotic or deviations from the "normal" majority culture (thus, the children of this culture feel like outsiders).

Teachers assess each child's progress toward the school's stated curricular goals, and they reflect on their practice to monitor the effectiveness of their teaching. They make changes to their teaching practice (environment, schedule, methods, etc.) as necessary to improve effectiveness for the group and for individual children.

○ Teachers do not regularly make use of assessment information to inform curriculum decisions.

Teachers connect curriculum topics with children's interests and with what children already know and can do. Young children learn best when the concepts, vocabulary, and skills they encounter are related to things they know and care about, and when the new learnings are themselves interconnected in meaningful ways.

○ Meaningful, connected learning is not a priority in the curriculum planning. Curriculum is not integrated across multiple learning domains.

Comments on effective implementation:

—Kindergarten teachers often do not have any say in the curriculum that is chosen by their school, district, or state. Despite this fact, teachers have the most important role to play in how effectively curriculum is implemented. In order to fully realize the curriculum's potential, teachers must have a clear idea of how learning experiences within the curriculum fulfill standards-based learning goals. By giving careful consideration to which standards are addressed by daily activities, teachers are able to better adapt curriculum in practice.

Planning Curriculum to Achieve Important Goals (cont.)

Physical Development

Health and Fitness

Teachers acquaint children with healthy habits in eating and exercise and introduce basic concepts of body functioning and physical health. Snacks are nutritious; sweets are never offered as an incentive. Teachers reinforce good hygiene habits.

○ Foods with low nutrition value and with high sugar or fat content are served. Children spend too much time sitting and do not get adequate exercise.

> Comments on health and fitness:
> —Children as young as kindergarten age are becoming obese in ever larger numbers. Even when children aren't dangerously overweight, being overweight at all negatively impacts children's current and future health, as a cycle of inactivity, tiredness, and decreased ability in and enjoyment of physical activity is established. It also affects children socially, as they may be excluded from active interactions with their peers.

Gross Motor Development

Children spend little time sitting; they are able to move around throughout much of the day. They have plenty of opportunities to use large muscles in balancing, running, jumping, climbing, and other vigorous movements, both in their play and in planned movement activities. Children play outdoors every day and have specialized instruction in physical education on a regular basis.

○ Children's opportunities for large muscle activity are limited, and there is no regularly scheduled time for specialized instruction in physical education. Recess time is limited, or there are no opportunities for gross motor activities when the weather is poor.

Adults teach children the pleasure and importance of physical activity, as well as body and spatial awareness and key movement skills (e.g., catching, jumping, balancing). Teaching of physical skills is sequential and adapted to accommodate children's various skill levels and special needs. Equal encouragement is given to girls and boys. Physical activities are integrated into various learning experiences throughout the day.

○ Teachers or other qualified adults are uninvolved during recess and free play times, except to provide basic supervision. Adults make little effort to involve less-active children and those lagging in physical skills or coordination and to help them develop the skills and confidence to engage in gross motor activities. Accommodations are not made to include children with special needs.

○ Physical activity areas have very limited equipment, so children lack variety of choices and/or must often wait quite a while to get a turn.

Planning Curriculum to Achieve Important Goals (cont.)

Gross Motor Development (cont.)

Comments on gross motor development:

—Kindergarten children need structured instruction in physical activity, unstructured time to play and exercise large muscles, and integration of physical activities throughout the day. However, less and less time in contemporary kindergarten classrooms is spent on planned acquisition of physical skills. In some districts, positions for specialist teachers in physical education have even been subject to budget cuts, and daily specialized instruction is rare. Unfortunately, this reduction comes at a time when it's more important than ever for children to be active, as our society becomes increasingly overweight.

—In light of reduced physical education programs and the needs of kindergarten children, many classroom teachers need to integrate physical development and learning into the day's activities. They need to familiarize themselves with the kindergarten standards in early physical education and plan activities to foster skill acquisition and link to learning in other domains. The PE Central website (www.pecentral.org) offers suggestions for classroom teachers who want to use physical activity to teach academic content, either in the classroom or in an outdoor play area.

Fine Motor Development

Teachers provide opportunities throughout the day for children to develop fine motor skills through working with suitable materials (e.g., pencils and markers, puzzles, playdough, beads, paper and scissors, small plastic interlocking blocks, buttons and zippers on clothing). As needed, teachers help children acquire such skills through scaffolding their efforts. Modifications and accommodations are made for children with physical disabilities.

○ Teachers give children fine motor tasks that are too difficult or hold them to an unrealistically high standard in executing tasks (e.g., expecting them to write letters with precision when they lack the necessary small muscle control).

○ The tools and fine motor experiences that teachers provide have insufficient variety to allow children at many different levels to progress in eye–hand coordination and motor control (e.g., there are only fat markers or brushes for the children to use). Assistive technology is not available for children with special needs.

Teachers provide opportunities and support for children to develop and practice self-help skills, such as putting on jackets, serving themselves snack or meals, washing hands, and cleaning up materials. Adults are patient when there are occasional spills, accidents, and unfinished jobs.

○ To save time and mess, adults often perform routine tasks for children. Children cannot get materials as needed, but must always ask adults for them.

○ Adults shame children or display irritation when spills or other accidents happen.

Planning Curriculum to Achieve Important Goals (cont.)

Fine Motor Development (cont.)

Comments on fine motor development:

—Although kindergarten children have longer attention spans than preschoolers and can focus more on fine motor tasks like writing and drawing, they often find it difficult to exert the necessary patience, time, and effort. Offering play-based activities with fine motor components (e.g., board games with game pieces and squares to land on) and especially open-ended learning opportunities (e.g., exploring and sorting a shell collection) is especially important in building children's abilities and tolerance for fine motor activity.

—Teachers need to take gender into consideration; in general, girls at the kindergarten level have more facility at fine motor tasks than boys (Berk 2008). This should be a factor in the selection of materials for fine motor activities—for example, manipulatives can include not only beads for stringing but also small interlocking blocks for construction, and both boys and girls can be encouraged to engage with all materials.

Language and Literacy

Listening, Speaking, and Understanding

To enhance children's listening skills, teachers create regular opportunities for children to actively listen to and converse with others and work together in small groups on projects or problem solving. They provide opportunities for children to listen and respond to stories and information books, follow directions, and listen attentively to others during group discussions.

○ Teachers focus on getting children to listen only for classroom management purposes.

○ Teachers stress the need for children to pay attention to them, providing little or no opportunity for response and discussion. They value passive rather than active engagement.

Teachers provide opportunities for oral response to stories and information books. Children are encouraged to describe events, retell stories or parts of stories, and give simple directions to others.

○ Little attention is given to intentional focus on developing children's speaking abilities in various situations. Children are largely viewed as the passive recipients of information.

○ Focused, guided opportunities for response and interactive discussion are limited.

Teachers engage in conversations with both individual children and small groups. Whenever possible these are sustained conversations (with multiple conversational turns, complex ideas, and rich vocabulary) and include decontextualized speech (talk about children's experiences beyond the here and now).

○ Teachers mostly ask children questions that call for brief or simple responses rather than elaborated speech.

○ Conversations with children are limited to the current context ("I'd like to hear about your picture").

Planning Curriculum to Achieve Important Goals (cont.)

Listening, Speaking, and Understanding (cont.)

Teachers attend to the particular language needs of dual language learners and children who are behind in vocabulary and other aspects of language learning. They engage the child more frequently in sustained conversations and make extra efforts to help her comprehend.

○ Teachers talk mostly with verbally skilled children, neglecting the children who most need language help—children who are quiet or hesitant, have communication difficulties, or are dual language learners.

○ When teachers talk to a child behind in language learning, they don't show the patience and attentiveness that the child requires in order to become a successful conversational partner.

Teachers support dual language learners in their home language (e.g., by gathering books and tapes/CDs/MP3s in each child's language, involving family members and other speakers of the language in various ways) as well as promoting their learning of English.

○ Teachers provide no support for children in maintaining their home language.

○ A policy (sometimes imposed from above) specifies that children and teachers use only English in the classroom.

Teachers help children use communication and language as tools for thinking and learning. For example, during group time teachers provide ways for every child to talk (e.g., talk to a peer, call out answers). Or teachers have children repeat aloud things they want to remember (e.g., "One plate, one spoon") or talk about what they will write before doing it.

○ During much of the day, children are expected to watch or be quiet. During group time teachers call on one child at a time to respond, making all the others wait, during which they may disengage mentally or become disruptive.

Comments on listening, speaking, and understanding:

—Using *decontextualized language* requires children and adults to use more explanation and description. Further, children will have to rely on printed language alone when reading, and experience with decontextualized language provides valuable preparation.

—Young children's language development progresses most when they are actively engaged in verbal interaction and teachers encourage them to extend their comments. Because many children have ground to make up in vocabulary and other language skills and/or English fluency, teachers need to use approaches in which children are talked *to* less and talked *with* more.

| Developmentally appropriate | In contrast |

Planning Curriculum to Achieve Important Goals (cont.)

Book Reading and Motivation

Every day, teachers read aloud to children in both small and large groups when possible. Books are accessible in a library area and other places conducive to their enjoyment and use. There is a good variety of high-quality books (e.g., suitable for kindergartners and reflecting the gender, cultural, racial, and social diversity of the group; storybooks and information books; varying reading levels). Children can listen to audiobooks and follow along in the printed book.

○ The classroom offers children only a small quantity and/or a limited variety of books.

○ For the most part, books are kept out of reach (i.e., handled only by teachers or available only at children's request), and thus children cannot freely explore them.

Teachers provide multiple copies of familiar kindergarten-level texts. Children are encouraged to return to books that have been read aloud to them for independent browsing. Special time is regularly set aside for independent reading of self-selected familiar texts.

○ Books in the literacy center rarely change. Multiple copies of books are unavailable for individual reading or reading with a partner.

○ Children are encouraged to read books on their own when time allows, but teachers do not set aside time for independent reading.

Teachers engage children in discussions about topics of interest and importance to them in books. Taking notes on individuals' comments and questions, teachers follow up on these in small groups or one-on-one.

○ Teachers do most of the talking when books are discussed.

○ When teachers ask questions, these are frequently at the recall level rather than at levels requiring children to make inferences, think critically, and express themselves through the use of new knowledge and vocabulary.

Comments on book reading and motivation:

—Fostering young children's interest in books and reading has an important positive influence on reading achievement. The more children read, the better they get at reading—and the more they want to read (Meiers 2004).

Phonological/Phonemic Awareness

Teachers introduce engaging oral language experiences (e.g., songs, poems, books, word games) that enhance kindergartners' phonological and phonemic awareness. Teachers assess and take into account where each child is in developing phonological awareness and tailor instruction accordingly.

○ Teachers give little or no attention to promoting phonological or phonemic awareness. Or they fail to tailor learning experiences according to what children need to progress.

○ Teachers spend too much time on structured phonemic awareness activities, continuing with such instruction even after children have mastered those particular skills.

Planning Curriculum to Achieve Important Goals (cont.)

Phonological/Phonemic Awareness (cont.)

Teachers continue to build on children's demonstrated understandings of phonological/phonemic awareness. For example, teachers move from phoneme identity (*What sound is the same in* sit, sip, *and* sun?) to phoneme categorization, or identifying the word in a set of words that has a different sound (*Which word doesn't belong:* doll, dish, toy?).

○ Teachers do not build on a logical progression of phonological and phonemic skills and concepts.

○ Teachers do not differentiate instruction to give students extra support where needed and offer appropriate challenges to those who are ready to move on.

Comments on phonological/phonemic awareness:

—Research has shown that children's awareness and ability to manipulate the sounds of spoken words—specifically, their phonemic awareness—is a strong predictor of their later success in learning to read (NRP 2000). Because many children do not automatically acquire such awareness and because it is vital for further progress, teaching phonemic awareness is a key role of the kindergarten teacher.

Writing

Teachers encourage and assist children in their own efforts to write (using letters, words, drawings) for different purposes such as signs, letters, lists, journals, and records of observations.

○ "Writing" is limited to completing workbook pages.

Teachers give children frequent opportunities to draw and write about topics that interest them. Emphasis is placed on helping children share their ideas through written communication. Teachers display children's writing, even if there are errors, for the ideas and expression they demonstrate.

○ Written composition for the purpose of expressing ideas is limited. Teachers view writing primarily as handwriting practice and copying, and they stress correct form and legibility above expression and communication.

○ Teachers control access to writing materials, and children must request them. Children rarely have opportunities to write on their own.

Children are encouraged to use conventional spelling for common or familiar words and also to apply their developing knowledge of sound/letter correspondences to spell independently (i.e., developmental spelling).

○ Correct spelling is highly valued. Little is done to encourage children's applications of their knowledge of sound/letter relationships in conjunction with the development of conventional spelling.

Comments on writing:

—*Developmental spelling* refers to young children's attempts to use what they already know about letters and sounds to attempt to write words. Research indicates that encouraging developmental spelling promotes children's understanding of the relationship between letters and sounds (Templeton & Bear 1992). Research also finds that developmental spelling does not interfere with children later becoming accurate spellers.

Developmentally Appropriate Examples to Consider

Planning Curriculum to Achieve Important Goals (cont.)

Letter, Word, and Print Knowledge

Much of the environmental print in the classroom is generated by and with children. It is purposeful and used by children in functional ways. For example, children refer to lists of helpers' responsibilities and things to do as part of their daily routines. Teachers encourage them to return (independently) to and reread charts that were developed collectively by the group.

○ Purposeless print clutters the environment (e.g., labels on many familiar objects) to the extent that children tune the print out.

○ Print is scarce or not placed where children can readily see and refer to it.

Teachers use various strategies to help children recognize that the sequence of letters in written words represents the sequence of sounds in spoken words. During shared writing, teachers model and/or engage children in figuring out sound/letter relationships in order to spell words. They track the print from left to write to reinforce the sequence of sound/letter relationships and encourage children to take risks and apply what they know about sounds and letters to form words.

○ Teachers do not actively engage children in making connections between the sounds of spoken language and the letters that represent them.

○ Teachers spend too much time focusing on the connections between letters and sounds.

○ Teachers are unaware of individual children's knowledge of sound/letter relationships because they do not collect and analyze children's written work samples.

Comments on letter, word, and print knowledge:

—Some children enter kindergarten knowing letters and sounds, recognizing some words, and understanding a good deal about print; others have considerably less of this knowledge. Teachers need to find out where all children are in their literacy learning and then differentiate instruction to help each child make optimal progress.

—As noted in comments on **Writing**, encouraging developmental spelling promotes children's understanding of the relationship between letters and sounds.

Building Knowledge and Comprehension

To broaden children's knowledge and vocabulary, teachers use a variety of strategies such as reading stories and information books rich in new concepts, information, and vocabulary; planning field trips and inviting class visitors to tell children about their work or interests; and providing experiences through technology (virtual field trips).

○ The books that teachers read to children cover a limited range of familiar topics and use mostly common, known words.

○ Teachers use materials and experiences primarily to entertain children or to occupy their time, thus overlooking many opportunities for learning.

Planning Curriculum to Achieve Important Goals (cont.)

Building Knowledge and Comprehension (cont.)

Children are prompted to link content (in text or in class instruction and discussion) to their own background experience while expanding their knowledge base. Teachers use questions and prompts that require children to problem solve and use new vocabulary.

○ Teachers give little attention to helping children connect new words or concepts to what they already know.

To help children develop comprehension strategies and monitor their own understanding, teachers engage them in guided discussion when listening or reading. They ask children to make predictions about story events, retell or dramatize stories, and notice when text does not make sense.

○ Teachers' questioning during and after read-aloud activities is restricted to low-level, recall questions. They rarely ask children to give their opinions about an event or character in the story or to respond to open-ended questions.

○ Teacher follow-up to reading activities is largely confined to assigning worksheets.

Comments on building knowledge and comprehension:

—Children from diverse backgrounds, including dual language learners, may have a difficult time grasping what they read or what is read to them, not simply because of the language barrier but because of their different life experiences. Teachers can help to bridge these gaps by becoming familiar with children's backgrounds and prior knowledge and drawing connections between these and the text or other classroom experiences.

—Children are better able to comprehend stories and other text when they are taught to make connections between what they know and what is being read to them. Children also learn vocabulary most effectively when teachers actively engage them in grasping word meanings (e.g., by explaining new words in everyday language, relating words to contexts and to other words children do know).

—Open-ended and distancing questions are most effective in promoting comprehension and vocabulary; these questions require children to think beyond the story and relate the events to something that happened to them in the past or might happen in the future.

Mathematics

Teachers recognize children's desire to make sense of their world through mathematics. They build on children's intuitive, informal notions and encounters relating to math, making a point to supply math language and procedures. In other words, teachers mathematize children's everyday encounters. For example, they help children learn and practice mathematics skills with block building, play with manipulatives, games, movement activities, and computers.

○ Teachers' own negative feelings about mathematics cause them to avoid teaching it.

○ The kindergarten day is marked by many missed opportunities for children to learn important mathematics content. Teachers fail to see the importance of introducing math concepts and infusing math vocabulary and methods into children's experiences (instead relying on what children may figure out on their own during play and other activities).

Planning Curriculum to Achieve Important Goals (cont.)

Mathematics (cont.)

Developmentally appropriate	In contrast
Every day, teachers provide focused math time that is interesting to children, using various instructional contexts (e.g., small group, large group, individual), and find opportunities to integrate mathematics learning with other curriculum areas.	○ So much time is devoted to literacy instruction that planned mathematics experiences are given short shrift. ○ Teachers teach math only to the whole group.
Because mathematics is a discipline in which mastering new concepts/skills requires having mastered earlier, foundational concepts/skills, the curriculum reflects a research-based progression of topics, and children gain an understanding of current concepts before they are moved on to a new topic.	○ The mathematics curriculum covers too many content areas superficially or doesn't follow a logical sequence; thus, children do not have the opportunity to master the foundational concepts and skills needed. ○ There is no organized mathematics curriculum.
Teachers build on children's current knowledge, making sure that children consolidate their understanding of a concept before moving ahead (e.g., children understand the link between number and quantity before moving on to addition or subtraction problems).	○ Teachers move along in the curriculum, even when children do not understand what has been covered. ○ Teachers spend too much time reviewing the same content over and over, boring children who have mastered it and are ready for new challenges.
Teachers use a variety of strategies to engage children in **reasoning**, **problem solving**, and **communicating** about mathematics (e.g., teachers talk about the problem, draw children into the process of investigating and solving it, and ask how they came up with their solutions).	○ Teachers focus heavily on children getting "the right answer" to a problem. Instead of giving children time and guidance to assist their reasoning and problem solving, teachers tell children the answers or solve problems for them. ○ Teachers stand back and leave children to solve problems on their own without any adult assistance or support, thus missing many opportunities to help children learn to think and reason mathematically.
The curriculum includes the major content areas of mathematics (NCTM 2006) and emphasizes the three that are most important for kindergartners: **number and operations**, **geometry**, and **measurement**. Teachers actively foster children's understanding of number and operations (representing, comparing, and ordering whole numbers; joining and separating sets). They engage children in thinking about and working with geometric/spatial relationships (describing shapes and space, ordering and comparing lengths of two objects).	○ Teachers focus only on teaching children about numbers and counting. ○ Teachers provide low-level, repetitive experiences, such as counting the days on the calendar or identifying common two-dimensional shapes (circle, triangle, square).

Planning Curriculum to Achieve Important Goals (cont.)

Mathematics (cont.)

Comments on mathematics:

—Economically disadvantaged children tend to enter kindergarten significantly behind their middle-class peers in understanding basic number concepts such as the relationship between number and quantity. With very few exceptions, all children are capable of learning complex mathematics. However, children from more affluent homes have more opportunities to learn math (e.g., through playing board games or using manipulatives) in situations at home or in preschool where adults make connections between children's experiences and mathematical language and concepts. In kindergarten, math teaching that focuses on building understanding of foundational concepts and skills is essential, or children will fall further behind in later grades.

—Covering too many topics interferes with children's gaining deep understanding of the concepts and skills important to prepare them for next steps in the mathematics learning. Consequently, the National Council of Teachers of Mathematics (2006) indicates that although each grade's curriculum should include all the major content areas of mathematics, there should be certain areas of focus each year. The emphases indicated in the columns above are based on the NCTM work.

Science

Teachers focus on kindergarten children's natural curiosity to emphasize inquiry in science experiences. Children are encouraged to observe and to ask questions about the natural world and to think about what might happen during various scientific processes. Teachers provide materials and offer experiences that teach about important scientific concepts and skills.

○ Teachers slight science under pressure to cover other subjects in the curriculum. Teachers may transmit factual information on scientific topics, but they do not engage children in doing science.

○ The science curriculum is only about exploration, and children do not acquire foundational concepts and knowledge.

The curriculum includes concepts not only from **life science/nature** but also from **physical science** (e.g., wheels, swings, levers) and **earth and space science** (e.g., sand and soil, the moon). Teachers use a variety of strategies to help children develop important scientific concepts and skills.

○ The curriculum is limited to one area of science or to a few isolated topics with which the teacher feels comfortable. Other areas receive scant attention, even when children ask questions and show interest in them.

Comments on science:

—Many kindergarten classrooms do not teach science in a meaningful, sustained way. Due to pressures such as the emphasis on literacy and math in accountability testing, science curriculum may be shortchanged. Even when science is integrated into the curriculum, kindergarten children often encounter only a limited range of topics (e.g., studying some aspects of the natural world but not physics). Further, for rich, in-depth learning experiences, children need opportunities for hands-on experimentation.

Planning Curriculum to Achieve Important Goals (cont.)

Technology

Teachers make thoughtful use of computers and other technologies in the classroom, not to replace children's experience with objects and materials but to expand the range of tools with which children can seek information, solve problems, understand concepts (e.g., rotating or transforming geometric shapes onscreen to gain a better grasp of them), and move at their own pace. Software is selected to emphasize thinking and problem solving.

○ Children spend a great deal of class time on computers and/or watching television or videos.

○ Computer software is primarily devoted to drills or to games with only a recreational purpose. Use of computers is a privilege, allocated as a reward or taken away as a punishment.

○ Teachers avoid use of computers and other technology in the classroom.

Teachers locate computers to foster shared learning and interaction—children talking about what they are doing, cooperating in solving problems, and helping one another. Teachers encourage children to use technology (e.g., cameras, video and audio recorders) to document their experiences and work. They invite children's exploration of the various operations and actions possible with the technology. Technology is used to document children's learning.

○ Computers are located only in an area outside the main learning environment (e.g., in a computer lab), so children have limited access to them.

○ Computers are in an accessible location, but children are never given the opportunity to work with partners or a small team on computer activities. Or due to a lack of equipment, children are always required to work at the computer with three or four peers (and consequently never gain individual experience with the technology).

○ Teachers do not adjust use of technology for children's different comfort levels and abilities (e.g., a math game is set at the same level for everyone). Children must progress at a single pace, even if some children struggle to keep up and some are bored and ready for the next thing.

The program provides enough equipment that a child can become engaged in technology-based activities in a sustained, deep way. Boys and girls have equal access and opportunity to use technology.

○ The school doesn't provide any technology, or provides so little that children get only very brief turns using a piece of equipment in order to allow everyone to have a chance. Boys dominate use of computers.

Planning Curriculum to Achieve Important Goals (cont.)

Social Competence; Social Studies

Kindergarten social studies curriculum is organized into broad topics of study. The content connects to children's lives, and study is integrated with other learning domains.

○ Teachers may convey facts relating to social studies, but the information is too remote from children's experience or too fragmented to be meaningful and interesting to them.

○ Rather than integrating learning experiences, teachers address each social studies standard individually with a separate activity or experience, and/or they separate social studies from other curriculum areas.

Teachers introduce projects and/or units that include basic aspects of geography, history, and civics/political science, and they draw connections between social studies knowledge and methods and everyday situations and events (e.g., having children vote on a decision such as the name of the class newsletter they produce together).

○ Teachers do not provide experiences that introduce children to basic concepts and ideas foundational for later learning in social studies. Or they lecture children on topics (e.g., values and ideals of civic engagement) without discussion or room for comment or disagreement.

Teachers actively foster children's understanding of democratic processes and attitudes in concrete, experiential ways that children are able to understand, such as making and discussing rules, solving together the problems that arise in the classroom community, and learning to listen to others' ideas and perspectives. When possible, children are involved in conflict resolution in the classroom through such vehicles as class meetings.

○ Teachers are the only decision makers in the classroom; they do not engage children in sharing ideas and solving their problems together. Children are never involved in conflict resolution or group decision making.

○ Teachers attempt to teach about democracy but in ways that are too abstract for young children to relate to (e.g., discussing the different branches of government).

Comments on social competence and social studies:

—Children have a wide variety of life experiences before entering kindergarten. While many have attended preschool, the type and quality of programs range widely; many children have no experience in educational group settings whatsoever. At the beginning of the year, some children will find merely sitting in a group and listening to others a challenge. As the year progresses, teachers' thoughtful planning to bolster children's social competence is interwoven with the social studies curriculum.

—Social studies appears in this section with social competence because up through the early grades, important aspects of the social studies curriculum are taught and learned through the everyday events of the classroom. For example, teachers foster kindergartners' abilities to participate in group decision making, establish rules and consequences, express opinions in a group setting, collaborate with others, and respect the rights of others in the classroom.

Planning Curriculum to Achieve Important Goals (cont.)

Creative Arts

Creative/Aesthetic Development

Classroom teachers (on their own or working with specialists) help children explore and work with various art and music media and techniques. Teachers convey an open, adventurous attitude toward the arts ("How about trying this?") that encourages children to explore available media and try new approaches and movements. The arts are integrated with other areas of the curriculum.

○ Art and music are taught as separate subjects once a week or less, and specialists do not coordinate closely with classroom teachers.

○ Teachers spend time preparing children for special performances or exhibits for families or the public rather than supporting children's active participation in the arts for the sake of their own creative expression, knowledge, and appreciation.

Teachers display children's art, as well as the work of artists, in the classroom and elsewhere in the program setting. Children have opportunities to experience music, art, and dance in the community.

○ Teachers emphasize the finished product or performance and single out for praise those children who are particularly gifted or trained in one of the arts.

○ The music and art in the environment reflect the teachers' own culture(s) and tastes but do not include the arts of the local community or the backgrounds of the children and their families.

○ The environment is heavily decorated with depictions of commercial media characters or other simplified, cartoon-like images.

Comments on creative/aesthetic development:

—Creativity and creative expression are not limited to the arts, but the arts are an excellent venue for fostering new ways of thinking. Kindergarten children love to explore with a wide variety of materials; when teachers include means for creative expression throughout the curriculum, children's interest in the subject matter is heightened. At the same time, teachers need to recognize that arts activities themselves fulfill important learning goals and have intrinsic value.

Planning Curriculum to Achieve Important Goals (cont.)

Visual Arts

Classroom teachers or specialized art teachers make available a wide variety of art media for children to explore and work with. They talk with children about their art. Teachers have children revisit projects and media, giving them opportunities to revise and expand their ideas and refine their skills.

○ Art materials are available, but children are not supported in moving beyond the exploration level.

○ Teachers introduce only the few art media and methods that they enjoy or know.

Teachers demonstrate new techniques or uses of materials to expand what children can do with them. When demonstrating techniques, teachers present information appropriate to children's developmental level (e.g., kindergartners are shown how black and white pastels can make gray but aren't expected to use shading in their pictures).

○ Children are allowed to use materials only under tightly controlled conditions. Or children have no conditions imposed on their artistic expression, as teachers believe this limits creativity; the result is a chaotic classroom in which children do not learn useful techniques.

Teachers do not provide a model that they expect children to copy.

○ Teachers provide a model and/or expect children to follow specific directions resulting in similar products. Emphasis is on group-copied crafts rather than individual artistic creations, and artworks are produced primarily to be pleasing to adults.

Comments on visual arts:

—In how they depict objects, people, relationships, and emotions on the page, children reveal their thoughts and feelings. Listening to what they have to say about their art can give teachers special insight. They often can describe their creations verbally in far greater complexity ("This is my sister, who has brown hair and laughs a lot") than they are able to achieve in their drawings.

—Teachers promote creative expression when they offer open-ended art experiences, in which children use their imaginations, for example, to consider a familiar story ("What do you suppose the Cat in the Hat's own house looks like?") (Jalongo & Isenberg 2006).

Planning Curriculum to Achieve Important Goals (cont.)

Music and Movement

Developmentally appropriate	In contrast
Teachers have a repertoire of songs to sing with children, who are mastering recall of both melody and lyrics. These include songs with predictable melodies and lyrics, as children enjoy repetition, and such songs give them opportunities to learn about pitch, rhythm, and melody.	○ Teachers rarely return to a song or dance once they have shared it with children, so children are unable to build up a repertoire of familiar music. Teachers do not introduce repetitive songs, and they do not sing with the children.
Teachers provide musical instruments for children to use. Songs and instruments from various cultures, especially those of the children in the group, are included.	
Whether or not there are specialist teachers for music, it is integrated with other areas of the curriculum, such as literacy (e.g., for teaching new vocabulary or phonological awareness) and mathematics (e.g., for counting beats or building spatial awareness).	○ Music is not integrated with other curriculum areas.
The joy of music is central in the experiences teachers share with children. In ways that don't interrupt that enjoyment, teachers highlight elements such as pitch, duration, tempo, and volume and engage children in varying and exploring these elements.	○ Teachers approach music in a didactic way, teaching specific terms and elements but not giving children integrated, enjoyable experiences in music.
	○ Teachers have a "performance orientation" and tend to single out those children most clearly gifted or trained in singing, dancing, or playing instruments and criticize or ignore the creative efforts of the other children. Teachers focus on performances to the exclusion of other musical curriculum.
Teachers introduce movement activities that engage kindergartners in recognizing and following rhythms. They give children opportunities to incorporate movement with music, both in responding to recorded music and in independent creation of music. Teachers encourage children to engage in full-body activities that require rhythm and timing (e.g., swinging).	○ Opportunities for moving to music are limited to clapping and other hand movements, which children can do while sitting. Teachers do not get up and move with children.

Comments on music and movement:
—Kindergartners enjoy call-and-response and echo songs. They can follow melodies and are able to grasp concepts such as higher or lower pitch, duration of sound, or tempo. Around age 5 or 6, children are learning to do two things at once, such as marching in a circle while playing a rhythmic instrument. Such music and movement experiences are also an important part of children's oral language learning, as they contribute to children's ability to separate syllables and analyze sounds.

Assessing Children's Development and Learning

Strategic and Purposeful

Developmentally appropriate	In contrast
Assessment is done for four specific, beneficial purposes: planning and adapting curriculum to meet each child's developmental and learning needs, helping teachers and families monitor children's progress, evaluating and improving teaching effectiveness, and screening and diagnosis of children with disabilities or special learning or developmental needs.	○ No systematic assessments of children's progress or achievements are done. ○ Assessments are done, but results are not used to provide information about children's degrees of understanding or to adapt curriculum to meet their needs. Doing the assessment takes an excessive amount of teachers' time and attention away from interacting with children. ○ Single-test assessment is used for high-stakes decision making (e.g., entry, special education referral).
Teachers use assessments in identifying children who might have a learning or developmental problem (in screening), typically at the beginning of the kindergarten year. When assessment identifies the possibility of a special need, appropriate referral to a specialist for diagnostic follow-up or other intervention occurs.	○ Developmental screening does not occur, or it (and the postscreening follow-up) occurs so late in the year that children go for months without receiving needed intervention or support. ○ Teachers diagnose or label a child after only a screening or one-time assessment. Test results are used to group or label children (e.g., as "unready" or "special needs").
Decisions that will have a major impact on children (e.g., entry, grouping, retention) are based on multiple sources of information. Sources include observations by teachers and specialists and also information from parents.	○ Eligible-age children are denied entry to kindergarten based on a one-time readiness or achievement test—that is, a test measuring what the child already knows and can do. ○ Overemphasis on assessing "readiness" or "achievement" causes some families to hold their kindergarten-age child out of school an extra year (redshirting). ○ Children are judged on the basis of inappropriate and inflexible expectations for their academic, social, or self-help abilities (e.g., whether they can write their name or go all day without a nap).

Assessing Children's Development and Learning (cont.)

Strategic and Purposeful (cont.)

Kindergarten assessment addresses key goals in all developmental domains (physical, social, emotional, cognitive) and in the areas of physical education and health, language and literacy, mathematics, science, social studies, and creative arts.

○ Programs and teachers don't think about which goals are important in each domain/area or how concepts and skills build on one another, so their assessments look at a limited set of skills in isolation.

○ Assessment focuses on certain domains/areas (e.g., math and literacy) and not others, ignoring important disciplines such as science, social studies, and social-emotional skills.

Comments on strategic and purposeful assessment:

—When a "readiness test" is an assessment of what sort of kindergarten experiences children are ready for and the results inform practice, then such a test can be both useful and appropriate (Gullo 2006a). Such assessments of children prior to kindergarten can play a useful role in helping teachers to plan kindergarten programming for the group and/or for individual children.

—Using a test to determine whether children are "ready" for kindergarten is inappropriate and can lead to detrimental decisions such as denial to kindergarten, required attendance in "developmental" instead of "regular" kindergarten, and retention in kindergarten or required attendance in a transitional year before first grade (Gullo 1994).

—Delaying children's kindergarten entry does not seem to help children and may actually be detrimental (Mehaffie & McCall 2002).

Systematic and Ongoing

There is an assessment plan that is clearly written, well organized, complete, comprehensive, and well understood by administrators, teachers, and families.

○ No plan for assessment exists.

○ The plan for assessment is not shared with or is not understood by the teachers who must execute it or the families whose kindergartners are assessed.

Regular health and developmental screenings are done by appropriate personnel to identify children who may need more in-depth, diagnostic assessment (e.g., vision and hearing screening upon kindergarten entry). Disabilities or other specific concerns not apparent at younger ages are a particular focus.

○ Screenings are not frequent enough in view of children's rapid growth and development as kindergartners.

○ When a child appears to be having difficulty (i.e., is outside the typical performance range), no individual assessment is done.

○ Teachers make diagnoses that should be done by specialists.

Assessing Children's Development and Learning (cont.)

Systematic and Ongoing (cont.)

Developmentally appropriate	In contrast
Information is collected at regular intervals throughout the year.	○ Assessments are rare and/or random. ○ Children's performance is assessed at the end of the year, when it's too late to affect learning outcomes.
Teachers have the time, training, and materials they need to do assessment properly and accurately.	○ Teachers are burdened with assessment requirements but not provided with adequate tools or appropriate professional development to use them accurately. Thus, assessing is a waste of teachers' and children's time and is likely to give misleading results.

Integrated With Teaching and Curriculum

Developmentally appropriate	In contrast
Assessment is consistent with the developmental and learning goals identified for children and expressed in the kindergarten curriculum.	○ Assessments look at goals not in the curriculum or content not taught to the children. ○ Assessments narrow and/or distort the curriculum (e.g., assessing in kindergarten only what will later be tested for accountability purposes).
Teachers use assessment to refine how they plan and implement activities. Teachers develop short- and long-range plans for each child and the group based on children's knowledge and skills, interests, and other factors.	○ There is no accountability for what children are doing and little focus on supporting their learning and development.
Teachers assess children on an ongoing basis (i.e., observe, ask, listen in, check). They collect and later reflect on documentation of children's learning and development, including written notes, photographs, recordings, and work samples. They use this information both in shaping their teaching moment by moment and in planning learning experiences.	○ Teachers don't determine where each child is in learning a new skill or concept, so they give every child the same learning experiences as every other child. ○ Assessment results (observation notes, work samples, etc.) go straight into a folder and are filed away. They are not reflected on to inform teachers how to help or challenge individual children.
Information about each child's learning and development is used to evaluate teaching effectiveness. This may lead to changes in schedule, curriculum and teaching strategies, room setup, resources, and so on.	○ Assessment results show that problems exist but do not indicate what needs to be changed. Or nothing changes because "that's how we've always done it" or it would be expensive or inconvenient for the school and/or teachers.

Assessing Children's Development and Learning (cont.)

Integrated With Teaching and Curriculum (cont.)

Teachers look at what each child can do independently but also assess collaborative work with peers and adults. Teachers assess as the child participates in groups and during other scaffolded situations.

○ Children are assessed only as individuals. Thus, teachers miss information about what children can do as members of a group or what tasks are just beyond their current capabilities and would benefit from adult support.

> Comments on assessment integrated with teaching and curriculum:
> —As much as possible, assessment should be woven into the act of teaching and interacting with children. However, there are times when the teacher needs to set up a special situation (e.g., clinical interview, structured task) designed to reveal a child's specific skill or understanding to get a fuller, more accurate picture of the child's thinking and abilities.

Valid and Reliable

Assessments are used only for acceptable purposes, where research has demonstrated they yield valid and reliable information among children of similar ages, cultures, home languages, and so on.

Only assessments demonstrated to be valid and reliable for identifying, diagnosing, and planning for children with special needs or disabilities are used for that purpose.

○ The school uses tests or other measures for which inadequate evidence of validity and reliability exists for the population assessed or for some segment(s) of that population.

Assessments include teachers' observations of what children say and do during center time, play, projects, discussions, movement games, and other learning experiences, as well samples of children's work and performance during teacher-guided tasks (e.g., categorizing words by their phonemes).

○ Teachers use methods not suited to kindergarten children (e.g., paper-and-pencil tests).

Assessments are matched to the ages, development, and backgrounds of the specific children. Methods include accommodations for children with disabilities.

Teachers use a variety of methods/tools, recognize individual variation among learners, and allow children to demonstrate their competence in different ways. They help children begin to reflect on their own learning.

○ Assessment assumes background knowledge that some or all of the children don't have. Methods prevent a child from demonstrating what he actually knows and is able to do (e.g., assessing addition with only a paper-and-pencil test when some children could accurately solve the problems with manipulatives).

Assessing Children's Development and Learning (cont.)

Valid and Reliable (cont.)

Developmentally appropriate	In contrast
Teachers gather information from families about children's health and development, including the skills, knowledge, and interests that children show at home.	○ Families are not considered a valid source of information.

Comments on valid and reliable assessment:

—Today's kindergartners are highly diverse, with an increasing number of dual language learners. In order to properly assess this population, assessment measures must take linguistic background into account and be free from cultural bias (NAEYC 2005). Using a variety of approaches to assessment is especially important with such children, as some indicators and sources of information may reveal more of a child's skills and abilities than others.

Communicated and Shared

Developmentally appropriate	In contrast
Teachers and families share information in ways that are clear, respectful, and constructive. Teachers and families make decisions together regarding learning goals and approaches to learning that are suitable for the individual child. Families are regularly informed about how their children are doing in all developmental domains.	○ Families are not kept informed about assessment results and children's progress. Teachers/ programs make important decisions unilaterally. ○ Schools provide families with information in ways that are not respectful or useful to them (e.g., written in educational jargon).
Within the limits of appropriate confidentiality policies, teachers exchange information about each child across ages/grades (e.g., kindergarten teachers with first grade teachers) and across areas (e.g., regular classroom teachers with "specials" teachers), so children are prepared for the next challenge and the next teacher knows each child's history.	○ Assessment information is not used to help ease transitions for children from one classroom and teacher to another.

Establishing Reciprocal Relationships With Families

Teachers, administrators, and school staff work to foster supportive relationships with families throughout the school year. Teachers solicit parents' knowledge about their children and input about their goals and concerns, and they use this information in ongoing assessment, evaluation, and planning. Families are offered venues for communication with teachers, such as email, a notebook that travels between home and school each day, and parent conferences.

○ Teachers and staff discount families' input, viewing them as of secondary importance in their children's education. Family members feel intimidated by teachers and by school policies, which makes them reluctant to become involved in school matters.

Teachers listen to parents, respecting differences in culture and goals while guiding families to participate in formal school procedures. When problems arise that necessitate communication with home, teachers see families as partners in finding solutions rather than obstacles. Teachers view children's education as a joint responsibility between parents and teachers.

○ Teachers view parental noninvolvement in school affairs as evidence that families do not care about their children's education, rather than taking into account cultural and linguistic differences or factors such as job schedules. When children have problems in the classroom, teachers assume that the home environment must be to blame.

○ Communication with families is used mainly to convey negative news.

○ The administration and teachers are too quick to accommodate parents' requests, even when these run counter to what is best for the child.

Families are welcome to visit the classroom as arranged with teachers, and they are encouraged to do so. Family members are offered opportunities to participate through various means, such as volunteering or observing in the classroom, accompanying children on field trips, and attending school events. Parents' work schedules are accommodated to the extent possible when planning events, conferences, and activities.

○ Families are not welcome in the school and parents are not encouraged to visit. Teachers are difficult to contact directly, and families are dissuaded from participating by a bureaucratic school culture.

○ Opportunities for parent participation, teacher–parent conferences, meetings, and other events for families occur only on rigid schedules. Conferences and meetings are held only during the day when many employed parents are unavailable.

Establishing Reciprocal Relationships With Families (cont.)

With parents who do not speak English, teachers/administrators seek strategies to facilitate communication, such as hiring bilingual staff or using translators at conferences or meetings.

○ Teachers and school staff take no action to enable families with limited English proficiency to understand written or spoken communications directed to them or to ask questions and convey any concerns they may have regarding their child or the program. Written communications are never translated. Families and children are penalized for incomplete or missing forms, though families cannot complete them due to language barriers.

○ Because of the challenges and potential awkwardness that may arise in meetings and other communication with family members who speak little or no English, teachers and school staff avoid having meetings, conferences, and other planned events with families.

Comments on establishing reciprocal relationships with families:

—Kindergarten teachers have a special opportunity and responsibility to establish positive, supportive school–family relationships at the outset of children's formal school experience. The quality of interaction between a child's kindergarten teacher and family helps to form a family's overall connection with school.

—Some cultures give teachers absolute authority over a child's education. When working with families from such cultures, teachers will need to let the relationship evolve gradually until those families become comfortable partnering with teachers.

The Common Core State Standards and Developmentally Appropriate Practices: Creating a Relationship

Susan Carey Biggam and Marilou Carey Hyson

Anna is a kindergarten teacher in a public school. Over the past year she has been hearing more and more about the Common Core. At the last faculty meeting, her principal announced that starting next year the school district will be using the Common Core State Standards for English language arts/literacy and mathematics in all classrooms, from kindergarten through grade 12. The principal told teachers to look for announcements of professional development meetings and other guidance about how to implement these new standards. Anna's friend Rochelle, who teaches in a local prekindergarten program, mentioned that her director has also been talking about these standards and how the Common Core might influence their curriculum.

At this point, Anna has many questions:

- What are these Common Core standards, anyway?
- Where did they come from, and what are they supposed to accomplish?
- What will they mean for me as a teacher and for the children I teach?
- What will they mean for programs for younger children?
- Will I have to neglect other aspects of the curriculum to focus only on English language arts/literacy and math?
- Will I be able to continue to use developmentally appropriate practices (DAP), including playful learning, or will these new standards dictate a radical change in how I must teach?

Susan Carey Biggam is associate director of research and development for the Vermont Reads Institute at the University of Vermont, and she served on the Smarter Balanced Assessment Consortium.

Marilou Carey Hyson, an early childhood consultant and former NAEYC associate executive director, is coauthor of *Why Early Childhood Education Matters* (Teachers College Press & NAEYC, 2014).

In this chapter, we try to answer these questions not only for kindergarten teachers like Anna, but also for teachers, principals, program directors, and other education leaders. We will

- Identify the essential features of the Common Core State Standards and their connections to the work of teachers and other early childhood professionals

- Increase practitioners' comfort and skill in implementing developmentally appropriate practices when addressing the Common Core standards

- Identify resources that may help practitioners understand, think critically about, and address the Common Core

- Provide a framework for action steps that will help you, the children you teach, and others with a stake in the Common Core

What the Common Core Is, and What It Is Not

What the Common Core Is: The Intended Benefits

In the past, each state had its own standards, or intended learning outcomes, for children from kindergarten through 12th grade. However, many education leaders thought that the United States, like most other countries, would benefit from a common set of expectations nationwide. The goal of the Common Core State Standards Initiative (www.corestandards.org) was to establish a common set of expectations for students who, when completing secondary education, would be "college and career ready." With this goal in mind, the developers of the Common Core (including researchers, teachers, and higher education professionals) started by defining what students should know and be able to do by the time they finished high school. The developers then wrote grade-level progressions to build solid foundations for each of these expectations.

As of this writing, 45 states, the District of Columbia, and three territories have already adopted these standards, but with varied implementation timelines.

What the Common Core Is Not: The Standards' Limitations

Just as it is important for early childhood educators to have a basic understanding of what the Common Core *is*, it's equally important to understand what it is *not*, and what it never was intended to be.

First, the Common Core is not a comprehensive description of everything children should know and be able to do. So far, the only content areas for which Common Core standards have been written are English language arts/literacy and mathematics. With

Criteria Used in Developing the Standards

According to the Common Core State Standards Initiative (NGA & CCSSO 2010), the standards were designed to give teachers and parents an understanding of what students from kindergarten through grade 12 should be expected to learn. To achieve that end, the developers tried to ensure that the standards

- Are aligned with college and work expectations

- Are clear, understandable, and consistent

- Include rigorous content and application of knowledge through higher-order skills

- Build upon strengths and lessons of current state standards

- Are evidence based

- Are informed by other top performing countries, so that all students are prepared to succeed in our global economy and society

Source: www.corestandards.org.

the needs of the whole child in mind, NAEYC and other organizations (ASCD 2012; NAEYC 2011; NAEYC & NAECS/SDE 2010) have expressed concern that the Common Core's exclusive focus may cause a narrowing of the kindergarten and primary grade curriculum, resulting in neglect of social and emotional development, approaches to learning, and other content areas such as science and the arts. Later in this chapter we will use classroom examples to show that this narrowing of curriculum can be avoided if educators are constructively critical and intentional about how the standards are implemented.

Second, the Common Core is not a curriculum and it is not a prescribed set of teaching practices. As emphasized in a position statement on early learning standards (NAEYC & NAECS/SDE 2002), standards describe desired results or outcomes for children, but they are not intended to provide detailed descriptions of the kinds of experiences and activities that are likely to lead to those outcomes, nor the methods that may be most effective. The developers of the CCSS are very clear on this point. For example, the Introduction to the English language arts and literacy standards notes that "The Standards define what all students are expected to know and be able to do, not how teachers should teach. For instance, the use of play with young children is not specified by the Standards, but it is welcome as a valuable activity in its own right and as a way to help students meet the expectations in this document" (NGA & CCSSO 2010, 6).

Third, the Common Core standards begin at kindergarten; they are not a description of what preschool children should know and be able to do. Those who design preschool programs need to know about higher-grade expectations, but teachers like Rochelle should focus on age-appropriate content and foundational experiences, rather than teaching content intended for older children. Many states are now working to coordinate or align their early learning guidelines with the Common Core, and some states have developed new literacy and math standards for their preschool programs specifically connected to the content of the K–12 Common Core. Seeing these connections between earlier and later learning can help teachers plan curriculum that keeps developmental progressions in mind, creating strong foundations while avoiding a "push-down" approach.

A Closer Look—The Common Core State Standards for Kindergarten

With that background, let's look specifically at the kindergarten standards. Because the English language arts/literacy and mathematics standards were developed by separate groups, they are not organized in the same way. However, both aim to provide clear descriptions of what the most important outcomes are—that is, what children's understanding and skills should be by the time they leave kindergarten.

"The Standards define what all students are expected to know and be able to do, not how teachers should teach."

The CCSS for Kindergarten in English Language Arts and Literacy

The big picture. Before describing the specific standards, it is important to know what the developers were thinking. They divided the standards into five categories: foundational skills, reading, writing, speaking and listening, and language. The categories are further divided into clusters.

The English language arts and literacy standards are available online at www.corestandards.org/ELA-Literacy.

The table below provides a few sample kindergarten standards. Some of these are probably familiar to you from your own state standards, but others may emphasize different things than you've been used to working on.

Areas/Domains, Clusters, and Sample Kindergarten Standards for English Language Arts and Literacy	
Area/Domain	**Cluster Headings/Sample Standards**

Foundational Skills	**Print Concepts**
	1. Demonstrate understanding of the organization and basic features of print
	   c. Understand that words are separated by spaces in print
	
	Phonological Awareness
	2. Demonstrate understanding of spoken words, syllables, and sounds (phonemes)
	   c. Blend and segment onsets [the part of the word before the vowel] and rimes [the vowel and what follows it] of single-syllable spoken words
	
	Phonics and Word Recognition
	3. Know and apply grade-level phonics and word analysis skills in decoding words
	   c. Read common high-frequency words by sight (e.g., *the, of, you, she, my, is, are, do, does*)
	
	Fluency
	4. Read emergent-reader texts with purpose and understanding

Reading (RL and RI): Reading (same clusters for literature [RL] and informational text [RI]. Some items are repeated.)	**Key Ideas and Details** **RL 3.** With prompting and support, identify characters, setting, and major events in a story **RI 3.** With prompting and support, describe the connection between two individuals, events, ideas, or pieces of information in a text **Craft and Structure** **RL 4.** Ask and answer questions about unknown words in a text **RI 4.** With prompting and support, ask and answer questions about unknown words in a text **Integration of Knowledge and Ideas** **RL 9.** With prompting and support, compare and contrast the adventures and experiences of characters in familiar stories **RI 9.** With prompting and support, identify basic similarities between two texts on the same topic (e.g., in illustrations, descriptions, or procedures)

Area /Domain	Cluster Headings/Sample Standards
	Range of Reading and Level of Text Complexity **RL 10.** Actively engage in group reading activities with purpose and understanding **RI 10.** Actively engage in group reading activities with purpose and understanding
Writing (W)	**Text Types and Purposes** **1.** Use a combination of drawing, dictating, and writing to compose opinion pieces in which they tell the reader the topic or the name of the book they are writing about and state an opinion or preference about the topic or book (e.g., *My favorite book is...*) **Production and Distribution of Writing** **5.** With guidance and support from adults, respond to questions and suggestions from peers and add details to strengthen writing as needed **Research to Build and Present Knowledge** **8.** With guidance and support from adults, recall information from experiences or gather information from provided sources to answer a question
Speaking/Listening (SL)	**Comprehension and Collaboration** **2.** Confirm understanding of a text read aloud or information presented orally or through other media by asking and answering questions about key details and requesting clarification if something is not understood **Presentation of Knowledge and Ideas** **6.** Speak audibly and express thoughts, feelings, and ideas clearly

Language (L)	**Conventions of Standard English**
	1. Demonstrate command of the conventions of standard English grammar and usage when writing or speaking
	  f. Produce and expand complete sentences in shared language activities
	2. Demonstrate command of the conventions of standard English capitalization, punctuation, and spelling when writing
	  a. Capitalize the first word in a sentence and pronoun "I"
	
	Vocabulary Acquisition and Use
	5. With guidance and support from adults, explore word relationships and nuances in word meanings
	  a. Sort common objects into categories (e.g., shapes, foods) to gain a sense of the concepts the categories represent

The CCSS for Kindergarten in Mathematics

The big picture. As with the English language arts/literacy standards, let's begin by understanding the general approach that was taken. The math standards developers based their approach on research about US children's mathematical competence, and about the deficiencies of many current practices in teaching mathematics. National reports and international comparisons (NRC 2001, 2009) have criticized math curricula that are a "mile wide and an inch deep," that cover too many topics in a scattered way, and that emphasize rote learning rather than comprehension. Additionally, children have often been expected (and expect themselves) to be "good at" math or not, with schools and families seeing mathematical competence more as a matter of innate ability than as a product of children's effort and the quality of teaching they receive. For these reasons the emphasis in the CCSS mathematics standards is on:

- Having greater focus and coherence in teaching mathematics

- Defining what children should understand and be able to do

- Giving all children opportunities to learn, including those with disabilities and other characteristics that may have limited their opportunities in the past

The standards for mathematical practice. Before presenting the grade-specific content standards, the developers described eight "standards for mathematical practice" that can be thought of as process standards, relevant to all levels of mathematics education. These are

1. Make sense of problems and persevere in solving them
2. Reason abstractly and quantitatively
3. Construct viable arguments and critique the reasoning of others
4. Model with mathematics
5. Use appropriate tools strategically
6. Attend to precision
7. Look for and make use of structure
8. Look for and express regularity in repeated reasoning

Although these may seem beyond the scope of kindergarten, teachers can lay the foundations in engaging ways—for example, Standard 4 can be addressed when children are encouraged to use many different ways to represent real-life problem situations (for example, showing combinations that make the number 5 by using toothpicks, drawing pictures, standing with their friends, and writing numerals). North Carolina's "unpacking" resource gives rich examples of how to implement the mathematical practice standards in kindergarten, http://www.dpi.state.nc.us/docs/acre/standards/common-core-tools/unpacking/math/kindergarten.pdf.

Kindergarten focus areas. In addition to the emphasis on standards for mathematical practice, the standards developers recommend that kindergarten mathematics should emphasize two focus areas:

- Representing, comparing, and operating on whole numbers—preferably with real objects

- Describing shapes and space

These topics are certainly familiar to kindergarten teachers like Anna. The difference is that the Common Core gives high priority to these areas, addressing them in greater depth, including attention to sets of critical outcomes within each area.

The mathematics standards are available online at www.corestandards.org/Math.

The specific standards for kindergarten mathematics outcomes. As shown in the table on the following page, math standards are grouped into five domains: counting and cardinality; operations and algebraic thinking; number and operations in base 10; measurement and data; and geometry. These domains represent the "big ideas," and each domain includes a group

Areas/Domains, Clusters, and Sample Kindergarten Standards for Mathematics

Area/Domain	Cluster Headings/Sample Standards
Counting and Cardinality (CC)	**Know number names and the count sequence** **3.** Write numbers from 0 to 20. Represent a number of objects with a written numeral 0–20 (with 0 representing a count of no objects). **Count to tell the number of objects** **4.** Understand the relationship between numbers and quantities; connect counting to cardinality. [Children understand that each number name refers to one larger than the previous one; the last number name tells how many were counted.] **a.** When counting objects, say the number names in the standard order, pairing each object with one and only one number name and each number name with one and only one object. **Compare numbers** **6.** Identify whether the number of objects in one group is greater than, less than, or equal to the number of objects in another group (e.g., by using matching and counting strategies).
Operations and Algebraic Thinking (OA)	**Understand addition as putting together and adding to, and understand subtraction as taking apart and taking from** **1.** Represent addition and subtraction with objects, fingers, mental images, drawings, sounds (e.g., claps), acting out situations, verbal explanations, expressions, or equations. **4.** For any number from 1 to 9, find the number that makes 10 when added to the given number (e.g., by using objects or drawings) and record the answer with a drawing or equation.
Number and Operations in Base 10 (NBT)	**Work with numbers 11–19 to gain foundations for place value** **1.** Compose and decompose (put together and take apart) numbers from 11 to 19 into ten ones and some further ones (e.g., by using objects or drawings), and record each composition or decomposition by a drawing or equation (e.g., $18 = 10 + 8$); understand that these numbers are composed of ten ones and one, two, three, four, five, six, seven, eight, or nine ones.
Measurement and Data (MD)	**Describe and compare measurable attributes** **2.** Directly compare two objects with a measurable attribute in common, to see which object has "more of"/"less of" the attribute, and describe the difference. For example, directly compare the heights of two children and describe one child as taller/shorter. **Classify objects and count the number of objects in categories** **3.** Classify objects into given categories; count the numbers of objects in each category, and sort the categories by count.
Geometry (G)	**Identify and describe shapes** **2.** Describe objects in the environment using names of shapes, and describe the relative positions of these objects using terms such as *above, below, beside, in front of, behind,* and *next to.* **3.** Identify shapes as two-dimensional (lying in a plane, "flat") or three dimensional ("solid"). **Analyze, create, compare, and compose shapes** **5.** Model shapes in the world by building shapes from components (e.g., sticks and clay balls) and drawing shapes. **6.** Compose (put together) simple shapes to form larger shapes. For example, "Can you join these two triangles with full sides touching to make a rectangle?"

of related standards. As in the English language arts/literacy standards, the math standards are grouped into clusters of related standards that logically go together (with one to three clusters in each domain). Each math standard is a statement of what children should typically know and be able to do by the end of kindergarten.

From What to How: Implementing the Common Core

These summaries show how the Common Core State Standards present the essentials of what children need to know and be able to do by the end of their kindergarten year in the domains of English language arts/literacy and mathematics. However, whether children will make progress in relation to these standards will be strongly influenced by what they experience in their kindergarten program. NAEYC's position statement on developmentally appropriate practice (www.naeyc.org/positionstatements/dap) gives practical recommendations about the opportunities and teaching methods that are most likely to result in positive outcomes, both in the CCSS domains and in other closely connected components of early development and learning.

Developmentally Appropriate Practice in Early Childhood Programs Serving Children From Birth to Age 8 and *Basics of Developmentally Appropriate Practice: An Introduction for Teachers of Kindergartners,* both from NAEYC, reiterate and provide new research support for five interrelated elements of high-quality practices in early childhood programs. As kindergarten teachers like Anna begin to think about and implement the CCSS, each of these elements is worth a fresh look with the Common Core in mind.

1. Creating a Caring Community of Learners

Relationships are the foundation of learning. With the CCSS in English language arts/literacy and mathematics, as in all other areas, children will make greater progress if they experience warm interactions with adults and spend their days with peers who care about one another. Many of the new Common Core standards are intentionally challenging, but they are achievable when teachers help children develop positive approaches to learning, including interest, initiative, persistence, and self-regulation. These learning behaviors are not inborn, but are developed over time through well-planned experiences at home and in early childhood programs (Hyson 2008).

2. Teaching to Enhance Development and Learning

Many of the recommendations within this element of developmentally appropriate practice will directly contribute to children's progress toward the outcomes in the CCSS. For example, a learning environment that encourages exploration, a daily schedule with blocks of time for both active and quiet times, a rich mix of teacher-guided and child-directed experiences, and an emphasis on playful learning will make it possible for kindergartners to benefit from engagement in CCSS-related activities.

3. Planning Curriculum to Achieve Important Goals

To be developmentally appropriate, curriculum should address all areas of development—which reminds teachers that much more is needed than the two CCSS content areas. The emphasis in developmentally appropriate practice on key concepts or "big ideas" in each discipline, and on sequences of skill development within content areas, is consistent with the Common Core's emphasis on greater depth and focus, especially (but not only) in mathematics. In planning CCSS-related activities, teachers can draw upon NAEYC's recommendations about connecting curriculum with children's interests, cultures, and prior experiences. Finally, the discussion of kindergarten curriculum includes many general recommendations in the domains of language and literacy and mathematics—recommendations that are likely to suggest more specific projects and learning activities linked to the CCSS outcomes.

4. Assessing Children's Development and Learning

States and school districts are working toward developing assessment systems that will help teachers track children's progress in relation to the Common Core. Two multistate consortia are helping with this task: Smarter Balanced Assessment Consortium and the Partnership for Assessment of Readiness for College and Careers. As this work moves forward, and as teachers like Anna think about their own practices, the recommendations on developmentally appropriate assessment, as well as the recommendations in a joint position statement on assessment (NAEYC & NAECS/SDE 2003), will be helpful. The key recommendation in both documents is that assessment must always be done for specific, beneficial purposes—the most important of which is to help improve teaching and promote children's learning, not to label or restrict children's access to later learning opportunities. Comprehensive developmental assessment—with information collected over time with varied, appropriate methods—can give teachers rich insight into each child's unique characteristics, strengths, and needs.

5. Creating Reciprocal Relationships With Families

The Common Core Standards Initiative intended the standards to help both educators and families understand and support important learning outcomes from kindergarten through the primary grades. With a strong emphasis on respectful relationships and shared responsibility for children's development, NAEYC's guidelines on developmentally appropriate practice can help teachers think about how to do this more effectively. As the guidelines emphasize, relationships with families are a two-way street. Teachers can share their understanding of the standards and their plans for helping all children make progress toward those outcomes, but parents and other family members are also valued sources of insight about their children's interests and strengths, including mathematical knowledge that teachers can tap into in the classroom—and about each family's goals, hopes, and dreams for their children. All of these insights, together with the four preceding elements of developmentally appropriate practice, help ensure positive results within and beyond the CCSS competencies.

Returning to Anna and the Common Core—
How Can Developmentally Appropriate Practice Help?

With a more specific idea of what the CCSS includes, and with guidance from NAEYC's developmentally appropriate practice framework, let's return to Anna's classroom. How might Anna incorporate the standards into her program in ways that engage the children; respond to their developmental, individual, and cultural needs; and result in solid learning outcomes? Here are some examples, first from English language arts/literacy and then from mathematics.

Anna, English Language Arts/Literacy, and Developmentally Appropriate Practice

Anna is very confident as a teacher of language arts and she has experienced a lot of high-quality professional development in this area. She is concerned that there are not enough informational books in the classroom library. In the Common Core there is a recommendation of 50 percent narrative and 50 percent informational material. How will she address this need in ways that are consistent with developmentally appropriate practice?

Here are some ideas Anna might think about.

- Organize the classroom library into different areas (e.g., picture books for science and math, picture books for social studies, art books, how-to books, fairy tales, big books) that are interesting and accessible to children, with areas for them to look at the informational books and magazines with their friends. Books can be introduced into other centers as well—for example, books about architecture in the block corner, or books about leaves in the science center.

- Talk to the curriculum coordinator, literacy coach, or principal about how to order more informational magazines. In doing this, Anna keeps in mind the interests, experiences, and cultures of the children, balancing familiar content with new material to pique their interest.

- Help the children with content-specific vocabulary from the informational texts—for example, by using Word Wizards, a child-friendly activity modified from the technique originally developed in the 1980s by Isabel Beck and colleagues and described in detail in the second edition of *Bringing Words to Life: Robust Vocabulary Instruction* (Beck, McKeown, & Kucan 2013). First, Anna can place a Word Wizards poster in an easily accessible location in the classroom. (Some teachers write the words on colored index cards so that the poster can be more or less permanent, though words change over time.) During read-aloud or other occasions when children notice interesting words, teachers select a few words to place on the Word Wizards poster. To be developmentally appropriate, words should be slightly challenging. Make sure that children can decode the word, and explain its meaning (in child-friendly terms) if you have not already done so. When introducing the approach, provide time for children to work in pairs or groups of three to practice using the words in meaningful sentences. Explain that we learn new words through practice, and the poster will provide a way to help us keep

Area/Domain	Cluster/Sample Standards	Sample DAP Approaches and Resources
Foundational Skills	**Phonological Awareness** Blend and segment onsets and rimes of single-syllable spoken words	**Head, Shoulders, Knees, and Toes** Give children a word with one to four phonemes (sounds). Have them stand up and touch their head, shoulders, knees, and toes as they are saying the sounds in words. For example, the word *cat* would be /c/ (head), /a/ (shoulders), and /t/ (knees). This is a great active, phonemic-awareness activity for helping children with segmenting, while balancing quiet times with more physically active ones.
Reading: Informational Text (RI)	**Integration of Knowledge and Ideas** 9. With prompting and support, identify basic similarities between two texts on the same topic (e.g., in illustrations, descriptions, or procedures)	**Interactive Read-Alouds** Interactive read-alouds give an opportunity to strengthen relationships between teachers and children. For example, the teacher and children can play Turn and Talk, a widely used strategy to help everyone participate in conversation with a partner and then share their responses: What's the same about the way these two books tell the story of Little Red Riding Hood? How are the stories different? How are the pictures different, and which do you and your partner like better?
Writing (W)	**Research to Build and Present Knowledge** 8. With guidance and support from adults, recall information from experiences or gather information from provided sources to answer a question	**Field Trips (e.g., library, farm, museum, store)** *What did we learn on our field trip? Can we write or draw something in our journals?* Here Anna is connecting the curriculum—and the standards—to children's prior experiences and interests.
Speaking/Listening (SL)	**Comprehension and Collaboration** 2. Confirm understanding of a text read aloud or information presented orally or through other media by asking and answering questions about key details and requesting clarification if something is not understood	**Voice Thread** Voice Thread (www.voicethread.com) can be used with kindergartners in separate towns, states, and across the world. Young children can ask questions, seek clarification, and communicate online, expanding their caring community of learners beyond their classroom.
Language (L)	**Vocabulary Acquisition and Use** 5. With guidance and support from adults, explore word relationships and nuances in word meaning. a. Sort common objects into categories (e.g., shapes, foods) to gain a sense of the concepts the categories represent.	**Sorting** Have children sort objects into boxes as they help clean up centers. Anna can scaffold conversation about how these materials are different and how they are the same—while simultaneously addressing math standards related to classification.

new words in mind so we can notice them when they are used. Any time a child hears the word, reads the word in a text, or uses the word appropriately in a sentence when speaking or writing, it receives a tally mark.

Every so often, the teacher should ask a child who adds a tally to the chart to describe or explain how the word was used. At the end of the week, count the tallies and declare one word the winner of the week. (Note that Anna can make this activity do double duty, addressing both literacy and math standards in engaging, developmentally appropriate ways.) Ask a child to take the words down and place them in a word winners box. This box becomes a repository of already-explored vocabulary words and a source of words that might be used for periodic review and classroom-based assessment.

- Engage the children with drawing, labeling, or writing about what they are reading in the informational books in the classroom library (e.g., the moon, snow, their town), Anna might help them write, label, or draw through journals and discussions.

These are just a few ways that Anna can support children's ability to engage with informational text as specified in one area of the Common Core. The chart on page 105 provides ideas for developmentally appropriate strategies that Anna might use for other, perhaps more challenging standards.

Anna, Mathematics, and Developmentally Appropriate Practice

As someone who has never had a lot of confidence in her math skills, Anna admits to herself that the Common Core standards in math seem intimidating. Of course, her program has always included math. In the past she has used a variety of enjoyable activities, often emphasizing a different math skill each week but without a clear sequence or progression. When Anna learned in district workshops that the Common Core emphasizes a smaller number of focus areas, she was happy to hear that. She decided that this year she would not feel as scattered in her approach to math. With that pep talk, Anna set out to plan experiences likely to give the children she teaches the kind of in-depth understanding that they need.

For example, Anna knows that the domain of geometry is one of the two recommended focus areas for kindergarten. One standard in particular, in the cluster on analyze, create, compare, and compose shapes, is something she's not thought about much: "Compose simple shapes to form larger shapes. For example, 'Can you join these two triangles with full sides touching to make a rectangle?'"

How can Anna help children take steps toward this outcome? Anna reminds herself that the standard isn't the curriculum—she does not have to sit the children down and quiz them about composing shapes. In fact, that is the kind of approach that's unlikely to lead to understanding, and it might also undermine children's interest and motivation in learning mathematics.

Guided by her knowledge of developmentally appropriate practices, Anna first thinks about incorporating this standard into experiences that the children already find engaging. Block building is a prime example. Instead of quizzing the children about shapes, Anna begins by watching groups of children as they are building together. She comments on what she sees them doing, and she challenges them to try out new ideas.

She then plans to implement some teacher-guided small group activities with a similar aim—again using children's existing interests and prior experiences as a springboard. The small group activities will also allow her to assess each child's knowledge so that she can plan additional experiences accordingly. Her assessment may also include photographs of what the children do with blocks and tangrams (geometric puzzles), resulting in a documentation board with a narrative constructed by Anna and the children (and strengthening CCSS in English language arts/literacy at the same time, while simultaneously promoting social competence as children work collaboratively on the project).

In addition to using block building, Anna plans to give children more in-depth learning opportunities with other materials that can be used to explore putting shapes together and taking them apart. One idea is to offer children small wooden shapes—triangles, squares, and rectangles—that can be put together in many ways. Anna intends to scaffold children's use of shape language by spending time with the children during this kind of activity. She encourages the children to talk about the shapes and what happens when they put them together. "Look, these two shapes have long sides so they might fit together. What happens when we put them together like this? Can you tell me what you did?" Anna might also create a shape curriculum that organizes the sequential introduction of different types of shapes and different types of activities with them. She sets up these activities to promote collaboration among children and to make adaptations for children like Robbie, who has a visual impairment but who will enjoy and benefit from this activity with support.

This is an example of the powerful array of developmentally appropriate approaches that can support children's progress on just one Common Core mathematics standard. The chart on the following page shows additional brief examples of developmentally appropriate approaches and resources that Anna might use for other mathematics standards—keeping in mind that multiple experiences, over time, are needed to build understanding and skills.

Tips for Teachers

The following are seven things that kindergarten and primary grade teachers can do to get ready for the Common Core.

- Take time to read and discuss the Common Core standards, getting as much help as you can to develop a practical understanding of what they mean.

- Review your English language arts/literacy and math curricula to ensure attention to CCSS priorities. What is missing or may need more emphasis?

- Identify developmentally appropriate strategies that will help children make progress toward the CCSS while supporting their holistic development.

- Access in-person and online professional development and other resources related to the Common Core.

- Work collaboratively with other teachers to brainstorm ways to address the more challenging, or newer, Common Core expectations.

- Talk with your curriculum coordinator or math or literacy coach to find appropriate resources (e.g., professional books, children's books, math manipulatives) related to the language arts and math standards.

- Carefully (and selectively) review what publishers are promoting to address the CCSS. There's a lot out there, but is it consistent with good early childhood practices?

Area/Domain	Cluster/Sample Standards	Sample DAP Approaches and Resources
Counting and Cardinality (CC)	**Compare numbers** **6.** Identify whether the number of objects in one group is greater than, less than, or equal to the number of objects in another group (e.g., by using matching and counting strategies).	**Question of the Day** On chart paper every morning, Anna writes a question that has two possible answers and then makes two columns on the paper. The question sometimes springs from the previous day's activity or something the children have been discussing—for example, "Did you walk to school or take the bus?" Children write their names or place an object on the chart, and at group time they work together to count and compare—which is more?
Operations and Algebraic Thinking (OA)	**Understand addition as putting together and adding to, and understand subtraction as taking apart and taking from** **1.** Represent addition and subtraction with objects, fingers, mental images, drawings, sounds (e.g., claps), acting out situations, verbal explanations, expressions, or equations.	**Putting Families Into a Mural** As part of a project on families, Anna asks the class to make mural showing each of the children's families. Within her comprehensive curriculum, Anna will challenge children to first create and cut out a drawing of themselves, and then add other people in their family. She will scaffold children's ability to do and understand addition by helping them count as they add more family members. Linking to literacy standards, children can also talk about their addition of family members and write a sentence about their family, incorporating some number language. And of course, family-related projects offer ways to develop many social and emotional understandings.
Number and Operations in Base 10 (NBT)	**Work with numbers 11–19 to gain foundations for place value** **1.** Compose (put together) and decompose (take apart) numbers from 11 to 19 into ten ones and some further ones (e.g., by using objects or drawings), and record each composition or decomposition by a drawing or equation [Note: kindergarten children should know what equations look like, but aren't expected to write equations] (e.g., $18 = 10 + 8$); understand that these numbers are composed of ten ones and one, two, three, four, five, six, seven, eight, or nine ones (separate into a group of ten objects, with leftovers).	**Nineteen Little Teddy Bears** Anna knows that her children are not ready to tackle place value this early in the year. She's building the foundation with activities like singing "Ten Little Indians" (but substituting teddy bears, dinosaurs, or bumblebees) using 11, 12, 13, etc. instead of 1–10. Her children love to sing together and they do this in Spanish as well as English. Anna also gives the children counting chips to put into a ten-frame, predicting whether they will all fit and having them set aside those that are left over when all the spaces in the ten-frame are filled. (North Carolina's unpacking resource has more examples and tips; see p. 112.)

Area/Domain	Cluster/Sample Standards	Sample DAP Approaches and Resources
Measurement and Data (MD)	**Classify objects and count the number of objects in categories** 3. Classify objects into given categories; count the numbers of objects in each category and sort the categories by count.	**Our Leaf Book** Anna has always used lots of classification activities with the children she teaches. This year she will be more intentional in discussing children's classifications with them and supporting them as they count the objects in each category. She plans to build more classification experiences into the art center (such as classifying collage paper by color or texture and counting how many in each category) and into some outdoor activities (classifying leaves by type, shape, or color and counting how many in each category). Again linking with literacy standards, children will be making class books with written descriptions of what they have found outdoors.
Geometry (G)	**Identify and describe shapes** 2. Describe objects in the environment using names of shapes, and describe the relative positions of these objects using terms such as *above, below, beside, in front of, behind,* and *next to.*	**Shapes at Home** Anna plans to use the children's work on this standard to make home–school connections. Children will take a card home asking them to engage their family in finding an object with a particular shape and describing where it was found, using some position words ("We found a round plate in the kitchen. It was next to a cup.") Children will report on their home objects in group time and will create drawings to illustrate what they found.

Multiplying the Benefits by Connecting Language/Literacy and Mathematics

So far we have discussed the two Common Core domains separately. However, Anna, Rochelle, and other teachers will find the benefits multiply when language/literacy and math are treated as partners and not as rivals for attention. "Math education is (in part) education in language and literacy" (Ginsburg, Boyd, & Sun Lee 2008, 4). For example, children who participated in one math curriculum not only gained better math knowledge but also better oral language skills than a comparison group (Sarama et al. 2012). In a supportive environment, children's language and literacy development can be enriched through mathematics and vice versa. Think about the way that interesting math projects can encourage children to talk together, using new words and challenging themselves to describe what they are doing. (Cara says, "Look, Eli, I put these two triangles together like this and made a square." "Cool!" Listening in, Cara's teacher might help her make a drawing of the block design and write a sentence about how she made the square.) When kindergarten teachers promote rich vocabulary of all kinds, they are helping children—especially dual language learners or those living in poverty—in all areas of their development, including the important ability to explain their mathematical reasoning (Pappas, Ginsburg, & Jiang 2003).

Although children need focused math experiences, other parts of the kindergarten schedule can expand the number of scaffolds for math and literacy.

Book-reading time is a great opportunity to strengthen children's interest and skill in both domains. Not only math books, but almost any storybook or informational book gives an opportunity to explore math concepts and apply mathematical practices: "How many ducks are on the boat now? Which is first and which is last? Are there more than there were on the page we just read? How would we find out? I wonder whether there will be more ducks on the next page: What do you think?" And finally, kindergarten teachers can use the power of play to further integrate learning across literacy and mathematics. In play, especially pretend play, children are motivated to stay engaged in and persist at challenging tasks—including mathematical challenges—and to use richer, more elaborate language. Making time for in-depth playful learning experiences pays off in every way (Bodrova & Leong 2003), within and far beyond the Common Core.

Taking Action—For Yourself, Young Children, and Others

The Common Core State Standards are here. Whether you are a kindergarten teacher like Anna, a preschool teacher like Rochelle, an administrator, or a professional development provider, these new expectations will surely affect your work in the years to come. As an intentional, empowered professional, there's much you can do to ensure that the CCSS become a positive component of quality early childhood programs and policies.

If you work in a kindergarten/primary setting, review the "Tips for Teachers" on page 107 and try implementing those that meet your needs the most. What will help build your knowledge, confidence, and competence to effectively integrate the new expectations into your practice? What will make you better informed and thoughtfully critical?

If you work with younger children, you, too, need to familiarize yourself with the CCSS. Through your NAEYC Affiliate and online resources (see p. 111), stay informed about steps being taken in your state or district to align early learning guidelines and other prekindergarten expectations with the Common Core. In working with children below kindergarten age, keep reminding yourself and others that "aligning" early learning guidelines with the Common Core should not mean pushing down standards that are supposed to apply to older children. Instead, your responsibility is to lay strong developmental foundations for later mastery of concepts and skills, and to provide children with the positive approaches to learning that will help them tackle challenging standards with enthusiasm, persistence, and initiative.

Whatever your early childhood role, take responsibility to advocate for developmentally appropriate implementation and integration of CCSS expectations into early childhood programs and policies. NAEYC's new resources (www.naeyc.org/topics/common-core) can help you communicate with policy makers, education leaders, and others as a knowledgeable professional who is prepared to describe the place of the CCSS within a holistic early childhood context.

Achieving these outcomes won't be easy, but everything is easier as a team. You and your colleagues can take the next steps together—for yourselves, the children you teach, and others with a stake in the Common Core.

Online Resources for the Common Core State Standards

These resources provide greater understanding, practical knowledge, and advocacy tools for implementing the Common Core State Standards.

ASCD: A Whole Child Approach to Education and the CCSS Initiative

www.ascd.org/ASCD/pdf/siteASCD/policy/CCSS-and-Whole-Child-one-pager.pdf

> ASCD (formerly the Association for Supervision and Curriculum Development) has adopted the "whole child approach" as a key component of its mission, not just for kindergarten but across all grades. This brief summarizes ASCD's position on the value of the CCSS initiative, but points out important issues to consider when schools try to implement the CCSS within a whole child framework.

CCSS for Kindergarten in English Language Arts/Literacy and Math

www.corestandards.org

> This link takes you to the CCSS home page, where you can download the kindergarten standards in literacy and math. The documents also include helpful explanations about what the Common Core standards are and are not.

Common Core Curriculum Maps

www.commoncore.org/maps/

> These were developed independently from the CCSS work, but they align closely with the CCSS. They may be downloaded, grade by grade, for a membership fee, or they may be purchased from the publisher. The first volume covers grades K–5.

Learning Progressions Frameworks Designed to Be Used With the Common Core

> Developed by Karin Hess of the National Center for the Improvement of Educational Assessment and teams of content experts, these documents describe specific learning targets aligned with the Common Core, and the research behind each.
>
> English Language Arts and Literacy: http://www.naacpartners.org/publications/ELA_LPF_12.2011_final.pdf
>
> Mathematics: http://www.nciea.org/publications/Math_LPF_KH11.pdf

NAEYC's Developmentally Appropriate Practice Position Statement

www.naeyc.org/positionstatements/dap

> The position statement describes specific practices, including those specifically for kindergarten, that help children learn in ways suited to their developmental, individual, and cultural characteristics.

New Jersey Kindergarten Implementation Guidelines

www.state.nj.us/education/ece/guide/KindergartenGuidelines.pdf

> Not specifically aligned with the CCSS, but a good guide to methods that combine active, playful learning with careful attention to content.

New Jersey Teacher Practices Related to Common Core State Standards for English Language Arts and Mathematics

English language arts and literacy: www.state.nj.us/education/ece/k/lal.pdf

Mathematics: www.nj.gov/education/ece/k/math.pdf

> These documents give kindergarten teachers practical support as they try to address the CCSS in developmentally appropriate ways, whether in New Jersey or elsewhere. This is not a curriculum, but suggests ways to emphasize the standards' outcomes within many everyday activities.

North Carolina Department of Public Instruction Resources

http://www.dpi.state.nc.us/docs/acre/standards/common-core-tools/unpacking/math/kindergarten.pdf

> North Carolina has developed wonderfully helpful instructional support tools, including "unpacking" documents that explain the underlying rationale and content of the CCSS, grade by grade, with suggestions for teaching strategies. The resources include an unpacking of the eight mathematical practices with kindergartners in mind.
>
> Like some other states, North Carolina also "crosswalks" the Common Core with its state standards and provides other resources for teachers: http://mcpublicschools.org/acre/standards/common-core-tools/.

State Consortia to Support High Quality Assessment for the Common Core

PARCC: www.parcconline.org/achieving-common-core

Smarter Balanced: www.smarterbalanced.org/k-12-education/common-core-state-standards-tools-resources/

> The Partnership for Assessment of Readiness for College and Careers (PARCC) and Smarter Balanced Assessment Consortium are two groups that are helping states develop high-quality assessment systems related to the Common Core. They are committed to using assessment to support educators, improve instruction, and help all students succeed.

YouTube and the CCSS

www.youtube.com/watch?v=RmLElb7yHDU

> This link will take you to many presentations that are designed to help educators understand and implement the CCSS. They vary in quality and appropriateness for kindergarten but are worth browsing. There is even a CCSS song (www.youtube.com/watch?v=X0mKVKxhMpQ)!

Vermont Department of Education Common Core Tools

ve2.vermont.gov/

> This is an example of one state's development of useful tools for teachers.

Young Children Articles

Integrating Science Inquiry With Reading and Writing in Kindergarten

Helen Patrick, Panayota Mantzicopoulos, and Ala Samarapungavan

Today is a science day in Debbie Hill's kindergarten class. Children are at three centers—some are reading a book about the life cycle of a chicken, a few gather to observe tadpoles, and others are writing in their notebooks what they want to know about caterpillars. They all are keenly interested and engaged, as is usual, and are sometimes noisy but rarely disruptive.

In Lorrie Newcomb's class next door, the kindergartners are drawing pictures of a chicken's life cycle. They are excited that a chick has hatched from one of the three eggs they have been observing.

These children are engaged simultaneously in science inquiry *and* in literacy activities—reading, writing, and talking about science content and the process of doing science. The teachers' lessons are aligned with the National Research Council's (NRC) science education framework (NRC 2012) whereby kindergarten teachers introduce ideas, concepts, and practices that are central to science. They are built on and revisited continually from kindergarten through 12th grade. The lessons are also in line with the Common Core State Standards for English Language Arts and Literacy (NGA & CCSSO 2010), which stipulate that half of K–5 reading should involve informational books in content areas such as science (Neuman & Roskos 2012).

Over the past three years we have worked with kindergarten teachers to develop study units with sequences of integrated science inquiry and literacy

> A range of integrated activities can flexibly support the learning of reading and writing while promoting scientific literacy.

activities appropriate for kindergartners. Our work is part of the Scientific Literacy Project (SLP) (Mantzicopoulos, Patrick, & Samarapungavan 2009; Samarapungavan, Mantzicopoulos, & Patrick 2011). The teachers did not work in the easiest circumstances—they taught classes of 20 to 28 children, many of whom started school speaking very little English. The schools serve ethnically diverse children and families predominantly with low incomes. The children in their schools generally score below the Indiana state average on state standardized tests once the testing program starts in third grade.

Our collaboration has been very successful. The children learned important science concepts and vocabulary, improved their language skills, developed more positive attitudes about science, and scored better, for example, on tests in both subjects than ethnically and socioeconomically similar children who did not participate in the science and literacy activities (Mantzicopoulos, Patrick, & Samarapungavan 2009). Teachers were enthusiastic. They could regularly include science in the curriculum without taking time away from reading and writing, and they saw the children learn and enjoy both.

The success of the Scientific Literacy Project is in the *approach* to science instruction, literacy instruction, and their integration, rather than the use of any particular book or activity. Teachers can apply this approach to any science topic, taking into account children's interests and the resources available. In this article, we outline the central ideas of the SLP, focusing on literacy-related activities. We present examples from many classes to illustrate how a range of integrated activities can flexibly support the learning of reading and writing while promoting scientific literacy.

Central Ideas of the Project

The SLP is grounded in the view that science involves asking questions about the world around us and seeking answers to those questions (Mantzicopoulos, Patrick, & Samarapungavan 2009; Samarapungavan, Mantzicopoulos, & Patrick 2011). Inquiry is central to science (Worth & Grollman 2003; NRC 2012). The process may involve making predictions, observing, taking measurements, recording what is seen or measured, comparing observations with predictions, summarizing, and communicating to others what was learned. Several key ideas guided the development of our activities:

- Science curricula and inquiry activities help children understand the big ideas in different science disciplines (for example, life sciences and physical sciences), rather than focus on collections of isolated facts

- Learning science through inquiry gives children insights into the nature of science

- Reading, writing, and quantification are integral to science

- Social interactions and science talk among children and adults center on shared activities that include book reading and stimulate children's interest and knowledge of science

We embed these central ideas in six study units. Three include (1) What Is Science?, (2) Tools, and (3) Force and Motion; each lasts one to two weeks.

This article was first published in *Spotlight on Young Children: Exploring Science* (Shillady 2013).

Helen Patrick, PhD, is a professor of educational psychology at Purdue University in West Lafayette, Indiana.

Panayota Mantzicopoulos, PhD, is a professor of educational psychology at Purdue University.

Ala Samarapungavan, PhD, is a professor of educational psychology at Purdue University.

The other units, (4) Living Things, (5) Life Cycles, and
(6) Marine Life, span four to six weeks. Each unit is built
around science topics and skills that link to Common Core
State Standards for English Language Arts and Literacy
(NGA & CCSSO 2010), as well as to NRC's framework for
science education (NRC 2012). We structure a cohesive
set of activities within each unit, and the content spirals
across the units so that children revisit concepts learned
earlier, such as characteristics of living things, adaptation
to habitats, or food chains.

Nonfiction Science Books

Reading high-quality and age-appropriate nonfiction science books is an essential part of the SLP approach. It
facilitates the development of distinct literacy skills,
such as making inferences, identifying key concepts, and
synthesizing and summarizing informa-
tion (Pappas 2006; Yopp & Yopp 2012).
Reading these books together also helps
children learn specific vocabulary in
context and enhances their conceptual
understanding of science. In addition, the
books' photographs of children encoun-
tering science—for example, while helping an adult in the kitchen or playing on
a teeter-totter—communicate that everyone, including children, can do science.

We chose books that fit each unit's
themes (see Mantzicopoulos, Patrick, &
Samarapungavan 2009). For example, in
the marine life unit, children read informational books about the ocean, characteristics of fish, creatures that live in
shells, kelp, ways that different fish are
camouflaged, and dolphins. The criteria we used to evaluate and select books
appropriate for each unit included content quality, accuracy, and currency;
the quality of illustrations; distinction of fact from fantasy; accurate portrayal
of time; race and gender equity; and correspondence with state and national
standards for science (Patrick & Mantzicopoulos 2013).

For each unit as a whole, we ensured that the range of books used comple-
mented each other and the classroom inquiry activities. We were attentive to
whether content, although not inaccurate, could potentially promote miscon-
ceptions. For example, some books support the common misconception that
plants take all their food from soil through their roots.

While reading with the children, teachers used different dialogic strategies,
such as asking open-ended questions, connecting children's comments to their

previous experiences (either within or outside the classroom), and extending children's statements (see Mantzicopoulos, Patrick, & Samarapungavan 2009). These strategies encourage children to predict what might happen, suggest reasons for events, and elaborate on the text (Early Learning Group 2004). In the process, children develop vocabulary, reasoning, and understanding—vital features of literacy and science.

Science Notebooks

Children build writing and reading skills as they participate in the activities. Across all units, teachers emphasize that as part of asking and answering questions, scientists must record what they want to know and what they find out so that they can remember what happened, compare what they see over time, and communicate their findings to others. Children document their questions, observations, and conclusions in their own science notebooks for each unit. The notebooks provide children with an authentic context for developing thinking and literacy skills. By highlighting the importance of writing as communication, teachers support young children's growing understanding of the meanings of reading and writing and the role of audience (Donovan & Smolkin 2011; Gerde, Bingham, & Wasik 2012).

Science notebooks work well for this age group because they are versatile in terms of individualizing learning, including meeting the needs of dual language learners (DLLs) and those with special needs, such as developmental delays. Despite the enormous variation typical within kindergarten classes (Donovan & Smolkin 2011), all children can use science notebooks. Notebook pages are relatively unstructured to allow flexibility in how different teachers use them, their appropriateness for various times of the year (for example, at the beginning or the end), and children's varying levels of literacy skills in the same class. Children with very different skills can, nevertheless, all succeed at writing. Over time, the children learn more and become better writers.

> Despite the enormous variation typical within kindergarten classes, all children can use science notebooks.

Children's Recordings in Their Science Notebooks

This section illustrates some of the many ways to use science notebooks with young children engaged in science inquiry and literacy activities. The examples represent children's work, from the first month of kindergarten to the end of the year.

Asking questions about butterflies. Children investigated the life cycle of the butterfly. At the beginning of all the study units, children recorded questions on topics they wanted to know about. This involved teaching children what questions are. Examples of their questions included, "What do baby butterflies look like?" and "How do butterflies eat?"

Investigating whether salt or beans dissolve in water. Making predictions and recording observations are important aspects of science. Sometimes children recorded both predictions and observations, such as when they investigated things that dissolve. In many classes the teacher introduced science at the beginning of the year by reading *Science Is Everywhere*, by Nancy Yu. Each child conducted an investigation shown in the book and the accompanying teacher guide, predicting, and then finding out, whether salt or beans dissolve when stirred in a cup of water.

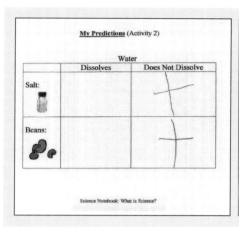

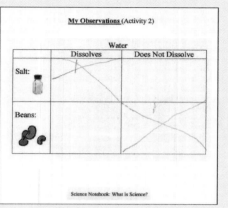

Because many kindergartners are learning to read, pictures accompanied the words *salt* and *beans* in their notebook charts and on the cups. The children made check marks in the appropriate column on their charts. With a large copy of the charts as a model, the teacher demonstrated what the children were to do: compare their predictions and observations. One child's notebook showed her prediction that neither salt nor beans would dissolve in water. She then observed and recorded her actual findings on the next notebook page.

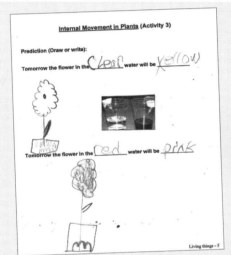

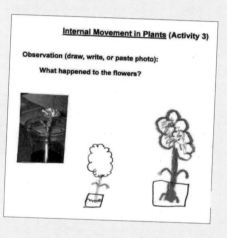

Comparing the appearance of white flowers in clear water and colored water. Children compared their predictions and observations as part of an investigation demonstrating that plants have movement—a characteristic of living things. Using two white carnations, children recorded their predictions about what the flowers would look like after one was placed in clear water and the other in colored water. On the following day, the children recorded the outcome, compared their predictions with their observations, and summarized what they learned. They drew pictures of the flowers and/or glued in photos, and they wrote descriptive words, if they were able.

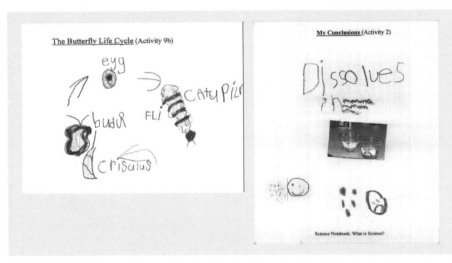

Recording observations from a nature walk. As part of the Living Things unit, the children and teacher took a nature walk outside. When they came inside, the children recorded the living things they had observed, using a combination of words, pictures, and drawings. One example, made after one month of school, includes digital photos taken by the teacher of a tree, grass, and two worms, as well as drawings. The child whose work appears in the second example labeled a drawing and photos of cattails and a squirrel and recorded fancifully that he saw a bat.

Summarizing what was learned about the butterfly life cycle and what dissolves in water. An important aspect of inquiry is having an opportunity to *summarize what was learned*. This helps children remember what they saw, clarify their thoughts, and think about what they learned. Two summaries by two children use a combination of pictures and words. In an example about the butterfly life cycle, a child uses drawings and invented spelling to document her learning after the class observed caterpillars change into butterflies. Another child's conclusion after the dissolving investigation shows a happy face beside salt crystals and a sad face beside beans, under the heading "Dissolves in [water]."

At the end of each science unit, children take their science notebooks home to share what they've learned with their families, which supports connections between school and home. The notebooks are records of children's progress through the year and reminders of their science inquiry concepts, vocabulary, and activities. The children are understandably very proud of their notebooks, and parents are usually delighted and often surprised at their children's learning.

Recording Promotes Literacy

Children's entries are personal and do not need to be the same in terms of specific content or skills used; many forms of recording promote literacy (Gerde, Bingham, & Wasik 2012). Children can keep records by using what-

Concepts and Guidelines for a Science Inquiry Project

- Science is the process of finding out about the world around us by asking questions, finding and recording conclusions, and communicating the conclusions to others. Science is not just learning facts.

- An inquiry approach to teaching science and integrating it with literacy involves addressing big ideas or themes in science. It can be used for any topic within the science learning standards and doesn't require specific activities, texts, or curricula.

- Some big ideas in science include (1) differences between living and nonliving things, (2) how living things adapt to their environment, and (3) interrelationships between living things (for example, food chains).

- Revisiting big ideas multiple times throughout the year, each time with greater complexity, leads to children's increased understanding.

- Young children easily learn the language of science when it is incorporated naturally in everyday classroom talk.

- Young children are fascinated by informational texts. Choose these texts carefully and read them more than once.

- Using loosely structured materials, like notebook pages rather than highly structured worksheets, gives children developmentally appropriate opportunities for learning writing and serves the needs of children with a range of skills and abilities.

- Keeping notebook pages together lets children look back at their previous thoughts and activities for comparisons and helps them remember what they have done and learned.

ever means works for them. They can complete the activity in a way that matches their developing skills and abilities. For example, children can draw pictures or paste in photos. They can dictate and have an adult write for them and perhaps copy in their own hand on top of or underneath the words. They can write their own words using invented spelling or copying from a word wall, paste in words, or add check marks to charts.

The notebooks also support assessment. They document children's developing skills throughout the year, so they serve as excellent records of changes in children's writing, vocabulary, spelling, and understanding. Thus, teachers are able to attain recommended goals for assessing children's "strengths, progress, and needs" (NAEYC & NAECS/SDE 2003, 10) in appropriate and valid ways that are tied to their daily activities.

Benefits for Dual Language Learners

During the science investigation process, as dual language learners participate in the reading, writing, inquiry, and discussion activities, they become familiar with key social communication skills that are fundamental to success in school. In addition, they develop important technical/academic vocabulary critical to success but less likely to be learned in DLL classes (Stoddart et al. 2002).

Being actively involved in literacy-rich science inquiry activities, especially in small groups, provides an exciting and real context for children to further both English and home language skills. For example, during the first weeks of school, Ernesto, who knew only Spanish, learned English words involving size, color, numbers, and position, and many nouns. He learned these while he searched for caterpillars on a milkweed plant, counted them, described their appearance, and compared their sizes with measurements he took on previous days.

In learning to write, children who are dual language learners benefit especially from the use of science notebooks. The loose structure allows children to express themselves pictorially or by writing in their home language while they learn English. This approach fits well with best practices for writing instruction (Gerde, Bingham, & Wasik 2012). Children can use science notebooks to build on their understandings, express what they know, and show teachers what they know and can do without relying on verbal skills (NAEYC & NAECS/SDE 2003). Teachers can use children's notebook entries to facilitate children's explanatory talk, such as when they explain verbally the records from an investigation in which the teacher simultaneously releases toy trains down two ramps with smooth and rough surfaces.

Common Core State Standards for English Language Arts and Literacy in History/Social Studies, Science, and Technical Subjects: Selected Standards for Kindergarten and Grade 1

Reading
- Read and comprehend informational texts
- Ask and answer questions about key ideas in a text
- Identify the main topic and key details
- Explain major differences between story and informational books
- Understand a variety of text features (e.g., table of contents, glossary)
- Describe the relationship between illustrations and the text
- Identify the reasons the author gives to support a point
- Identify similarities and differences between two texts on the same topic

Writing
- Use a combination of drawing, dictating, and writing to state an opinion, compose informative texts, and narrate an event including details and sequence
- Participate in shared research and writing projects
- Recall information from experiences or gather information from provided sources
- Respond to questions and suggestions from peers, and add details

Speaking and listening
- Participate in collaborative conversations, and build on others' talk
- Describe people, things, and events while giving details
- Speak audibly, and express thoughts and ideas clearly

Adapted from NGA & CCSSO (2010).

Conclusion

Integrating reading and writing about science with inquiry activities is a particularly effective and efficient way to teach meaningful science in kindergarten as well as the early grades. This approach establishes a cohesive context in which children can develop skills and knowledge important for both literacy and science. Primary grade teachers do not need specialized materials or workbooks to provide meaningful and developmentally appropriate learning experiences for all their children. Both teachers and children in this project were overwhelmingly positive about the activities.

The teachers had a way to meet science standards for kindergarten while also authentically fulfilling English language arts standards. They recognized that the children learned a considerable amount in both subjects, a finding supported by scores on both researcher-administered literacy tests and science tests. The test scores were higher than the scores of ethnically and socioeconomically similar children whose teachers did not use this approach (Mantzicopoulos, Patrick, & Samarapungavan 2009). In addition, the children were excited about "being scientists" and developing real science and language skills and knowledge.

Science Education Framework: Selected Practices, Concepts, and Ideas

Scientific practices
- Ask questions
- Plan and carry out investigations
- Analyze and interpret data
- Construct explanations
- Obtain, evaluate, and communicate information

Crosscutting concepts
- Cause and effect
- Scale, proportion, and quantity
- Structure and function
- Stability and change

Disciplinary core ideas
Life sciences
- Structures and processes
- Unity and diversity

Physical sciences
- Motion and forces

Adapted from NRC (2012).

Young Authors: Writing Workshop in Kindergarten

Kathryn M. Brown

"Can we write our books today?"
"Can I share the book I wrote?"
"I finished another book!"

These are things one would hear in a primary writing workshop. Would you believe that kindergartners are saying this?

In January of my first year as a kindergarten teacher, I decided to introduce writing workshops to the class. After teaching third grade for four years, I was passionate about this approach to writing. However, I wasn't sure that kindergartners, just learning to read and write, were ready.

I teach in a suburban elementary school in Fairfax County, Virginia. Most of the children enter the half-day kindergarten having already attended a community preschool, and many come with knowledge about writing and books. But not everyone has the same knowledge, and there are vast differences in children's literacy levels.

During that first kindergarten year, writing time consisted of journal writing and individual teacher–child conferences. The children would draw in their journals, then write about their drawings. When they finished, they would either share their journal entry with a buddy or have a conference with the teacher to talk about their writing. I saw a lot of "Me and Kristine r plaing" and "I luv my mom," and I felt that the children could do more.

Because the journaling approach was not personally meaningful, the children's writing was short on content, creativity, and spark. I missed the writing workshop I had taught in third grade. During that workshop, the children created meaningful, creative pieces of writing. I was perplexed about how I could incorporate the workshop techniques that I loved in the primary grades into kindergarten writing instruction.

Writing Workshop for Kindergartners

Because this was my first year teaching kindergarten, I had asked my graduate school professor for a list of must-read books for kindergarten teachers. It was in this list that I came upon Ray and Cleveland's *About the Authors: Writing Workshop With Our Youngest Writers* (2004). The book explains how to use writing workshop ideas with younger children—just what I wanted to do.

The workshop approach allows children blocks of time to write, focusing not on a finished product, but rather on the act of writing itself. Children do not have to complete a piece every day. They put unfinished writing in their folders to continue the next day. When they do finish a piece, they begin the writing process again.

Ray and Cleveland's writing workshop for young children uses the same processes as the upper grades: drafting, editing, revising, and publishing—all in the context of making books. This idea aligns with developmentally appropriate teaching practices, which recommend "daily opportunities and teacher support to write many kinds of texts for different purposes" and "writing experiences that allow the flexibility to use nonconventional forms of writing at first (invented or phonic spelling) and move to conventional forms" (IRA & NAEYC 1998).

The writing workshop differed drastically from the journaling the children had been doing. Instead of having time constraints, the time in which to complete a book was unlimited. Instead of being confined to one page in a journal, the number of pages in a book was the writer's decision. I wondered once again whether these young children could handle such an open-ended program.

This article was first published in the January 2010 issue of *Young Children*.

Kathryn Brown, MA, is a kindergarten teacher at A. Scott Crossfield Elementary School in Fairfax County, Virginia.

Introducing the Workshop

All year we had been reading quality children's literature about anything and everything. Good literacy instruction begins with immersing children in diverse texts—"we need to marinate students in literature so that, over time, it soaks into their consciousness and, eventually, into their writing" (Fletcher 1993). So to open the new writing program, I wanted the children to take a close look at books and follow up with a discussion.

I randomly distributed a variety of books on the floor in the group meeting area. Before having the class explore the books, I asked the children to keep in mind the question, "What do you notice about books?"

They loved how the books were spread over the floor, beckoning them to dive in and explore, and they loved having an opportunity to just talk about books. When the children completed their book investigations, we made a class chart to synthesize their learning. They noticed (with little prompting from me) that books have a title, authors/illustrators, pages, words, illustrations or

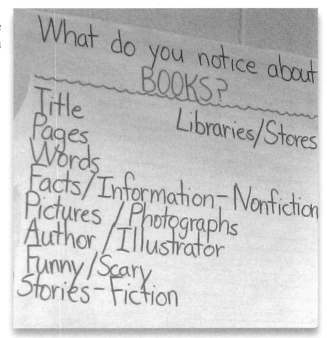

photographs, stories, facts, and more—all the things I had hoped they would notice. We called the chart, "What Do You Notice About Books?"

I told the class that writing workshop would be a time to make books. I showed the children the blank books they would write in—blank sheets of paper stapled together—and the writing folders where they would keep their works in progress and some of their finished books. I emphasized that the books they created should include all the elements they noticed during their explorations—that they were authors setting out to write books like the many books we had read in the classroom.

Knowing that some children would have trouble coming up with a topic, I invited a few to share their topics with the class, hoping that it would inspire others. Then all the children eagerly put pencil (and crayon) to paper and began making books.

The Children Plunge In

The children wrote titles on the front page, and some even wrote "by" and "illustrated by" (looking at the class chart to spell *illustrated*). The myriad of ideas and topics showed the diverse interests and knowledge of the class. There were nonfiction stories about snakes, outer space, cars, and lizards. There were fiction stories about missing teachers and dog adventures. One author modeled her book on a counting book. She titled it "Ducks," and on three consecutive pages she wrote, "1 ducks," "2 ducks," "3 ducks."

When I ended writing time that first day, the children did not want to stop. They were deeply engaged and could not wait to come back and continue working on their books. Some asked if they could work on them during center time. I helped them file their work in their writing folders and told them that they could continue working on the books the next day.

I was a little skeptical about whether 5- and 6-year-olds would even remember their books the next day, much less want to continue writing in them; but they did. Some children worked diligently on the same books for several days. The children worked with a feeling of confidence in their writing and ideas that I had not expected.

Being a class of 29 children, they engaged in much talk and sharing of ideas and stories every day. Each morning numerous children came up to share with their classmates and me ideas and information about what was happening in their lives. This may have played a part in the success of the writing workshop approach. Lamme and colleagues find that the foundation of a writing program is "a classroom rich with talk, where children are encouraged to tell about events in their own lives" (2002, 74).

Focus on Kindergartners

When Is a Book Finished?

In mini-lessons I gradually introduced new information about writing. Mini-lessons are short lessons given every day before the class begins independent writing. Mini-lessons use modeling and interactive and shared writing to teach writing conventions. The first mini-lesson was about knowing when a book is finished.

We referred to the list we had made on the first day of writing workshop—what the children noticed about books. We then talked about what finished books should look like. One child said that they needed to add the date stamp, like we had done all year with the journals. Another mentioned that they needed to add their names, just like real books have the author's name on the front. With some prompting from me, the children checked the chart and discussed the importance of filling books with illustrations and writing.

We created a new chart, "I Know I'm Finished When . . .", listing this information. The children could look at this chart when they thought their book was complete, before coming to the teacher for a conference.

While I wanted the children to work toward completing their books, we also talked about how writers do not have to finish one piece before they begin another. The children could work on multiple pieces at one time or abandon a piece they were no longer passionate about, because that is what writers do. They could always go back to the abandoned work and finish it later. In writing workshop, the most important thing for the teacher is to keep the children writing enthusiastically, working toward a finished product and experiencing the joy of writing.

During writing conferences, the young authors and I referred to the new chart to check that they had done everything necessary to complete their books. Then we discussed the next steps to take—sitting in the Author's Chair to share finished books with their classmates, sharing with a friend, and putting the book in the classroom library or taking it home. These important steps bring a sense of closure to a piece as well as celebrate the work a child has done. In *Writing Essentials*, Routman believes that "we are much more apt to do optimum work when we know our best efforts will be supported and celebrated and when we believe we can succeed" (2005, 18).

Expectations for Kindergarten Writers

Using the writing workshop approach in kindergarten, I have found that approximations and authentic writing experiences are the cornerstones of good writing instruction. By *approximations* I mean children's representations of adults' conventional writing. Authentic writing experiences provide the impetus for these young children to become writers—with appropriate approximations.

My advice to teachers who try the writing workshop approach with young children is not to expect perfect penmanship, spelling, or a well-crafted story line. A kindergarten book will most likely have some illustrations with a line or two of approximated writing. Teachers have to look beyond what may or may not be there and see how the children have made kindergarten versions of books.

Learning More About Books and Writing

The content of subsequent mini-lessons concerned making really great illustrations, matching illustrations to words, adding dedications, and focusing on one big idea. When I held a mini-lesson about a new aspect of writing, we looked at examples in other books (written by children or professional authors). I encouraged the children to try the new ideas in their writing and share their experiences and results with each other. One mini-lesson that really took off was about adding a dedication.

We first went back and looked at the dedications in the books we'd read in class throughout the year. I then encouraged the children to think about whom they would like to dedicate their own books to. Many children who had chosen to write bird books (the theme for the week) dedicated their books to the teaching aide, who had been sharing her love of birds all week. Another child dedicated her book on the five senses to her little brother. She wrote in her dedication, "To Campbell to learn about the five senses."

When it comes time for the authors to share, I frequently choose writers who have tried out new ideas. When they take the Author's Chair, the pride shines in their faces. It is just the encouragement the rest of the class needs to take risks in their writing. Showcasing the work of young authors who try something new in their writing is the best way to encourage others to try it.

Conclusion

I was very surprised by how easily the class took to the writing workshop approach and began writing. Looking back, I see that all year I had worked to instill in the children the sense that they were writers, no matter what their developmental level. And for months before I introduced writing workshop, we had read excellent books every day, which helped the children understand books and enabled them to use the books as models for their writing. When it came time for the children to write their own books, the foundation had been laid.

By the end of the school year, my kindergarten class was full of writers. In a short time, the children had become authors, writing authentic, meaningful texts. Granted,

some books you could not read without the author's help, but the children were beginning to see the world through the eyes of a writer, and they were excited.

The book-writing approach took the class to another level of learning faster than the previous five months of journal writing. And more important, in their first year of formal schooling, these kindergartners were learning to love the act of writing.

Humpty Dumpty and Rosa Parks:
Making Space for Critical Dialogue With 5- and 6-Year-Olds

Candace R. Kuby

The summer program did not officially start until 8:00 a.m., so when I arrived at 7:30 I put out wooden blocks, ramps with marbles, and other manipulatives for children to explore and build with as they entered the room. "Humpty Dumpty" played on a CD as everyone arrived. As the 5- and 6-year-olds came into the room, they returned class library books and found new books to take home.

I was walking around the room preparing materials when Annie, who is White, stopped me to ask some questions about Rosa Parks. She was having a hard time understanding why White people would create a law that forbade African Americans from sitting where they wanted to sit on a bus. We looked together at the Rosa Parks biography that I had read to the class the previous day. I pointed out some of the photographs that showed separate water fountains for Whites and Blacks. We discussed the photographs of African American people with angry faces. As the conversation continued, Annie kept asking why a law would be created that separated people.

The vignette above—taken from my experience teaching 5- and 6-year-olds in a summer enrichment program—demonstrates a young child's curiosity about social justice issues. As a teacher, I do not always find it easy to know how to talk with children about such critical topics. As I spoke with Annie, I found myself wondering, How much do I tell her about segregation? What history does she already know? Do I share my own beliefs about racial segregation?

It seemed ironic that "Humpty Dumpty" was playing on the CD while Annie and I discussed Rosa Parks. The song seems lighthearted, while a conversation about racial segregation is so weighted. This comparison mimics the tensions I felt as a teacher discussing critical issues with young children.

128

Critical Inquiry Curriculum

Using a critical inquiry curriculum is about teaching children to read the word and the world (Freire [1970] 2000). Early childhood teachers apply this theory by helping children question events and texts they interact with in their communities. For example, teachers can help children understand why certain events happened, including whose voices may have been excluded. This helps young children learn about positions of power and how people can make changes to balance this power. Critical inquiry with children is important because they live in a world filled with injustices and need to discuss what they experience and witness. This type of curriculum involves looking carefully at power structures in the world, specifically how they relate to children's lives.

Several teachers have written about their experiences learning along-side young children as they think critically, problem solve, and explore injustices (Comber & Simpson 2001; Cowhey 2006; O'Brien 2001; Sahni 2001; Souto-Manning 2009, 2010; Vasquez 2001, 2004, 2005). These educators offer detailed accounts of teaching children and how children's curiosity about injustices in the world led to stimulating critical inquiry curricula. Critical inquiry curriculum starts with children's personal experiences. By observing children's interactions with and questions about the world, teachers and children cocreate curriculum. Jointly teachers and children decide on inquiry topics, sources of information, ways of representing children's learning, and avenues for social change. I considered situations the children observed that were unfair and prompted discussions about social injustices.

I believe that teachers should embrace children's experiences and use them as a springboard for a critical inquiry curriculum (Kuby 2010). Teachers must acknowledge that young children can (and do) question the injustices of the world and are eager to problem solve. In this article, I share insights and suggestions based on my discussions with 5- and 6-year-olds about an incident that happened on our playground, coupled with connections I made to Rosa Parks.

> Teachers must acknowledge that young children can (and do) question the injustices of the world and are eager to problem solve.

The Playground Bench: Inquiry Begins

One day, some teachers told children in my class they could not sit on a playground bench during recess because benches are for adults only. I was unsure how to respond to this instruction because I was not aware of such a rule. As I watched the children's facial expressions and sluggish body movements when they got up from the bench, I sensed they felt powerless in the situation. Someone with more power and authority made a rule that some children felt was not fair. Reflecting on this experience, I wanted the children to think critically about the incident and to problem solve, but I struggled about what to do next.

During the next day's morning meeting, I shared with the children what I had witnessed on the playground and asked them how they felt about what happened. From this, I made a connection to Rosa Parks, who was arrested in the 1950s in Montgomery, Alabama, for violating a bus segregation law. I am not equating what happened to Rosa Parks with what happened to the children, but I felt that discussing bus segregation would provide a historical

This article was first published in the September 2011 issue of *Young Children*.

Candace R. Kuby, PhD, is an assistant professor of early childhood education at the University of Missouri, Columbia.

Overview of a Critical Inquiry Curriculum for a Summer Program

Week

1 Got to know each other: conducted interviews and created self-portraits

2 Discussed playground incident: made a chart stating the problem and possible solutions if it happened again

Introduced Rosa Parks: printed information from the Internet about Rosa Parks to help answer children's questions

3 Read *Richard Wright and the Library Card,* by William Miller; Marybeth Lorbiecki's *Sister Anne's Hands;* and Jacqueline Woodson's *The Other Side,* to help children understand the concept of segregation

Recorded key points from our discussions about segregation on chart paper

4 Read Anthony Browne's *Voices in the Park* and used the structure of the text to write and illustrate our own class book, *Voices on the Bus* (the text described the perspectives of four groups of riders who were on the bus during Rosa's arrest)

5 Created a timeline to look at the history of segregation

Read *Henry's Freedom Box,* by Ellen Levine, for a historical perspective of slavery

Used a wall-size world map to discuss how people from different countries and continents came to America

6 Read *This Is the Dream,* by Diane Zuhone Shore and Jessica Alexander, and Peggy Moss's *Say Something,* as a way to discuss injustices that happen in the lives of children

Illustrated unfair situations in our own lives and ways to respond

Circled back to discuss the incident on the playground

example to help process and understand power relations. The children asked questions about Rosa, such as, "Why was she arrested?" This began our summer critical inquiry, in which we researched racial segregation in juxtaposition with the perceived injustice on our playground. Through reading children's literature, creating class books, and role-playing, we wrestled together with issues of segregation and coconstructed understanding. Not only were the children working to find out answers to their questions, I was also a learner, struggling to come to terms with the history of racial bus segregation. Together we were making inquiries about social issues at our school (the playground bench) and society at large (bus segregation). (See "Overview of a Critical Inquiry Curriculum for a Summer Program.")

I made a decision to foster children's critical thinking regarding the perceived injustice on our playground, although the curriculum could have gone in many different directions. For example, we could have explored other questions in response to the playground incident (Kuby 2011), like, How do we show respect for teachers/adults? And although we talked about bus segregation, we didn't specifically go into depth about questions such as: What defines an injustice? Can something be perceived as an injustice for one person but not another? Can segregation ever be good?

Insights on Critical Inquiry

The heart of this article is sharing practical strategies that help create opportunities to engage children in critical dialogue. I elaborate on three insights I gained from teaching:

1. Persistent questions guide a critical inquiry curriculum and teach us that young children can think in sophisticated ways about critical issues

2. It is important to foster verbal, spontaneous role play, which allows children to take on multiple perspectives

3. Fissures, or unexpected moments, are productive opportunities and teach us that sometimes children's critical thinking and problem solving goes in an unexpected direction that is rich for new learning

These three insights taught me how a curriculum of uncertainty is necessary in fostering space for problem solving and critical conversations with children.

Persistent Questions Guide Inquiry Curriculum

When I read aloud Lola Schaefer's *Rosa Parks* biography, the children asked questions such as, Is she dead? Is she still under arrest? How old is she now? As described in the opening vignette, Annie approached me with lots of questions about Rosa Parks while looking at the biography book.

Candace (teacher): Do you remember that the other day we talked about how people who were African American were not allowed to go to the same restaurants or drink out of the same water fountains as White people? See here in the book how it says "colored"? That means people who were not White had to drink out of this water fountain.

Annie: What did the White people drink out of?

Candace: They got a separate one by themselves. What do you think about that?

Later in our conversation, Annie asked more about Rosa Parks:

Annie: How come Rosa Parks didn't give up her seat for the White man?

Candace: Why do you think? What do you think was going on in her head when the White man [*a policeman*] came and asked her to get up? What do you think she was thinking?

Annie: She was thinking not to.

Candace: Why? What would be her reason?

Annie: Because she wanted to keep her spot because that was her spot and I think she knew that you shouldn't share your spots, because whoever gets there first gets to ride the bus in that seat.

Candace: So she decided to say no, huh? And when she decided to say no, they put her in jail. 'Cause they thought because she was African American that she did not deserve to have a seat on the bus.

Annie: Why not?

Candace: I'm not sure why not. I think that the White men felt like they had more power. What do you think?

Annie ended our conversation with some questions:

Annie: I want to talk a little more today.

Candace: Right now? Or with everybody else?

Annie: With everybody else.

Candace: What would you like to ask? What do you still want to know from other people?

Annie: How come Rosa Parks had to give up her seat?

Candace: Why did she have to give up her seat? You want to see if anybody else can help us figure that out?

Teachers encourage critical thinking by asking questions to help children role-play and take on multiple perspectives.

Throughout the conversation, Annie persistently asked questions about Rosa Parks and bus segregation. As teachers, we do not always find it easy to follow the lead of children when we have a planned curriculum. But when I let go of my agenda and truly listened to Annie, I was able to see how curious she was and what she found most intriguing.

Embracing children's questions allows space for critical thinking and dialogue. It was Annie's main question that guided the rest of our research over the summer: Why would a law be created to separate people?

Verbal Role Play Helps Children Take on Multiple Perspectives

During our conversations, I began to notice children taking others' perspectives through role-playing when critically thinking and trying to problem solve. I did not plan activities for role-playing, although I wish I had. However, educators advocate for this in critical inquiry teaching (Boal [1979] 2000; Medina & Campano 2006). As I observed the children's behavior, I embraced their spontaneous, verbal role play as a strategy children can use to process critical topics.

Candace: Why do you think a man or woman would make a law segregating people on buses?

Annie: Hmm, I don't really know.

Candace: Does it sound like something that would be fair? If you got on a bus and saw that all the African American people had to sit in the back, how would you feel about that?

Annie: If I was the White people?

Candace: Yes.

Annie: I would let them sit in my spot.

Candace: You think so? What if you were an African American person?

Annie: Hmm.

Candace: How would you feel?

Annie: Sad.

Candace: You might feel sad to sit in the back. Do you think that's how they felt back here [*pointing to a picture of the back of the bus*]?

By listening carefully to children's questions, teachers can make space for conversations about sociopolitical issues and encourage social action. I was surprised that Annie took on someone else's position. Through her talk, she began to role-play the various perspectives of people on a segregated bus.

Teachers encourage critical thinking by asking questions to help children role-play and take on multiple perspectives. Lewison, Flint, and Van Sluys (2002) write that teachers need to create spaces where children can disrupt commonplace assumptions, interrogate multiple viewpoints, focus on sociopolitical issues, and take action to promote social justice. Young children can take action by writing a petition, creating and performing a play for others about an issue, writing a letter to a policy maker, or even interacting differently with others.

> Teachers can be on the lookout for events or experiences that can serve as a springboard for critical inquiry and problem solving.

Fissures Are Productive Curricular Spaces

Fissures are cracks or unexpected moments in interactions. It was a fissure when the children in my class were told they could not sit on the playground bench. I did not know it would take place, nor did I expect to witness the children's emotional responses. As I *kidwatched*, or carefully observed children and their interactions (Kuby 2011; Owocki & Goodman 2002), it was evident that this surprising event deserved some space for a conversation during our daily class meeting.

Many times, fissures are seen as interruptions or "off task" comments. (Initially, I perceived the fissures in our conversations as just that—off task—and repeatedly tried to get back to my agenda or lesson plan.) Teachers can be on the lookout for events or experiences that can serve as a springboard for critical inquiry and problem solving.

Another fissure, an unexpected interaction, happened during a one-on-one conversation with Logan. He was painting a picture about his experience of being told to get off the playground bench. We were discussing what he could do if it happened again. All of a sudden, he introduced a fissure in our discussion with a story about his cousin:

Candace: If you think something is unfair, it is hard to say something to a grown-up because you don't want to be disrespectful or rude, do you?

Logan: Yeah. Like one of my cousins, I think. We wrestled and I got him down a couple of times. Then somebody jumped on me and my sock came off. I had to put it back on and I got pushed right down on the ground.

Candace: I bet that was hurtful.

Logan: He got me on the ground about 300 times.

Candace: Is he bigger or older than you? Like an adult?

Logan: Yeah, he's 8.

Candace: Oh, he's a little bit older than you. All right, so what did you think about what you can say next time if this happens again?

Logan: We can both sit on the bench.

Candace: You could say, "We can both sit on the bench."

Logan: Yeah, I never want that to happen again.

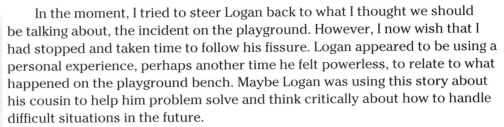

In the moment, I tried to steer Logan back to what I thought we should be talking about, the incident on the playground. However, I now wish that I had stopped and taken time to follow his fissure. Logan appeared to be using a personal experience, perhaps another time he felt powerless, to relate to what happened on the playground bench. Maybe Logan was using this story about his cousin to help him problem solve and think critically about how to handle difficult situations in the future.

Many times I think teachers may feel too busy to embrace these "one time" stories from children. As educators, how can we become more comfortable in embracing fissures? What support might we need from administrators to follow a child's lead in the moment and to value these fissures as productive catalysts for curriculum?

Embrace a Curriculum of Uncertainty

When a teacher embraces persistent questions, engages in role play, and responds to fissures, the curriculum can feel a bit uncertain. To help with the cocreated, uncertain curriculum, I used an *audit trail* to guide our learning (and my planning) (Harste & Vasquez 1998; Vasquez 2004). An audit trail is a collection of writings, drawings, questions, transcribed conversations, book covers, timelines, and any materials related to an inquiry. These items are displayed to document a learning process. As Harste and Vasquez (1998) write, an audit trail includes the following aspects:

- Child-made drawings and writings as well as outside sources that document a learning process

- Flexibility so that it always has the potential to change

- Construction whereby children and teachers deciding together what is displayed

- A window into the life of a classroom for others to witness

The audit trail allowed me to follow the children's lead and their questions in our critical inquiry investigation, while at the same time documenting our process to inform families and administrators. Using an audit trail also helped me embrace the idea of critical inquiry as lived (Vasquez 2001, 2004). Vasquez discusses critical inquiry as lived, in that it is not an addition to the curriculum but the curriculum itself. This concept requires teachers to follow the children's needs, lives, and choices for learning. Using an audit trail allowed us to live out the critical inquiry for others to see and provided a tool to guide our daily questions and investigations. Living out critical inquiry also means that the curriculum is not scripted or prepackaged, but instead arises from children's lives. This approach views critical inquiry as a way of life and learning for both teachers and children. I encourage teachers to embrace a curriculum of uncertainty, negotiating inquiries with children so problem solving can flourish.

The photograph of the chart illustrates the starting issue for our critical inquiry as documented on the audit trail. This chart captures the problem we experienced on the playground bench and possible ways to respond if it happened again. The photograph of our learning wall shows the entire audit trail (starting on the left side with the chart), documenting the journey through the books we read (photocopied covers), printed information from the Internet, questions and comments from children, and drafts of a class-made book, *Voices on the Bus*.

> When I began the process of critical inquiry with the children, I had to first ask myself what assumptions I had about teaching and learning in early childhood.

Putting It Back Together Again? Humpty Dumpty as a Metaphor for a Curriculum of Uncertainty

As I described in the opening vignette, "Humpty Dumpty" was playing in the background as Annie and I discussed racial segregation and Rosa Parks.

Humpty Dumpty sat on a wall,
Humpty Dumpty had a great fall.
All the King's horses,
And all the King's men,
Couldn't put Humpty together again.

While this song seems neutral and innocent, upon reflection it serves as a strong metaphor for what was happening in my interactions with the children. There were many times that I felt Humpty Dumpty had fallen off the wall in our critical inquiry curriculum, times when I couldn't follow the connections children were making or times when fissures seemed to get us off task from what I had hoped to teach. Just as the King couldn't put Humpty together again, metaphorically I couldn't always either. However, the times I embraced the children's questions, role play, and fissures and followed their lead, our discussions were productive. By not trying to fix Humpty Dumpty, we used our social interactions as a way to understand the social injustices in our world.

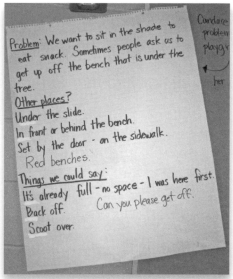

There is no set way to do critical inquiry with children, but teachers can use the strategies in this article to foster spaces for critical thinking and problem solving. As Gerald Campano writes, "One of our first challenges as teacher researchers is to inquire into and often call into question our own taken-for-granted assumptions about teaching and learning" (2007, 12). When I began the process of critical inquiry with the children, I had to first ask myself what assumptions I had about teaching and learning in early childhood. Perhaps that is the first step in teaching young children to think

critically and to problem solve: We must each dig deep into our lives and wrestle with ingrained beliefs about early childhood and social justice issues. Learning alongside the children opened my eyes to specific ways I could create spaces for critical dialogue and problem solving.

Put it back together again? No! I say embrace the uncertainty and give a critical inquiry curriculum room to flourish. Don't young children deserve to at least have space in schools to talk about what they experience and witness in their world?

The Inside-Out Project: Illustrating the Complexity of Relationships in Kindergarten and First Grade

Eva L. Essa, Jennifer M. Kirn,
Julia M. Pratt, and Shari A. Roberts

A group of six children from our kindergarten/first grade class in a Reggio-inspired program were involved in a four-month project to design an outdoor area in which indoor materials could be used. Student teachers Jennifer and Julia were in charge of the Inside-Out project, working closely with Shari, the head teacher of the class, and Dr. Essa, who taught the preschool curriculum class in which the student teachers were enrolled. Facilitated by teachers and student teachers, projects provide a venue for children's integrated, developmentally appropriate learning (Bell 2010; Fraser & Gestwicki 2001; Helm & Katz 2011). Because they integrate so many ways of addressing a common topic, projects are a way for children to meet multiple standards (Helm & Katz 2011). They provide an appropriate learning tool for preschool as well as elementary school-age children, as the following discussion illustrates. Furthermore, projects in general, and this one in particular, highlight the importance of relationships with others in a school community.

Project Initiation

Initially, Shari noticed children's misuse of materials outside and their boredom. She thought that creating more opportunities for the children to use a variety of materials outside would create more productive play and help to foster each child's interests. Shari wanted the children to expand their thinking about where materials could be used—for example, as long as children take care of books, they can read them outside. Julia and Jennifer decided to pursue this concept. They introduced the idea to the class and asked who would be interested in working on a project. They selected six

children—Cindy, Jessica, Sarah, Tanner, and Vinnie (kindergartners) and Luke (a first-grader)—based on their interest in the topic and their abilities, behavior, and friendships. When the group first met, Julia and Jennifer engaged them in a discussion about who would be affected by this project. Julia and Jennifer

asked, "Is this just for you, or will others be affected?" A lively discussion helped the children realize that the other classroom in the facility, a mixed-age preschool, would also be affected by changes to the playground. The teachers encouraged the children to think about how to get input from the other children in their own kindergarten/first grade class, as well as from the younger children downstairs in the mixed-age preschool class and the adults who work in the facility. Gradually, the teachers guided them to consider the best ways to elicit others' ideas.

Cindy said, "Let's get the sign-in sheets so we have everyone's names." Soon the group decided that each of them would be in charge of interviewing a subgroup of children. Jennifer and Julia facilitated this complex discussion, ensuring that all group members—both the outspoken and the quiet—had ample opportunity to share ideas. The children wanted to be sure that each of them had an equal number of other children to interview, with no overlaps. They did not yet know how to divide, but they came up with their own unique method. Julia and Jennifer allowed the children to test out their strategy. One child would put the letter of her first name next to a name on the list and pass it to the next group member until the names on the sheet ran out. Then, the children counted how many children they each had to interview by counting their initial and making sure they each had an equal number. Once everyone in the group had the same number, the children began to write the names of those they needed to interview on a piece of paper, leaving room for answers.

Next the children decided what to ask in the interview. After lengthy discussion, the children recognized that they needed to gather consistent information. They decided to ask one common question: "What would you like to bring outside?" Each child wrote this question at the top of his or her list of names. They spent time practicing how to ask the question and then set out, armed with clipboards, pencils, and their list of names. The group members wrote the children's answers next to the interviewees' names.

The next challenge involved deciding how to use the information they had gathered. Julia asked, "We have all these lists. What do we do with them?" Several children suggested bringing all the items on the lists outside. After further discussion, the children began to see the impracticality of this idea. Tanner proposed, "Why don't we tally the answers?" Luke added, "The ones that have the most tallies are the ones we bring outside." The children worked out a system. They agreed to put all of their lists together. One child at a time would read the items on his or her list while another child would tally the items on a master list. The children took turns until all lists had been accounted for. Some items had multiple votes while others had only one or two. "I have

This article was first published in the November 2012 issue of *Young Children*.

Eva L. Essa, PhD, is professor emerita of human development and family studies at the University of Nevada, Reno.

Jennifer M. Kirn is a kindergarten teacher and University of Nevada, Reno, graduate.

Julia M. Pratt graduated from University of Nevada, Reno, with a BS in early childhood education, and is currently a developmental specialist for early intervention.

Shari A. Roberts, MEd, taught kindergarten at the Child and Family Research Center at the University of Nevada, Reno, for 12 years.

an idea," said Sarah. "We'll choose the top seven—
one for each of us and one for Jennifer and Julia!"
Everyone liked this idea, and so seven items from the
master list made the final cut.

The children selected books, drawing materials, stamps, large LEGO bricks, small Legos, writing
tools, and painting materials to take outside. These
items were among the children's favorite indoor
materials, and they wanted to enjoy them outdoors.
The group gathered the materials from the student
teachers, the head teachers, and the classrooms and
organized them in hanging baskets and buckets on a
shelving unit to take outside.

Luke, who had been learning about graphing,
said, "We can show how many people voted for
each of the seven items with a graph." He explained
the process to the group and suggested that each
item should be represented by a different color.
Each child and the student teachers picked a color.
The children decided to use a bar graph to show
fellow classmates and parents the voting results
for the items to be taken outside. Jennifer and
Julia prepared the grid for the graph, and the children colored squares in the
appropriate columns, double-checking their work for accuracy. Several children expressed their concern that the preschoolers would not understand the
graph, so they wrote a letter to the preschool class, explaining how to interpret
the graph.

Later steps in the project included more shared decision making. The children decided where to place the objects on the playground. They also talked
about storing the items, measuring the available space, organizing a cleanup
day, and writing and posting rules for use of the Inside-Out area, making sure
all the children understood the rules. Both children and adults shared the project with families.

What the Children Learned

The four-month project offered many opportunities for children to practice
multiple skills, including math, literacy, science, problem solving, leadership,
public speaking, learning from and teaching each other, and both critical and
reflective thinking. Multiple learning standards were met through this project (Helm & Katz 2011; Mitchell et al. 2009) and the children used the seven
essential life skills described by Ellen Galinsky (2010)—self-control, perspective taking, communicating, making connections, critical thinking, taking on
challenges, and self-directed learning. Children were clearly motivated to learn
through active engagement in this project (Stipek 2011). Most important, the
children were encouraged to view their work in the context of relationships.
They took into consideration the perspectives of the children and teachers

Julia and Jennifer
asked, "Is this just
for you, or will oth-
ers be affected?"
A lively discussion
helped the children
realize that the other
classroom in the
facility, a mixed-age
preschool, would
also be affected
by changes to the
playground.

with whom they shared common space as they discussed the implications of their decisions on others. At this age children begin "to realize that others also have a sense of self and can perceive and think differently" than they think (Gallagher & Sylvester 2009, 223). The Inside-Out project illustrates powerful and interrelated outcomes in terms of children's social-emotional and cognitive development, a connection that is confirmed by research, and emphasizes the vital role of relationships in the learning process (e.g., NSCDC 2007; Thompson & Twibell 2009). This project also shows many practical applications of best practices, for both children and adults as learners and teachers. These strategies can be generalized to many settings and activities.

Strategies for Working With Children

Here are some practical strategies for working on a project with a group of children.

While working with the full group and in pairs, the children engaged in collaboration, an important aspect of building positive relationships.

Encourage children to test their hypotheses. Jennifer and Julia allowed the children to test their own ideas and inquiries and find the answers themselves. For instance, when the children wanted to build a shed to store the inside materials outside, the teachers encouraged the children to think critically about their ideas and answer several questions: Why did they need a shed? Was building one realistic? Was there room in the available space? On their own, the children came up with a realistic solution that worked very well—to store the materials in bins on an outside shelf.

Help children challenge one another through conversation. Julia and Jennifer's goal was to help guide discussions and thought processes in a way that promoted finding solutions through conversation. The children were able to problem solve and discuss details with their small group. They also worked through options with their peers in the larger class and discussed the need to use simpler words when talking with the preschoolers. There were challenges as well, for example, Jessica's reluctance to talk in front of the class, and Vinnie's and Sarah's insistence on voicing their opinions and not wanting to compromise. Jennifer and Julia's task was to redirect conversation and talk about how these differences affected the children's communication.

Teach collaboration both in the whole group and in pairs. Jennifer and Julia acknowledged the importance of collaboration among the group, and moved on only when all the children agreed, voted on the next steps, or talked through disagreements. At times, working with all six children on one task at the same time became challenging. Because the project encompassed many different responsibilities, Jennifer and Julia sometimes paired children by the activities they were drawn to. While working with the full group and in pairs, the children engaged in collaboration, an important aspect of building positive relationships.

Bring together children of different ages. Because the outdoor environment was a shared space, collaboration among everyone in the school was important. The group realized early on that not only should other children in their class have a say, but the younger preschool children had a stake in the project as well. The Inside-Out group had many meetings with the preschool children: they initially informed them about their project, they interviewed and polled them, they discussed the top seven results, they wrote letters to the preschool class, and they invited the children to be a part of cleanup day. These relationships helped group members become proficient in communicating with children of different ages, from the older first-graders in their own classroom to the 3- and 4-year-olds in the mixed-age preschool class.

Encourage children to share expertise and knowledge. During the project, the children relied heavily on each other's knowledge and came to realize that the answers were within the group. By encouraging children's unique skills, a positive classroom environment, and group discussions about each challenge, Jennifer and Julia helped the children learn to use each other's strengths. Luke was able to show the group his graphing skills and share his mathematical knowledge. Vinnie shared his understanding of measuring with inches, which the children applied to see if the storage containers would fit in the outside space. Cindy, an excellent writer, helped Sarah write a letter. Vinnie took charge when public speaking was called for, and Jessica and Cindy shared helpful information about the preschool classroom's resources.

Support children working on different parts of the project, based on their strengths and interests. All children learn, think, and process information differently and have different needs, wants, and interests. The six children in the Inside-Out group possessed different strengths. Jennifer and Julia took these into account when individualizing each child's role in the project. While all the children contributed to the project, they could work on different tasks. As the project progressed, Jennifer and Julia often split the group, so some of the children took responsibility for measuring and sorting while others wrote letters or illustrated posters. Because of the relationships that developed over the course of the project, children recognized and respected each other's contributions as important to the project's success.

Guide children to reflect on what they have done. Several times throughout the project, Julia and Jennifer made a conscious effort to bring the group of children together to discuss and share what they had learned, what they had accomplished, and what still needed to be done. At first, reflection was a difficult concept for the children to understand and do, but as Jennifer and Julia modeled reflection by talking about their own thinking processes, gradually the children began to reflect. Teachers and children frequently reviewed documentation of important parts of the project together. Seeing photographs of their activities, the children could think back, remember, and talk about activities that led up to that particular point in time. Reflection reinvigorated the children, and they became excited about the work they had

accomplished and the tasks remaining to finish their project. Such reflection also supported and reinforced the importance of communication and relationships.

Recognize that hands-on activities give meaning to what children do. The teachers realized the children would value very little if they were not immersed in the project's activities. They gave the children challenges—to organize and find space outside for the indoor materials, design their own graph, gather information, write letters, design an aesthetically pleasing environment, and be responsible for the space they created. These hands-on activities helped children stay engaged.

Strategies for Working With Adults

Here are some practical strategies for working on a project with teachers and adult students.

Model how to work effectively with small groups of children. Julia and Jennifer spent the first semester of their curriculum class observing the children, their environment, and the head teacher. Coupled with instruction in the preschool curriculum class, these experiences helped them understand the program's teaching philosophy and laid the foundation for building relationships with the children and Shari, the head teacher. Shari modeled how to work with a small group of children with varying abilities, ask open-ended questions, bring out each child's individual strengths, collaborate with the group, and get the children to collaborate with each other. The students learned basic classroom management skills and how to find a balance between teacher-directed and child-initiated ideas.

Encourage adults to test their own hypotheses and take risks. As Jennifer and Julia took control of the project, Shari took a backseat to support them. After an activity, she encouraged them to take risks and make adjustments according to what worked and what did not. For example, Shari suggested that they include math tasks related to the items the children selected to take outside, but she left it up to the student teachers and the children to make any final decisions. After the children polled the classes, they posted their tally sheet on the classroom wall. Shari encouraged the student teachers to make sure the posted tally sheet was easily understood by anyone entering the room. With Julia and Jennifer's guidance, the children decided to add a brief explanation along with a colored graph that could easily be read by both children and adults.

Revisit the project and make changes as necessary to move forward. Jennifer and Julia regularly revisited the work they had done with the children, reminding them about the project's purpose and the progress they had made. Revisiting the project helped the student teachers decide on the next step. For example, they reflected on which items children brought outside and why the children seemed interested in them.

Once the items were placed in the outside space, the group conducted a trial run with the rest of the school. After observing the children who were not part of the project group using the materials and space, the group met with Julia and Jennifer and concluded that they needed a place to hang paintings to dry and a place to save unfinished work. The adults and children came up with solutions for these issues and put them in place the following day.

Think reflectively about purpose and process. Teachers need to take time to reflect on their work with children and on their work with each other (Darling-Hammond & Richardson 2009). Shari helped Jennifer and Julia think about their decisions and keep their focus on the project. She encouraged them to examine the process as well. Although the children sometimes wanted an immediate solution, the adults would slow down and focus on the process with the children. Shari, Julia, and Jennifer frequently met after working with the children to discuss what worked well, what didn't work well, and what steps should come next. This allowed the student teachers to make better decisions about the children's future learning, based on their past work.

Allow children to take charge of their own learning. Shari worked with Jennifer and Julia to create a balance between teacher-directed and child-initiated input. Although the student teachers wanted the children to take the lead on the project, the children still needed adult guidance. Shari provided suggestions about when to step in. For instance, she encouraged Julia and Jennifer to ask the children why an item they proposed for outside use was important. The ensuing discussion helped the children focus and think about the intent of each suggestion and whether it was possible to implement it. This eliminated suggestions that were not feasible, and also helped the student teachers to be intentional in their teaching approach (Epstein 2007).

Provide opportunities for adults—students, teachers, and faculty—to communicate on a regular basis. Head teachers met formally and informally with the college students whenever time was available. In addition, head teachers, preservice teachers, and faculty met once a week during the students' curriculum class. They often used email as well to communicate the steps involved in the project.

> Shari modeled how to work with a small group of children with varying abilities, ask open-ended questions, bring out each child's individual strengths, collaborate with the group, and get the children to collaborate with each other.

Summary

The Inside-Out project provided children many meaningful experiences. It also offered multiple learning opportunities for the student teachers who facilitated the project. As the student teachers learned to ask appropriate questions, the children recognized that they should reach out to others. The children's comments showed their growing awareness and inclusion of others' needs and wants:

How do we include everyone's ideas?

The preschoolers can't read. How can we make sure they understand the rules?

We should ask all the teachers what they want to have outside.

By thinking from the perspectives of the children and adults with whom they shared the facility, this small group of kindergarten and first grade children gained valuable relationship-building skills.

Joyful Learning and Assessment in Kindergarten

Kim Hughes and Dominic Gullo

The bar for today's kindergarten has been raised. With more children enrolled in prekindergarten programs and state academic kindergarten standards becoming more prevalent, expectations for both kindergarten children and their teachers have risen (Graue 2006). Since 2001–02 the total enrollment for state-funded prekindergartens has increased by 73 percent for 4-year-olds and 45 percent for 3-year-olds. More than 80 percent of all 4-year-olds attend some kind of pre-K program (NIEER 2008). In addition, over the last 30 years a trend has developed to establish an earlier-in-the-year cutoff date for kindergarten entry (Colasanti 2007). In 1975, 9 states required children to have turned age 5 by September or earlier to enter kindergarten; in 1990, 28 states made this a requirement; and by 2005, 33 states had made the requirement.

Entering a kindergarten classroom today, we are more likely to see academically oriented teacher-directed instruction than active learning based on socialization, imagination, and creativity. The kindergarten curriculum now emphasizes content-oriented, skill-based learning that teachers assess with conventional measures such as worksheets or other paper-and-pencil tests to determine what skills or knowledge children have attained.

Kindergarten is looking more and more like the primary grades, yet the fundamental developmental characteristics of kindergartners and how they construct knowledge, problem solve, and interact socially have not changed. And although teachers often assess children as if they should all know the same things at the same time, the fact remains that not all kindergartners learn at the same rate or in the same way (Berk 2006; Tomlinson 2009).

Many early childhood professionals blame assessment for inappropriate practices in kindergarten. Some teachers "teach to the test"—meaning that they focus only on those areas in which children will be tested. Others rely on drill and practice to ensure that children's performance on tests meet predetermined standards, whether appropriate or not.

But assessment doesn't have to be that way. Developmentally appropriate assessment can be a means of maintaining and regaining joyful learning. Assessment can inform teaching so that developmentally and culturally appropriate practices are preserved *and* academic standards are met (Gullo 2006). What follow are some assessment guidelines and examples of actual classroom practices that demonstrate how assessment can ensure accountability in an atmosphere of joyful learning.

Assessment is a continuous process. Ideally, assessment describes the progress of a child's learning not just after a single test but over time. There

> According to Webster, *joyful* means "experiencing well-being, success, or good fortune." We who touch the lives of young learners believe that children deserve kindergarten experiences that foster a sense of well-being; that all children should experience success; and that all children must have opportunities for good fortune—all this, while making certain that all kindergartners meet the academic standards that foster future school and personal success.

is no beginning, middle, or end to learning, so it follows that assessment of children's learning should not be limited to measurement only at the end of an instructional unit. It is important that we identify the learning sequences that children are mastering. We should also recognize that children progress *individually* through learning sequences. Learning is a continuum, and assessment can help teachers identify where each child is on this continuum. The following vignette describes how a kindergarten teacher uses her awareness of children's learning to assess their understanding of pattern construction over time and in multiple ways.

> As Charles and Vamsi skip into their kindergarten classroom, they see the Question of the Day has to do with constructing an AABB pattern. Last week their teacher, Mrs. Wasserman, introduced the idea of AABB patterning to the class with a game that involved stacking color blocks, followed by a guided discovery lesson on creating AABB train cars with Unifix cubes. Since then, Mrs. Wasserman has reinforced the notion of patterning through a variety of engaging and enjoyable experiences, such as organizing the children in AABB patterns of boy–boy–girl–girl. She is careful to informally jot down on sticky notes and blank computer labels her observations about the many ways the children demonstrate their knowledge about patterning. Later, she transfers this information into each child's math-learning portfolio to document progress toward mastery.

In this vignette, as Mrs. Wasserman observes these activities, she assesses the kindergartners' knowledge of the newly introduced concept. She uses frequent, embedded assessments to guide instruction and monitor progress. Mrs. Wasserman understands instructional sequences and is acutely aware of the continuum of learning in each curricular area. In her classrom, assessment forms the basis for education decision making. She learns about children's progress and needs through her observations. She selects materials that match various learning styles and developmental levels, with the hope of aligning the curriculum content and instructional strategies with children's success.

Assessment is a comprehensive process. It can measure many aspects of learning. How well does a kindergartner understand patterning? How does she use what she has learned about patterns as she arranges colored blocks? Can she apply what she has learned to other situations? Assessing only in one way or in one context does not tell us the whole story. We need to consider the many ways children learn and the many ways they can show what they know. In the following vignette, Mrs. Wasserman continues to assess children's understanding of patterning, demonstrating how varied assessment contexts and procedures add to her understanding of children's learning.

> Whenever possible, Mrs. Wasserman uses naturalistic assessment procedures when she observes children in classroom learning settings. She asks each kindergartner to create a unique ABAB pattern using cutout shapes. She notices Vamsi asking a peer, "What is an ABAB pattern?" During Discovery Time, she invites Vamsi and a few other children to the Math and More Center to explore pattern blocks. After Vamsi spends time with varied manipulative materials that invite "messing around," Mrs. Wasserman steps in to facilitate his increased understanding about patterns. As

Learning is a continuum, and assessment can help teachers identify where each child is on this continuum.

This article was first published in the May 2010 issue of *Young Children.*

Kim Hughes, a former kindergarten teacher and North Carolina Teacher of the Year, trains, coaches, and mentors kindergarten teachers via Conscious Connections.

Dominic Gullo is a professor of early childhood education and associate dean for research in the School of Education at Drexel University in Philadelphia.

Mrs. Wasserman, the kindergarten teacher in the vignettes, is based on Kim's classroom experiences.

they sort and transform several patterns, she asks open-ended questions (such as, "How are these two patterns different?") to encourage Vamsi to create a variety of ABAB patterns.

Days later, during Discovery Time, Mrs. Wasserman makes note of several ABAB patterns that Vamsi created with multicultural figures as he "pattern chatted" with himself at the sand table. Then, she overhears him tell a classmate that the lunch line is an ABAB pattern of boy–girl–boy–girl–boy–girl. After observing several examples of Vamsi's mastery of the ABAB pattern, Mrs. Wasserman is now confident that he has a basic foundation for the concept and is ready for the next level of sequenced learning.

Assessment is an integrative process. The curriculum's stated learning goals should guide our assessment process. Ideally, children should be assessed while engaged in the process of learning. This results in two benefits: (1) teachers can use assessments as tools to modify the curriculum to meet individual children's strengths and needs; and (2) teachers can use assessments as a measure of curriculum effectiveness. Below, Mrs. Wasserman shows how she assesses children while they are learning and how she uses this information to guide future planning.

In Mrs. Wasserman's class, Together Time is a daily experience that brings the children together to connect, respond, share, and react to various topics of conversation and exploration. Today the children will play Guess My Pattern. Mrs. Wasserman separates the children into small groups and hands each group a specific pattern to create by using their bodies. The first group of giggling 5-year-olds brainstorms and begins building an AABB pattern: one-color shirt—one-color shirt—multicolored shirt—multicolored shirt. At their turn, the children enlist four additional classmates to join them and continue the pattern. At first the other children are stumped. Then Jasmeka exclaims, "I know! I know! I see an AABBAABB pattern! Can you see it? It is plain shirt—plain shirt—lots-of-colors shirt—lots-of-colors shirt . . . That's a super tricky one!"

In this vignette, Mrs. Wasserman plans activities that respond to her kindergartners' interests, experiences, and skills and at the same time confirm that her curriculum is effective. She gathers data to drive instruction by asking thought-provoking questions that extend children's interest, thinking, and learning. Observation, careful questioning, respectful listening, and detailed record keeping give her insight into each child's capabilities. She seizes teachable moments to create a springboard for future instruction and to reinforce children's progress along the continuum of comprehension.

Maintaining academic standards in kindergarten does not mean sacrificing developmentally appropriate teaching. Appropriate assessment can lead to joyful learning *and* joyful teaching.

Learning is personal, active, and genuine; *discovery* invites mastery and empowerment; *delight* feeds passion and a quest for more; and *determination* nurtures confidence and creates a sense that learning is forever.

It is possible for kindergartners to experience success and well-being as they learn the things that will foster both school and personal achievement. A joyful kindergarten does not mean that academic standards are not being met. Maintaining academic standards in kindergarten does not mean sacrificing developmentally appropriate teaching. Appropriate assessment can lead to joyful learning *and* joyful teaching.

Learn to Say Yes! When You Want to Say No! to Create Cooperation Instead of Resistance: Positive Behavior Strategies in Teaching

Katharine C. Kersey and Marie L. Masterson

It is human nature to be resistant when someone tells us no. Children are no exception. Nevertheless, when teachers are frustrated with children's behavior, they may resort to saying no (Lane et al. 2007). Often the child responds, "Why?" or resists.

What teachers really seek are strategies to help children in preschool and the early primary grades learn how to be respectful and cooperative. They want to encourage children to trust their guidance, take their lead, and willingly follow directions.

Reframing the Equation to Understand the Power of *Yes*

If the goal is to create cooperation and reduce resistance, it helps to replace *no* with strategies that redirect behavior successfully. Effective strategies can turn resistance into cooperation even for children with whom the teacher typically struggles. Saying yes often empowers success and weakens the setup for resistance. Situations that make us want to say no can become opportunities to say yes.

Children's interactions with teachers (negative or positive) provide a lasting blueprint for the way children feel about learning and themselves, teachers, and their peers, now and in the future (Cozolino 2007; Miles & Stipek 2006). Positive interactions are the hallmark of high-quality educational environments and provide an essential framework for motivation,

learning, and development (Fantuzzo et al. 2007; Haynes 2008; NICHD-ECCRN 2005). Outcomes of responsive practices include increased social skills, greater emotional regulation, and ongoing motivation for children (Emmer & Stough 2001). In addition, positive relationships support resiliency, compensate for stress experienced at home, and help children achieve their full potential (Hamre & Pianta 2005; Raver et al. 2008).

Even though research advocating the benefits of positive interactions in early childhood (birth to age 8) is compelling, teachers may need fresh approaches to create this kind of climate and help children find healthy solutions to challenges. In an engaging, supportive classroom environment, teachers can develop strategies that encourage respectful, effective communication and ensure children's success (Miller & Sawka-Miller 2007).

Four Strategies for Replacing *No* With *Yes*

The following strategies encourage behavioral changes in ways that support children and teachers.

1. The Make-a-Big-Deal Strategy

List all the positive qualities you hope children will develop. When you see children demonstrating those qualities, say,

"I saw you sharing! That was so thoughtful."

"I saw you helping your friend."

"I heard the two of you discussing the rules of the new board game. What did you decide?"

"I noticed the story you were writing. Can you tell me about it?"

When you give attention, thanks, specific and effective praise, and recognition for a job well done, children feel proud of their contributions and know their responsibility is valued. This draws their attention to important traits that will serve them well now and throughout life. The behaviors you focus on will grow!

In *My Stroke of Insight,* Jill Bolte Taylor (2008) says that human brains are designed to focus on anything we are looking for. If we seek red in the world, then we will find it everywhere. The longer we concentrate on it, the more we see it. Shifting our attention to behaviors we want to see more often is as important for adults as it is for children (Miller & Sawka-Miller 2007). When we look for the positive in the classroom, our eyes and ears become trained

This article was first published in the July 2011 issue of *Young Children.*

Katharine C. Kersey, EdD, is a professor of early childhood education and director emerita of the Child Study Center at Old Dominion University, in Norfolk, Virginia.

Marie L. Masterson, PhD, is an assistant professor of early childhood education at Dominican University, in River Forest, Illinois.

to find, emphasize, and reinforce the respectful behaviors children need to possess.

Choose a child who is less likely to be on task or who tends to require a great deal of support. Take every opportunity to make a big deal about this child's positive contributions:

"I'm amazed you remembered all of the chapter we read yesterday."

"You can really figure out things so quickly."

"I saw how kind you were to Jules when she bumped into your lunch tray."

"You worked so hard to get the blocks picked up. That was a good solution to sort first and then carry them over to the shelf."

This child will soon feel connected to you in positive ways. He will likely be less resistant and more cooperative. He will learn to use the actions and behaviors that lead to satisfying results.

It takes practice to notice children when they are behaving appropriately. Speaking positively yields a huge payoff. The truth is, what we respond to positively will grow. Like a plant that is fed and watered, the behavior that gets our positive attention will thrive.

> Focusing on what we want, instead of putting our energies into what we don't want, results in higher cooperation and more time spent on learning.

2. The Incompatible Alternative Strategy

When trying to stop an undesired behavior, it's necessary to replace it with something else. Give a child something appropriate to do that ends the inappropriate behavior. For example, if a child is running around the room, ask her to pass out books. You will discover quickly how easily this encourages cooperation. Instead of saying no (or "Don't do that"), tell the child what *to do*. When a child is distracting a friend and keeping him from writing in his journal, you can say, "Please show me how your writing or picture is progressing."

Redirecting behavior with incompatible alternatives is highly effective (Tiger, Hanley, & Hernandez 2006). Instead of expending energy emphasizing what is not working, think about a desired behavior. For example, rather than ask a child to stop running, suggest something positive, such as "Use your walking feet" or "Come tiptoe behind me." Teachers will be surprised how quickly the child responds to the new suggestion (Masterson 2008).

3. The Choice Strategy

Choice gives a child alternatives. The teacher states a desired goal and then gives the child two choices for accomplishing it; both are positive and acceptable.

"We need to be quiet in the hall. Would you rather tiptoe or sneak along like a mouse?"

"It's time to go back inside. Would you rather help carry the bag of balls or the hoops?"

The strategy behind choice is that children learn there are different ways to accomplish a goal. Using two positive choices increases cooperation and helps children become creative and thoughtful (Kersey 2006; Masterson 2008).

"It's time to clear off our desks. Do you want to do it in one minute or two? I will set the timer."

If the child suggests a third alternative, the teacher needs to remain firm.

"One minute or two? You choose or I'll choose."

Adding "You choose or I'll choose" softens even the most resistant child, because he will want to decide for himself.

"It's chilly outside. Will you wear your coat or your sweater?"

If you offer a specific choice and the child hesitates, then choose one while quickly making cheerful conversation about what is going to happen next. It is important to move on. Practicing making choices with a teacher gets children in the habit of looking for positive alternatives when they can't have what they originally wanted.

4. The When/Then Strategy

"When you put your books on the shelf, then you may put on your coat."

"When you finish putting away the playdough, then you may choose a partner for the game."

Using the principle of *when/then* is a strategy that links a specific expectation to a positive outcome. When/then uses a logical contingency and communicates expectations (Kersey 2006). It is important to say "when" rather than "if." The word *if* may cause a child to think or respond, "Suppose I don't?" But the word *when* communicates your trust that the child will follow through.

"When you clean up, then you may have lunch."

"When you come, then we'll choose a book to read together."

"When your table is clear, then you may go to the library."

Children handle transitions more easily when they understand expectations. Saying "if" invites a power struggle. Saying "when" invites cooperation.

Until the child completes the first responsibility, of course, she loses out on the promised outcome, such as a new activity. "When you put away your markers, then you may go to the sand table." If she doesn't put away the markers, she can't go on to the next center. We want to say and communicate to children what we ourselves would want to hear—respectful, positive words about what needs to be done. The when/then principle communicates respect and gives children a consistent opportunity to be successful.

What we respond to positively will grow. Like a plant that is fed and watered, the behavior that gets our positive attention will thrive.

Ensuring Positive Outcomes

Teachers may use the four strategies for positive redirection alone, in succession, or combined as needed to invite children's cooperation and responsibility.

"You and Tabitha used great teamwork to read sooner!" (make-a-big-deal strategy)

"Can you arrange the blocks in order by size?" (incompatible alternative strategy)

"Would you like her help, or can you do it yourself?" (choice strategy)

"When you have put away the tray of sorting blocks, then you may sit with Tabitha." (when/then strategy)

These four strategies help teachers and children to shift direction, refocus attention, and say yes when they might otherwise say no.

Creating a *yes* environment provides an excellent setting for children's exploration and mastery (Anderson 2009). Focusing on what we want, instead of putting our energies into what we don't want, results in higher cooperation and more time spent on learning. We want to say yes as often as we can, knowing that we are teaching children skills that will serve them well in school and in life.

Get Started Using the Four Strategies

- Begin with one new strategy.

- Use the strategy until you feel comfortable. Add the others one at a time.

- Record your reflections in a journal: What happened or led up to the interaction? Which strategy did you use? How did the situation turn out? How did the child respond? What did you learn?

- Practice until the strategies become second nature. The strategies model skills that help children to become responsive and cooperative.

Family Involvement: Challenges to Consider, Strengths to Build On

Mariana Souto-Manning

Educators have long known that family involvement is vital to children's success in school. Yet many teachers struggle to find effective ways to involve families in their classrooms. Often, the dilemma is due not to families' lack of interest (Souto-Manning & Swick 2006) but rather to time constraints and differing cultural expectations about the roles of teachers and families.

In today's fast-paced society, teachers and families face competing demands for their time, energy, and resources (Anderson & Sabatelli 2007). For an ever growing number of families, adults work and children attend early education programs. In trying to reach out to families and make classrooms inclusive places, caring and well-intentioned educators may unknowingly place additional demands on families. In fact, research shows time demands and cultural mismatch as two prevalent challenges to family involvement (Souto-Manning & Swick 2006).

To respond to these challenges, this article explores ways in which teachers can involve families while respecting the demands on their time and the expectations of diverse cultures. While this is not an exhaustive list of ideas, it provides a foundation for teachers to start imagining how to involve families in their children's educational settings. I hope to inspire educators to reenvision family involvement and work toward building on families' strengths.

Volunteering Time and Expertise

For many adults who work full time, it may be impossible to volunteer in their children's classrooms. Work schedules often preclude engaging in such traditional activities as making bulletin board displays or reading with children during the school day. Such roles are valuable and can help make the classroom routines run more smoothly, but there are other ways families can play

meaningful roles in their children's early childhood education. A few key components are important to successful family involvement programs.

Invite Families and Set Clear Expectations

Introduce family involvement opportunities as invitations, not as obligations. *Inviting* families' involvement in contrast to *expecting* it is a subtle yet important difference. Sending an invitation acknowledges that family involvement in children's education varies across cultures. Include a place where parents can indicate the best way to be contacted and the days and times that are most convenient for them to contribute to the classroom.

Calling family members, helping them feel at ease, and setting clear and mutually agreed on expectations (Epstein 2001) are important first steps toward family involvement. When parents know what to expect, they are likely to feel less anxious about getting involved. Teachers can follow up with parents to jointly plan for the family's contributions. Having a conversation together lets teachers and family members discuss their interests, propose ideas for a project or visit, and work out further details.

Many parents may not be able to come to the classroom on a regular weekly basis. It is more likely that they could visit once or twice a year. Outlining some contributions that do not require classroom visits (e.g., recording books on tape) lets all families feel included. Schools may have a ready-made activities list (e.g., caring for a school garden, talking about one's occupation or area of expertise, taking pictures of community landmarks for illustrating class books and posters, or arranging for the class to visit his or her workplace). Often the list includes short descriptions of the time and tasks involved.

Family engagement is likely to be more successful if teachers tailor the list to the interests and expertise of family members. Provide a blank space on the invitation, allowing families to suggest other activities. Teachers can ask families for activity suggestions at enrollment or orientation. Collaborating on a new list each year ensures that activities represent the unique characteristics of the families that make up the classroom.

Draw on Families' Expertise

To make the most of the times when families can visit the classroom, be sure to let them know how their contributions will support the children's education in unique ways. When family members see themselves as part of the learning that goes on in the classroom, they are more likely to further their involvement. Inviting families to talk about treasured cultural artifacts and share the knowledge that underlies their everyday household activities and traditions—what educators call *funds of knowledge*—is an engaging way to help families feel comfortable, competent, and involved (Gonzalez, Moll, & Amanti 2005).

Educators can incorporate the idea of funds of knowledge in their planning and programming as they invite all families to share experiences and skills that encourage learning. Nieto and Rolón (1997) suggest that teachers build on family motifs (values, traditions, and talents that shape a family) and emphasize how important families are in the education of young children.

Research shows time demands and cultural mismatch as two prevalent challenges to family involvement.

This article was first published in the March 2010 issue of *Young Children*.

Mariana Souto-Manning, PhD, is an associate professor of early childhood education at Teachers College, Columbia University.

Outlining some contributions that do not require classroom visits lets all families feel included.

Remember to include *all* families (Nieto 1999). Leaving out any family sends a message of exclusion—that only some, not all, families have something to give to the classroom or school. Part of a teacher's role is to acknowledge families and their communities as meaningful partners in promoting learning (Nieto 1999) and to recognize that all families have important contributions to make.

Build on Family Strengths

Parents will feel more involved if their family expertise, such as literacy practices, continues in the classroom after their visit is over or their contribution is received. This can serve to validate families and also to better address the educational needs of their children by providing relevant background knowledge. Family literacy practices are home-based, cultural ways of negotiating meaning and can be meaningfully embedded in the curriculum (Gregory, Long, & Volk 2004).

In the past, literacy was defined as linking letters with sounds and decoding words. Today, not only does literacy mean the ability to read and write in the traditional sense, but it also "entails the ability to use these skills in a socially appropriate context. The very notion of literacy is also evolving to include the skills required to function in a technological society" (Caspe 2003, 1). It is the ability to function within and across worlds that indicates literacy.

The following examples present the idea that learning is synergistic. When children in multilingual, multicultural contexts have opportunities to interact purposefully and in a comfortable environment that values them and allows them to draw on what they know, they use their knowledge to create new spaces for learning and teaching.

Make a place for meaningful peer interaction. For example, dual language learners may support each other's language learning in a classroom in which they have opportunities to enact cultural roles through dramatic play, are celebrated for use of their home language and English, feel comfortable taking risks to translate and clarify meanings for each other, and can take on the role of expert (Long 2004).

Create classroom conditions that parallel community settings. If families are involved with church, teachers may learn from the conditions and characteristics of the children's experiences (Haight & Carter-Black 2004; McMillon & Edwards 2004). Storytelling, an example of the rich oral traditions in which some children and families participate in at church, can support learning in many ways—by creating spaces for students to relate content to their own lives and extend and understand abstract concepts by creating connections to their lives, by building relationships, and by engaging children. "Understanding the value of diverse practices from community settings ... can help us strengthen the teaching of all children. Storytelling is just one of those practices" (Haight 2006 2).

Import Family Meaning Making

Family literacy includes the meaning-making processes and social practices in which families engage every day. Children participate in these family literacy practices in their homes and communities. For example, families might write

156

a shopping list before going to the grocery store, and the children match products on the list with those on the shelves. Such family practices are highly transportable to the classroom. A teacher can build on families' strengths by including their home literacy practices in the classroom. A family could tell stories, dance as they interpret music or lyrics, engage in call-and-response like a congregation answering the preacher or rabbi during a religious service, or compose hip-hop lyrics.

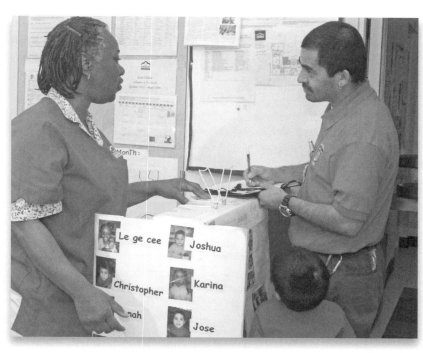

The absence of such meaning-making practices in schools can impede children's learning. Researchers (Heath 1983; Rogers 2003) have documented the contrast between children's literacy proficiency in their homes/communities and the way their literacy skills are perceived in school settings. When educators ask, "But what kind of home literacy practices might a family have if the family members have little education and may themselves be illiterate? Do they still have something that could be considered a literacy practice?," the answer is yes. For example, bringing oral storytelling traditions—which can be prominent in African American households—to classrooms may lead to successful involvement for many families.

When these practices enter the classroom, children are more successful and family members feel honored (Allen 2007; Gregory, Long, & Volk 2004). Nieto (1999) proposes the need to value the kinds of knowledge and literacy practices that children bring to school. For example, oral traditions may provide more syntactically complex sentences than the written word. Delpit and Dowdy (2002) pinpoint that children feel excluded and have lower perceptions of their knowledge and competence and may end up failing in school when classroom practices do not honor and involve their cultural legacies.

Understanding Different Cultural Expectations

Often, teachers and families have different cultural expectations about children's development and schooling. These differences may become obstacles to forging strong classroom and family ties. The answers to seemingly simple questions, such as whether teachers view a family member or parent's visit to a classroom as a sign of support or criticism, may vary across cultures (Souto-Manning & Swick 2006). As a result, instead of relying on common sense, which is heavily informed by one's cultural assumptions, teachers need to learn about cultural expectations held by children's families.

The best way to do this is to position oneself as a learner and embark on a journey of documenting children's home and community practices (Gregory,

Instead of relying on common sense, which is heavily informed by one's cultural assumptions, teachers must learn about cultural expectations held by children's families.

Furthering Literacy Practices of Families at Home

Families may not recognize the complex literacy practices in which they engage every day (Rogers 2003). Early childhood teachers can encourage families to continue engaging in home-based literacy practices. Suggesting additional types of activities sends families the message that the school values and honors what happens at home and wants to collaborate on further activities. Hydrick (1996) offers several home-based literacy ideas.

- Tell your children a story about when you were young. Adapt your story for engaging an audience of young children. Choose a story that reveals something about your own culture. Or share a story about something unusual that happened at work that day. You may leave off the ending and ask your children to add an ending in their own words.

- Make a book of collected family stories handed down from generation to generation. Record favorites retold about family events, such as a reunion, a holiday, or memories of places where the family has lived.

- Post a list of foods to buy at the grocery store. Have the children add to the list, read the list, find the items at the store, read package information, and check off items on the list while shopping.

- Keep a family calendar in a central place. Look for a calendar with large boxes for each day of the month so children can write in special events or draw pictures as reminders. The calendar can also work as a family message center (in any language).

Long, & Volk 2004). Teachers can incorporate strategies and practices they learn from families for teaching (mentoring, teaching by doing, active participation, teaching by example), using knowledge from children's community members. This is an essential step in creating environments that are inviting, fully inclusive, and respectful of family diversities.

In the following sections, I list a few issues for educators to consider as they seek to forge strong relationships with *all* families, especially those whose linguistic and cultural backgrounds differ from their own.

Consider and Respect Families' Cultural Backgrounds

Young children are active members of different groups at home and at school (Gregory, Long, & Volk 2004). Their development occurs within a cultural context (Rogoff 2003). If the cultural context at home differs significantly from the dominant culture at school, a child's development can be hindered. Teachers are key players in understanding how children function as members of different groups (home, school, and community) and in facilitating their transition between home and school. Bringing home literacy practices into the classroom, as discussed earlier, is one way to create a bridge between these various contexts.

Successful family involvement relies on teachers' respect for and understanding of children's and families' cultural backgrounds and practices. For example, in some countries females of a certain age wear a veil or cover their hair with a *hijab*. Teachers can learn about and consider families' previous experiences with schools in their own or other countries where they have lived. In Brazil, for instance, my mother would never have visited my classroom because it was considered a sign of criticism. In the United States, staying away could be mistaken as a sign of a family's disinterest.

Through the classroom environment or a specially created school space, teachers can show they recognize and value diversity in the school. One way of doing this is by creating spaces in classrooms and schools for children to reinvent classroom practices as they draw on their own experiences and knowledge. For example, Volk (2004) describes the networking role of Puerto Rican siblings in literacy learning, as many older siblings bring together school and home practices in flexible, hybrid, and promising ways. Volk (2004) found that older siblings, as knowledgeable members of school communities, often engage in teaching younger siblings (and helping them with schoolwork). This invites us to rethink the multiple networks of support young children may have

beyond their parents. In addition, it is important to let parents and families know their involvement is welcome and provide some ideas on the roles they might play.

Learn About Families and Communities and Share Ownership of Knowledge

When teachers foster respect and understanding, they blur the line between teacher and learner (Freire 1970) and share the ownership of knowledge. Visiting children's homes and communities and talking with parents and family members from a learner's perspective can forge strong relationships. One caution in home or community visits is to keep the focus on conversation and knowledge exchange to avoid slipping into a parent-education role. Telling parents and family members what they need to do with their children can cause tension in family–school ties. Educators who position themselves as learners communicate a genuine interest in the family.

Home and community visits let teachers become familiar with the child's home environment, the community setting, and cultural practices. Teachers learn better how they might incorporate appropriate home practices in the classroom. Such visits help a child's teacher develop rapport with the family and build a family's motivation to visit and participate in the classroom. Home and community visits can allow a more personal time to discuss how the family would like to be involved in their child's care and education. The Office of Head Start offers helpful guidance. Staff should

> work closely with parents to ensure that goals and experiences are congruent with the family's culture; build on children's interests and abilities; promote curiosity and positive views about themselves and about learning; and use responsive interactions as the primary vehicle for learning. (US DHHS 2008, 10)

Foster True Dialogue

Culturally responsive teachers and schools meet with families to engage in true, authentic dialogue instead of merely passing on information or communicating school decisions (Allen 2007). By doing so, all involved can construct knowledge and arrive at decisions together. This approach lets families know that the educator and the school respect their contributions and perspectives and want to get to know all children and their families. To be fully inclusive, schools can further develop decision-making policies that rely on true dialogue.

How teachers and families work together affects the quality of programming children receive. Children often perceive and may reflect their family's attitudes toward school, so it is valuable to listen to the children and foster in them positive attitudes toward what goes on in the classroom.

Establish regular times for talking with families. During these conversations, exchange information with each other about the child's development, learning, interests, and successes. Teachers can try strategies such as these:

- Set up "Help Us Get to Know Your Child" times in the beginning of the school year. During these conversations/meetings, teachers position themselves as learners. This is a time to reach out to parents and families and invite them

Home and community visits can allow a more personal time to discuss how the family would like to be involved in their child's care and education.

to describe their child. Teachers will gain different kinds of information than they would from talking to a child's previous teachers or reading the information in a child's file. Provide some prompts, if needed, such as "Tell me some things [child's name] likes to do," or ask questions such as "What are your child's favorite foods?" Teachers may ask family members about their hopes and expectations for their child's progress in the coming year or if they have concerns or questions. This approach can help teachers and families feel comfortable with each other in addition to providing an invaluable learning opportunity for teachers.

- Develop some "talking" meetings to which families are invited. These meetings are not academic conferences. In such meetings, each family joins their child's teacher(s) to engage in shared conversation—an authentic dialogue that leads to change and transformation (Allen 2007; Freire 1970). The goal of these talking meetings is to exchange information and ideas and learn from each other how to meet the needs of the child in culturally relevant ways and to build on the child's strengths and interests.

- Use parent–teacher conferences to communicate information regarding learning standards or curriculum plans, but allowing enough time for two-way communication and authentic dialogue.

- Send home to each family an ongoing parent–teacher newsletter (or use other ways to engage in ongoing communication) featuring their child. Share conversation-style classroom news and updates about the child's experiences at school. These may include photos. For example, Phillip Baumgarner and Anjanette Russell, teachers at the Child Development Lab at the University of Georgia, used photofolios—portfolios documenting children's everyday experiences in the classroom in photos—sent to parents weekly. These documents become treasured by families. They can serve as a way for teachers and families to communicate and as conversation starters for children, who often volunteer to recount to family members the action portrayed by the snapshots.

Conclusion

It is imperative for early childhood educators to consider family involvement in children's education within the context of competing demands and varying cultural expectations. Finding creative ways to address some of the challenges of family involvement is essential throughout the year. Most important is recognizing that family involvement is critical to children's developmental and educational progress, even when conceived of differently across cultures and family structures and responsibilities.

Classroom Bird Feeding: Giving Flight to the Imaginations of 4- and 5-Year-Olds!

Deanna Pecaski McLennan

Little did I know on that frosty morning in October, when I first hammered the pole into the ground and affixed the plastic, gazebo-style bird feeder on top, that I was lighting the imaginations of the children in my classroom. Always an avid backyard bird-watcher, I hoped to sneak peeks through the classroom windows at the feathered visitors that might come during the school day. The almost 80-year-old school had well-established, diverse landscaping in the yard. Just outside the classroom's three-tiered windows stood a round formation of evergreens and tall shrubs, perfect for attracting and protecting birds at a feeder.

A Perfect Place for Bird Feeding

Despite being an architectural beauty, the school was designated by our school board as eligible for special funds and services because of its high levels of student transience, low socioeconomic levels, numerous dual language learners, and high rates of student absenteeism. At the time, I taught a large class of 27 4- and 5-year-olds. Many were new immigrants who were likely to quickly transfer to other sections of the city once their families became established. The children differed greatly in their abilities and interests, which made our program and daily interactions exciting and engaging. There was never a dull moment.

The education program was primarily a play-based, emergent approach to learning. Children engaged in self-directed and collaborative, exploratory, arts-based activities for most of the day. Although I enjoyed integrating elements of nature into learning centers, I admit that I first set up the bird feeder for personal purposes. I expected that some children might show an interest in it, but I had no intention of including it in the regular classroom curriculum. I simply hoped to continue a hobby to which I devoted much of my spare time.

What was once just talk of the birds slowly evolved into a more sophisticated, personal dialogue, full of philosophical references to life and personal interests.

I was correct in my earlier assumption that a wealth of established greenery would attract a variety of birds to the feeder, but to my amazement the children's interest in the bird feeder was instantaneous! The day I erected the feeder, our discussion focused on what it was and how it would attract birds. I learned that many children had never experienced hanging an outdoor feeder. Most of the children lived in cooperative, subsidized housing or large apartment buildings and didn't have access to a big yard with large trees. As that first day with the feeder progressed, many hopeful faces spent their choice time (a block of time when the children select their activities) standing at the windows, waiting for our first guests to arrive. According to Lewin-Benham (2006), children are often eager to learn about the environment, and an emergent, inquiry-based approach is ideal for capitalizing on these interests and engaging them in environmentally friendly practices that will hopefully last a lifetime.

Within a few weeks, the feeder attracted some colorful local birds—house finches, goldfinches, sparrows, and even a few blue jays. As new birds arrived, we consulted birding websites on the Internet or asked the teacher–librarian in our school for help finding reference materials to identify the birds and what they liked to eat. Researching the birds together with the children allowed them to see me as a fellow learner who wanted to continue to expand her own knowledge. I was modeling lifelong learning (Wien 2008).

Classroom visitors would think that a superhero had arrived by the level of excitement and noise that ensued when the children noticed a new bird. Surprisingly, many children continued to spend choice time watching the feeder, and they often called out to their peers when they spotted a new arrival. Every child appeared interested in the activities at the feeder, and no one missed the opportunity to see a new bird.

An Enriched Literacy Program

Autumn gave way to winter and the birds continued to excite the children. What had begun as a personal activity for me was now the focal point of our classroom, providing inspiration for child-led inquiry and discussion. The colder weather brought numerous birds to the feeder, and they usually ate one large bag of seed each week. Children began to incorporate their observations into their play in other classroom centers. Many children who usually were not motivated to engage in language activities began to draw pictures and attempt emergent writing to describe the birds and the changing seasons. During visits to the school library, the children checked out nature books, and at their request I read many fiction and nonfiction books about birds at story time.

As the children noticed more varieties of visiting birds, they became intrigued with bird names and characteristics. This inspired them to write a class letter to a nature sanctuary during our shared writing time. We requested information on local wildlife. The sanctuary wrote back to us and included a large poster depicting native Ontario birds, which we promptly posted on the wall next to the window. As we spotted new birds, we recorded their names and the date on a chart. All winter the children kept a log of what they

This article was first published in the November 2012 issue of *Young Children.*

Deanna Pecaski McLennan, PhD, is an elementary educator at the full-day kindergarten program in Amherstburg, Ontario, Canada.

Bird-Related Resources for Children

1. *About Birds: A Guide for Children,* by Cathryn Sill
2. *Don't Let the Pigeon Drive the Bus!,* by Mo Willems
3. *Backyard Birding for Kids,* by Fran Lee
4. *A Mother for Choco,* by Keiko Kasza
5. *Two Blue Jays,* by Anne Rockwell
6. National Geographic Backyard Birding: http://animals.nationalgeographic.com/birding
7. Project FeederWatch: www.birds.cornell.edu/pfw
8. NWF Garden for Wildlife: www.nwf.org/How-to-Help/Garden-for-Wildlife.aspx

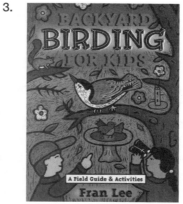

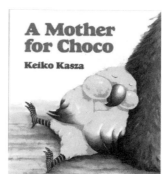

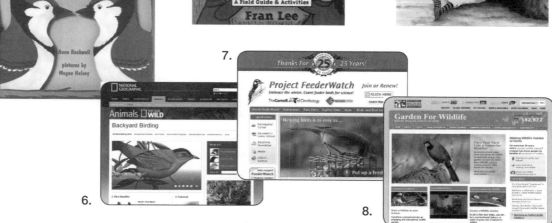

noticed—similar to winter birding counts conducted by serious birdwatchers. Along with the poster came informational brochures on local wildlife, which I placed in the language center; many children became engrossed with the detailed pictures of new animals. This nonfiction material supplemented our reading program well, as the children were incredibly motivated to conduct their own research by analyzing the brochures and then creating their own brochures about birds in the language center.

By midwinter the children still spent much of their choice time watching the feeder, aided by the new binoculars that hung next to the window. I noticed a gradual change in the conversations children were having at the windows.

What was once just talk of the birds slowly evolved into a more sophisticated, personal dialogue, full of philosophical references to life and personal interests. Children engaged in rich discussions about what they loved about the birds and how the birds had inspired them to engage in other activities in the classroom. They elaborately planned for what they would play together during outside time and how they could continue to watch the birds during these activities. They dreamed of the possibilities of flying like our birds and visiting exotic lands. They were beginning to have *real* conversations with one another. Children stood by the windows, engaged in meaningful verbal exchanges. The bird watching had achieved what I had tried earlier to develop through planned circle time discussions. The communal experience of bird watching provided a natural, secure atmosphere for children's discussions to grow and flourish.

Mathematics and Science Connections

Just as the birding had inspired numerous literacy activities, the children also used this information in authentic, meaningful math and science investigations during activity times. A few children analyzed the information from the bird count sheet and created a pictograph to represent how many of each variety they had spotted at our feeder. This child-guided initiative led to a discussion one day about which seeds our birds preferred to eat. After doing Internet research on what seeds birds liked to eat, the children proposed placing different types of seed in the feeder to observe if the number and variety of birds changed as a result.

For a number of weeks in the winter, we experimented with black oil sunflower seeds, striped sunflower seeds, mixed bird seed, and peanuts to see what worked best. I was amazed at the depth of student connection and interest. Never before had I observed the children taking such an active role in devising their own mathematical and scientific investigations. At the conclusion of our experiment, we noted that the birds ate the seeds regardless of the variety, with the exception of peanuts, which only the blue jays and woodpeckers preferred. The peanuts, however, opened a new world of possibility for us as a hungry squirrel took notice of them one day in December and began to visit the feeder. As a result, we placed a separate feeder a few feet away from the bird feeder, and each week filled it with peanuts for the squirrels. The children never tired of watching them climb up the feeder's pole and cling to the side. The squirrels carefully held on with one paw and used the other to open the lid and remove a peanut before scampering off to a branch to eat. I loved watching this spectacle as well.

The snowy winter also provided the perfect opportunity for us to investigate the size and shape of bird and animal tracks under the feeders. Some days we ventured outside with measuring tapes, pencils, and sketch pads to record what we found. Children delighted in seeing the variety of prints left in the snow, and they were intrigued by the markings we did not recognize. The children also examined and measured the differences in length between the tracks. We experimented by moving in the snow to observe how long our strides were when running and walking. We never did discover which other

Children delighted in seeing the variety of prints left in the snow, and they were intrigued by the markings we did not recognize.

animals were eating the seeds discarded on the ground. Upon returning to the classroom, some children were inspired to paint animal tracks at the art easel, replicating what they noticed outdoors and hypothesizing as to what mysterious creatures had left them.

An Authentic, Collaborative Experience

As the weather warmed and spring arrived, children slowly lost interest in the feeders. They became more interested in bugs and butterflies, and they eagerly anticipated once again playing on the outdoor climbing equipment. Although classroom discussions and explorations ceased to revolve around the feeder activities, I was forever changed as an early childhood educator by this experience. Although that school year was a little hectic at times, I look back on it as one of my most rewarding and enjoyable. Never before in my classroom had children taken such initiative for directing their learning in so many collaborative and holistic ways. The birds sparked a natural curiosity in the children, who then spent much of their time engaged in authentic, child-centered projects and activities.

As the school year progressed, children returned time and time again to the communal experience of observing the birds, adding new personal insights to help deepen and shape their understandings. The children explored and expressed their learning collectively through literacy, mathematics, and scientific engagement. I guided the direction their inquiries took and how they researched information about birds and their behavior. Through critical thinking and collaboration, the children used different centers in the classroom to demonstrate and showcase their learning. Placing that bird feeder outside the classroom windows on that cold autumn morning was a catalyst for capturing and inspiring the children's imaginations. This empowered them to explore self-directed activities that resulted in meaningful, collaborative learning for most of the school year and hopefully instilled a love of and respect for nature for their entire lives.

References

AAAS (American Association for the Advancement of Science). 2008. *Benchmarks.* www.project2061.org/publications/bsl/online/index.php?home=true.

Achenback, T.M., & C. Edelbrock. 1991. *National Survey of the Problems and Competencies Among Four- to Sixteen-Year-Olds.* Monographs of the Society for Research in Child Development, vol. 56, no. 3, serial no. 225. Chicago: University of Chicago Press.

Allen, J. 2007. *Creating Welcoming Schools: A Practical Guide to Home–School Partnerships With Diverse Families.* New York: Teachers College Press.

Anderson, C. 2009. "Respect: What It Means to James L. Hymes Jr." *The Educational Forum* 73: 298–305.

Anderson, S., & R. Sabatelli. 2007. *Family Interaction: A Multigenerational Perspective.* 4th ed. Boston: Allyn & Bacon.

Anglin, J.M. 1993. *Vocabulary Development: A Morphological Analysis.* Monographs of the Society for Research in Child Development, vol. 58, no. 10, serial no. 238. Chicago: University of Chicago Press.

ASCD. 2012. A Whole-Child Approach to Education and the Common Core State Standards Initiative. Alexandria, VA: ASCD. http://www.ascd.org/ASCD/pdf/siteASCD/policy/CCSS-and-Whole-Child-one-pager.pdf.

Bagwell, C.L., M.E. Schmidt, A.F. Newcomb, & W.M. Bukowski. 2001. "Friendship and Peer Rejection as Predictors of Adult Adjustment." Chap. 2 in *The Role of Friendship in Psychological Adjustment,* eds. D.W. Nangle & C.A. Erdley, 25–49. San Francisco: Jossey-Bass.

Barbour, N.H., & C. Seefeldt. 1993. *Developmental Continuity Across Preschool and Primary Grades: Implications for Teachers.* Wheaton, MD: Association for Childhood Education International.

Beck, I.L., M.G. McKeown, & L. Kucan. 2013. *Bringing Words to Life: Robust Vocabulary Instruction.* 2nd ed. New York: Guilford.

Bell, S. 2010. "Project-Based Learning for the 21st Century: Skills for the Future." *The Clearing House* 83 (2): 39–43.

Berk, L.E. 2006. "Looking at Children in Kindergarten." Chap. 2 in *K Today: Teaching and Learning in the Kindergarten Year,* ed. D.F. Gullo, 11–25. Washington, DC: NAEYC.

Berk, L.E. 2008. *Infants and Children: Prenatal Through Middle Childhood.* 6th ed. Boston: Pearson/Allyn & Bacon.

Bickart, T.S., J.R. Jablon, & D.T. Dodge. 1999. *Building the Primary Classroom: A Complete Guide to Teaching and Learning.* Washington, DC: Teaching Strategies.

Birch, S.H., & G.W. Ladd. 1998. "Children's Interpersonal Behaviors and the Teacher-Child Relationship." *Developmental Psychology* 34 (5): 934–46.

Blair, C., & R.P. Razza. 2007. "Relating Effortful Control, Executive Function, and False Belief Understanding to Emerging Math and Literacy Ability in Kindergarten." *Child Development* 78 (2): 647–63.

Bloom, L. 1998. "Language Acquisition in Its Developmental Context." In *Handbook of Child Psychology, Vol. 2: Cognition, Perception, and Language,* 5th ed., eds. D. Kuhn & R.S. Siegler, 309–70. New York: Wiley.

Boal, A. [1979] 2000. *Theatre of the Oppressed.* Trans. by C.A. McBride & M.-O.L. McBride. New York: Theatre Communications Group.

Bodrova, E., & D. Leong. 2003. "Chopsticks and Counting Chips: Do Play and Foundational Skills Need to Compete for the Teacher's Attention in an Early Childhood Classroom?" *Young Children* 58 (3): 10–17.

Bodrova, E., & D.J. Leong. 2008. "Developing Self-Regulation in Kindergarten: Can We Keep All the Crickets in the Basket?" *Young Children* 63 (2): 56–58.

Bransford, J., A.L. Brown, & R.R. Cocking, eds. 2003. *How People Learn: Brain, Mind, Experience, and School.* A Report of the National Research Council. Washington, DC: National Academies Press.

Bransford, J.D., A.L. Brown, & R.R. Cocking, eds. 2000. *How People Learn: Brain, Mind, Experience and School.* Report of the National Resource Council, Committee on Developments in the Science of Learning, Commission on Behavioral and Social Sciences and Education. Washington, DC: National Academies Press.

Bredekamp, S., ed. 1986. *Developmentally Appropriate Practice.* Washington, DC: NAEYC.

Bredekamp, S., ed. 1987. *Developmentally Appropriate Practice in Early Childhood Programs Serving Children From Birth Through Age 8.* Exp. ed. Washington, DC: NAEYC.

Bredekamp, S., & C. Copple, eds. 1997. *Developmentally Appropriate Practice in Early Childhood Programs Serving Children From Birth Through Age 8.* Rev. ed. Washington, DC: NAEYC.

Bronson, M.B. 1994. "The Usefulness of an Observational Measure of Children's Social and Mastery Behaviors in Early Childhood Classrooms." *Early Childhood Research Quarterly* 9: 19–43.

Bronson, M.B. 2006. "Developing Social and Emotional Competence." Chap. 5 in *K Today: Teaching and Learning in the Kindergarten Year*, ed. D.F. Gullo, 47–56. Washington, DC: NAEYC.

Brooks, A.M. 1913. "The Value of Outdoor Kindergartens." *Journal of Education* 78 (5): 121.

Bruer, J.T. 1999. *The Myth of the First Three Years.* New York: Free Press.

Bukowski, W.M. 2001. "Friendship and the Worlds of Childhood." Chap. 5 in *The Role of Friendship in Psychological Adjustment,* eds. D.W. Nangle & C.A. Erdley, 93–105. San Francisco: Jossey-Bass.

Burhans, K.K., & C.S. Dweck. 1995. "Helplessness in Early Childhood: The Role of Contingent Worth." *Child Development* 66 (6): 1719–38.

Burns, M.S., P. Griffin, & C.E. Snow. 1999. *Starting Out Right: A Guide to Promoting Children's Reading Success.* A Report of the National Research Council. Washington, DC: National Academies Press.

Bush, G., P. Luu, & M.I. Posner. 2000. "Cognitive and Emotional Influences in the Anterior Cingulate Cortex." *Trends in Cognitive Sciences* 4: 215–22.

Campano, G. 2007. *Immigrant Students and Literacy: Reading, Writing, and Remembering.* New York: Teachers College Press.

Case, R. 1998. "The Development of Central Conceptual Structures." In *Handbook of Child Psychology, Vol. 2: Cognition, Perception, and Language,* 5th ed., eds. D. Kuhn & R.S. Siegler, 745–800. New York: Wiley.

Case, R., & Y. Okamoto, eds. 1996. *The Role of Central Conceptual Structures in the Development of Children's Thought.* Monographs of the Society for Research in Child Development, vol. 61, nos. 1–2, serial no. 246. Chicago: University of Chicago Press.

Caspe, M. 2003. *Family Literacy: A Review of Programs and Critical Perspectives.* Cambridge, MA: Harvard Family Research Project.

Caspi, A. 1998. "Personality Development Across the Life Span." In *Handbook of Child Psychology, Vol. 3: Social, Emotional, and Personality Development*, 5th ed., ed. N. Eisenberg, 311–88. New York: Wiley.

CCNY (Carnegie Corporation of New York). 1998. *Years of Promise: A Comprehensive Learning Strategy for America's Children.* www.carnegie.org/sub/pubs/exec-sum.html.

Clements, D.H. 2001. "Mathematics in the Preschool." *Teaching Children Mathematics* 7 (4): 270–75.

Colasanti, M. 2007. *Kindergarten Entrance Ages: A 30-Year Trend Analysis.* Denver: Education Commission of the States.

Colorín Colorado. 2007. *Reading Comprehension Strategies for Content Learning.* www.colorincolorado.org/educators/content/comprehension.

Comber, B., & A. Simpson, eds. 2001. *Negotiating Critical Literacies in Classrooms.* Mahwah, NJ: Erlbaum.

Coplan, R.J., K. Prakash, K. O'Neil, & M. Armer. 2004. "Do You 'Want' to Play? Distinguishing Between Conflicted Shyness and Social Disinterest in Early Childhood." *Developmental Psychology* 40: 244–58.

Copple, C., & S. Bredekamp. 2006. *Basics of Developmentally Appropriate Practice: An Introduction for Teachers of Children 3 to 6.* Washington, DC: NAEYC.

Copple, C., & S. Bredekamp, eds. 2009. *Developmentally Appropriate Practice in Early Childhood Programs Serving Children From Birth Through Age 8.* 3rd ed. Washington, DC: NAEYC.

Cost, Quality, and Child Outcomes Study Team. 1995. *Cost, Quality, and Child Outcomes in Child Care Centers.* Technical report. Denver: University of Colorado, Center for Research in Economics and Social Policy.

Cowan, N., L.D. Nugent, E.M. Elliott, I. Ponomarev, & J.S. Saults. 1999. "The Role of Attention in the Development of Short-Term Memory: Age Differences in the Verbal Span of Apprehension." *Child Development* 70 (5): 1082–97.

Cowen, E.L., A. Pedersen, H. Babigian, L.D. Izzo, & M.A. Trost. 1973. "Long-Term Follow-Up of Early Detected Vulnerable Children." *Journal of Consulting and Clinical Psychology* 41: 438–46.

Cowhey, M. 2006. *Black Ants and Buddhists: Thinking Critically and Teaching Differently in the Primary Grades.* Portland, ME: Stenhouse.

Cozolino, L. 2007. *The Neuroscience of Human Relationships: Attachment and the Developing Social Brain.* New York: Norton.

Cratty, B.J. 1986. *Perceptual and Motor Development in Infants and Children.* 3rd ed. Englewood Cliffs, NJ: Prentice Hall.

Darling-Hammond, L., & N. Richardson. 2009. "Teacher Learning: What Matters?" *Educational Leadership* 66 (5): 46–53.

Dearing, E., H. Kreider, & H.B. Weiss. 2008. "Increased Family Involvement in School Predicts Improved Child-Teacher Relationships and Feelings About School for Low-Income Children." *Marriage & Family Review* 43 (3–4): 226–54.

Delpit, L., & J. Dowdy, eds. 2002. *The Skin That We Speak: Thoughts on Language and Culture in the Classroom*. New York: The New Press.

Dempster, F.N. 1993. "Resistance to Interference: Developmental Changes in a Basic Processing Mechanism." In *Emerging Themes in Cognitive Development, Vol. 1: Foundations,* eds. M.L. Howe & R. Pasnak, 3–27. New York: Springer-Verlag.

Denham, S.A., & A.T. Kochanoff. 2002. "Parental Contributions to Preschoolers' Understanding of Emotion." *Marriage and Family Review* 34: 311–43.

Dodge, D.T., L.J. Colker, & C. Heroman. 2002. *The Creative Curriculum for Preschool*. 4th ed. Washington, DC: Teaching Strategies.

Dodge, K.A., J.E. Lansford, V.S. Burks, J.E. Bates, G.S. Pettit, R. Fontaine, & J.M. Price. 2003. "Peer Rejection and Social Information-Processing Factors in the Development of Aggressive Behavior Problems in Children." *Child Development* 74 (2): 374–93.

Donovan, C.A., & L.B. Smolkin. 2011. "Supporting Informational Writing in the Elementary Grades." *The Reading Teacher* 64 (6): 406–16.

Downer, J.T., K. Driscoll, & R.C. Pianta. 2006. "Transition From Kindergarten to First Grade." Chap. 14 *K Today: Teaching and Learning in the Kindergarten Year*, ed. D.F. Gullo, 151–60. Washington, DC: NAEYC.

Duda, M., & V. Minick. 2006. "Easing the Transition to Kindergarten: Demonstrating Partnership Through Service Learning." *Mentoring & Tutoring: Partnership in Learning* 14 (1): 111–21.

Dunn, J. 1988. *The Beginnings of Social Understanding*. Cambridge, MA: Harvard University Press.

Dunn, J., J.R. Brown, & M. Maguire. 1995. "The Development of Children's Moral Sensibility: Individual Differences and Emotion Understanding." *Developmental Psychology* 31: 649–59.

Early Learning Group. 2004. "Read Together, Talk Together." Program guide. New York: Pearson.

Eder, R.A., & S.C. Mangelsdorf. 1997. "The Emotional Basis of Early Personality Development: Implications for the Emergent Self-Concept." Chap. 9 in *Handbook of Personality Psychology*, eds. R. Hogan, J. Johnson, & S. Briggs, 209–40. San Diego: Academic Press.

Edwards, C.P., L. Gandini, & G. Forman, eds. 1998. *The Hundred Languages of Children: The Reggio Emilia Approach—Advanced Reflections*. 2nd ed. Greenwich, CT: Ablex.

Eisenberg, N. 2003. "Prosocial Behavior, Empathy, and Sympathy." In *Well-Being: Positive Development Across the Life Course*, eds. M.H. Bornstein & L. Davidson, 253–65. Mahwah, NJ: Erlbaum.

Eisenberg, N., & R.A. Fabes. 1992. "Emotion, Regulation, and the Development of Social Competence." In *Review of Personality and Social Psychology, Vol. 14: Emotion and Social Behavior*, ed. M.S. Clark. Newbury Park, CA: Sage.

Eisenberg, N., & R.A. Fabes. 1998. "Prosocial Development." In *Handbook of Child Psychology, Vol. 3: Social, Emotional, and Personality Development*, 5th ed., ed. N. Eisenberg, 701–78. New York: Wiley.

Eisenberg, N., R.A. Fabes, & S. Losoya. 1997. "Emotional Responding: Regulation, Social Correlates, and Socialization." Chap. 5 in *Emotional Development and Emotional Intelligence: Educational Implications*, eds. P. Salovey & D. Sluyter, 129–63. New York: Basic.

Eisenberg, N., & P.H. Mussen. 1989. *The Roots of Prosocial Behavior in Children*. Cambridge: Cambridge University Press.

Elias, C., & L.E. Berk. 2002. "Self-Regulation in Young Children: Is There a Role for Sociodramatic Play?" *Early Childhood Research Quarterly* 17 (1): 216–38.

Ely, R. 2005. "Language and Literacy in the School Years." In *The Development of Language*, 6th ed., ed. J.B. Gleason, 395–443. Boston: Allyn & Bacon.

Emmer, E., & L. Stough. 2001. "Classroom Management: A Critical Part of Educational Psychology, With Implications for Teacher Education." *Educational Psychologist* 36 (2): 103–12.

Entwisle, D.R., & K.L. Alexander. 1998. "Facilitating the Transition to First Grade: The Nature of Transition and Research on Factors Affecting It." *Elementary School Journal* 98 (4): 351–64.

Epstein, A.S. 2007. *The Intentional Teacher: Choosing the Best Strategies for Young Children's Learning*. Washington, DC: NAEYC.

Epstein, J.L. 2001. *School, Family, and Community Partnerships: Preparing Educators and Improving Schools*. Boulder: Westview.

Espinosa, L.M. 2007. "English Language Learners as They Enter School." In *School Readiness and the Transition to Kindergarten in the Era of Accountability*, eds. R.C. Pianta, M.J. Cox, & K.L. Snow. Baltimore: Brookes.

Espinosa, L.M. 2008. "Challenging Common Myths About Young English Language Learners." *Foundation for Child Development Policy Brief, Advancing PK–3* 8.

Fabes, R.A., N. Eisenberg, L.D. Hanish, & T.L. Spinrad. 2001. "Preschoolers' Spontaneous Emotion Vocabulary: Relations to Likability." *Early Education and Development* 12: 1127.

Fantuzzo, J., R. Bulotsky-Shearer, P. McDermott, C. McWayne, D. Frye, & S. Perlman. 2007. "Investigation of Dimensions of Social-Emotional Classroom Behavior and School Readiness for Low Income Urban Preschool Children." *School Psychology Review* 36 (1): 44–62.

Flavell, J.H., P. Miller, & S. Miller. 2001. *Cognitive Development*. 4th ed. Upper Saddle River, NJ: Prentice Hall.

Fletcher, R. 1993. "Roots and Wings: Literature and Children's Writing." In *Pen in Hand: Children Become Writers*, ed. B. Cullinan, 7–18. Newark, DE: International Reading Association.

Foy, J.G., & V. Mann. 2003. "Home Literacy Environment and phonological Awareness in Preschool Children: Differential Effects for Rhyme and Phoneme Awareness." *Applied Psycholinguistics* 24: 59–88.

Fraser, S., & C. Gestwicki. 2001. *Authentic Childhood: Exploring Reggio Emilia in the Classroom.* Clifton Park, NY: Delmar.

Freire, P. [1970] 2000. *Pedagogy of the Oppressed.* 30th ann. ed. New York: Continuum.

Freire, P. 1970. *Pedagogy of the Oppressed.* New York: Continuum.

Galinsky, E. 2010. *Mind in the Making: The Seven Essential Life Skills Every Child Needs.* Washington, DC: NAEYC.

Gallagher, K.C., & P.R. Sylvester. 2009. "Supporting Peer Relationships in Early Education." In *Handbook of Child Development and Early Education: Research to Practice*, eds. O.A. Barbarin & B.H. Wasik, 223–46. New York: Guilford Press.

Gallahue, D.L. 1995. "Transforming Physical Education Curriculum." In *Reaching Potentials, Vol. 2: Transforming Early Childhood Curriculum and Assessment*, eds. S. Bredekamp & T. Rosegrant, 125–44. Washington, DC: NAEYC.

Gartrell, D. 2004. *The Power of Guidance: Teaching Social-Emotional Skills in Early Childhood Classrooms.* Clifton Park, NY: Thomson Delmar Learning.

Gelman, R., & K. Brenneman. 2004. "Science Learning Pathways for Young Children." *Early Childhood Research Quarterly* 19: 150–58.

Gerde, H.K., G.E. Bingham, & B.A. Wasik. 2012. "Writing in Early Childhood Classrooms: Guidance for Best Practices." *Early Childhood Education Journal* 40 (6): 351–9.

Ginsburg, H.P., J. Boyd, & J. Sun Lee. 2008. "Mathematics Education for Young Children: What It Is and How to Promote It." *Social Policy Report* 22 (1): 1–23.

Golbeck, S.L. 2006. "Developing Key Cognitive Skills." In *K Today: Teaching and Learning in the Kindergarten Year*, ed. D.F. Gullo, 37–46. Washington, DC: NAEYC.

Gonzalez, N., L. Moll, & C. Amanti, eds. 2005. *Funds of Knowledge: Theorizing Practices in Households, Communities, and Classroom.* Mahwah, NJ: Erlbaum.

Graue, M.E. 2006. "This Thing Called Kindergarten." Chap. 1 in *K Today: Teaching and Learning in the Kindergarten Year,* ed. D.F. Gullo, 3–10. Washington, DC: NAEYC.

Greer, T., & J.J. Lockman. 1998. "Using Writing Instruments: Invariances in Young Children and Adults." *Child Development* 69 (4): 888–902.

Gregory, E., S. Long, & D. Volk, eds. 2004. *Many Pathways to Literacy: Young Children Learning With Siblings, Grandparents, Peers, and Communities.* London: Routledge.

Gullo, D.F. 1994. *Understanding Assessment and Evaluation in Early Childhood Education.* New York: Teachers College Press.

Gullo, D.F. 2006a. "Assessment in Kindergarten." Chap. 13 in *K Today: Teaching and Learning in the Kindergarten Year*, ed. D.F Gullo, 138–47. Washington, DC: NAEYC.

Gullo, D.F., ed. 2006b. *K Today: Teaching and Learning in the Kindergarten Year.* Washington, DC: NAEYC.

Haight, W. 2006. "Stories as Tools for Teaching: Lessons From Sunday School at an African American Church." *School Talk* 11 (4): 1–2.

Haight, W.L., & J. Carter-Black. 2004. "His Eye Is on the Sparrow: Teaching and Learning in an African American Church." In E. Gregory, S. Long, & D. Volk, 195–207.

Halfon, N., E. Shulman, & M. Hochstein. 2001. "Brain Development in Early Childhood." *Policy Briefs* 13: 1–4. Los Angeles: UCLA Center for Healthier Children, Family and Communities, California Policy Research Center.

Halford, G.S., & G. Andrews. 2006. "Reasoning and Problem Solving." Chap. 13 in *Handbook of Child Psychology, Vol. 2: Cognition, Perception, and Language*, 6th ed., eds. D. Kuhn & R. Siegler, 557–608. Hoboken, NJ: John Wiley & Sons.

Hamre, B.K., & R.C. Pianta. 2001. "Early Teacher-Child Relationships and the Trajectory of Children's School Outcomes Through Eighth Grade." *Child Development* 72 (2): 625–38.

Hamre, B.K., & R.C. Pianta. 2005. "Can Instructional and Emotional Support in the First Grade Classroom Make a Difference for Children at Risk of School Failure?" *Child Development* 76 (5): 949–67.

Harnishfeger, K.K. 1995. "The Development of Cognitive Inhibition: Theories, Definitions, and Research Evidence." In *New Perspectives on Interference and Inhibition in Cognition*, eds. F.F. Dempster & C.J. Brainerd, 176–204. San Diego: Academic Press.

Harris, P.L. 2006. "Social Cognition." Chap. 19 in *Handbook of Child Psychology, Vol. 2: Cognition, Perception, and Language*, 6th ed., eds. D. Kuhn & R. Siegler, 811–59. Hoboken, NJ: Wiley.

Harste, J., & V. Vasquez. 1998. "The Work We Do: Journal as Audit Trail." *Language Arts* 75 (4): 266–76. http://php.indiana.edu/~harste/recpub/workwedo.pdf.

Hart, B., & T.R. Risley. 1995. *Meaningful Differences in the Everyday Experience of Young American Children.* Baltimore: Brookes.

Hart, B., & T.R. Risley. 2003. "The Early Catastrophe." *Education Review* 17 (1): 110–18.

Harter, S. 1996. "Developmental Changes in Self-Understanding Across the 5 to 7 Shift." Chap. 10 in *The Five to Seven Year Shift*, eds. A.J. Sameroff & M.M. Haith, 207–36. Chicago: University of Chicago Press.

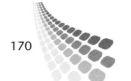

Harter, S. 2003. "The Development of Self-Representations During Childhood and Adolescence." Chap. 30 in *Handbook of Self and Identity*, eds. M.R. Leary & J.P. Tangney, 610–42. New York: Guilford.

Hartup, W.W. 1996. "The Company They Keep: Friendships and Their Developmental Significance." *Child Development* 67 (1): 1–13.

Haynes, M. 2008. "Building State Early Learning Systems: Lessons and Results From NASBE's Early Childhood Education Network." *The State Education Standard* (June): 12–19.

Heath, S.B. 1983. *Ways With Words: Language, Life, and Work in Communities and Classrooms*. New York: Cambridge University Press.

Helm, J.H., & L. Katz. 2011. *Young Investigators: The Project Approach in the Early Years*. 2nd ed. New York: Teachers College Press.

Hoffman, M.L. 1983. "Affective and Cognitive Processes in Moral Internalization." Chap. 10 in *Social Cognition and Social Development: A Sociocultural Perspective*, eds. E.T. Higgins, D.N. Ridale, & W.W. Hartup, 236–74. Cambridge: Cambridge University Press.

Howes, C. 1988. "Relations Between Early Child Care and Schooling." *Developmental Psychology* 24 (1): 53–57.

Howes, C., & C.C. Matheson. 1992. "Sequences in the Development of Competent Play With Peers: Social and Social Pretend Play." *Developmental Psychology* 28: 961–74.

Howse, R.B., S.D. Calkins, A.D. Anastopoulos, S.R. Keane, & T.L. Shelton. 2003. "Regulatory Contributors to Children's Kindergarten Achievement." *Early Education and Development* 14 (1): 101–19.

Hudson, J.A., B. Sosa, & L.R. Shapiro. 1997. "Scripts and Plans: The Development of Preschool Children's Event Knowledge and Event Planning." In *The Developmental Psychology of Planning: Why, How, and When Do We Plan?*, eds. S.L. Friedman & E. K. Scholnick, 77–102. Mahwah, NJ: Erlbaum.

Huttenlocher, P.R. 2002. *Neural Plasticity: The Effects of Environment on the Development of the Cerebral Cortex*. Cambridge, MA: Harvard University Press.

Hydrick, J. 1996. *Parents' Guide to Literacy for the 21st Century: Pre-K Through Grade 5*. Urbana, IL: National Council of Teachers of English.

Hyson, M. 2004. *The Emotional Development of Young Children: Building an Emotion-Centered Curriculum*. 2d ed. New York: Teachers College Press.

Hyson, M. 2008. *Enthusiastic and Engaged Learners: Approaches to Learning in the Early Childhood Classroom*. New York: Teachers College Press.

IRA (International Reading Association) & NAEYC. 1998. *Learning to Read and Write: Developmentally Appropriate Practices for Young Children*. Joint position statement. Washington, DC: NAEYC. www.naeyc.org/files/naeyc/file/positions/PSREAD98.PDF.

Jablon, J.R., A.L. Dombro, & M.L. Dichtelmiller. 1999. *The Power of Observation*. Washington, DC: Teaching Strategies.

Jalongo, M.R., & J.P. Isenberg. 2006. "Creative Expression and Thought in Kindergarten." Chap. 11 in *K Today: Teaching and Learning in the Kindergarten Year*, ed. D.F. Gullo, 116–26. Washington, DC: NAEYC.

Jones, E., & J. Nimmo. 1994. *Emergent Curriculum*. Washington, DC: NAEYC.

Karmiloff-Smith, A., J. Grant, K. Sims, M. Jones, & P. Cuckle. 1996. "Rethinking Metalinguistic Awareness: Representing and Accessing Knowledge About What Counts as a Word." *Cognition* 58: 197–219.

Katz, L.G., & S.C. Chard. 2000. *Engaging Children's Minds: The Project Approach*. 2nd ed. Norwood, NJ: Ablex.

Katz, L.G., & D.E. McClellan. 1997. *Fostering Children's Social Competence: The Teacher's Role*. Washington, DC: NAEYC.

Kersey, K. 2006. *A Guide to Positive Discipline: The Facilitator's Guide*. Distance learning publication. Norfolk, VA: Old Dominion University Child Study Center.

Kochanska, G., & A. Knaack. 2003. "Effortful Control as a Personality Characteristic of Young Children: Antecedents, Correlates, and Consequences." *Journal of Personality* 71: 1087–112.

Koestner, R., C. Franz, & J. Weinberger. 1990. "The Family Origins of Empathetic Concern: A 26-Year Longitudinal Study." *Journal of Personality and Social Psychology* 58: 709–16.

Kontos, S., & L. Keyes. 1999. "An Ecobehavioral Analysis of Early Childhood Classrooms." *Early Childhood Research Quarterly* 14 (1): 35–50.

Kuby, C.R. 2010. "Understanding an Early Childhood Inquiry Curriculum Through Crystallizing Autoethnography, Practitioner Research, and a Performative Analysis of Emotion." PhD diss., Indiana University. ProQuest.

Kuby, C.R. 2011. "Kidwatching With a Critical Eye: The Power of Observation and Reflexive Practice." *Talking Points* 22 (2): 22–28.

Kupersmidt, J., & J.D. Coie. 1990. "Preadolescent Peer Status, Aggression, and School Adjustment as Predictors of Externalizing Problems in Adolescence." *Child Development* 61 (5): 1350–62.

Ladd, G.W. 1999. "Peer Relationships and Social Competence During Early and Middle Childhood." *Annual Review of Psychology* 50: 333–59.

Ladd, G.W., S.H. Birch, & E.S. Buhs. 1999. "Children's Social and Scholastic Lives in Kindergarten: Related Spheres of Influence?" *Child Development* 70 (6): 1373–400.

Ladd, G.W., E.S. Buhs, & M. Seid. 2000. "Children's Initial Sentiments About Kindergarten: Is School Liking an Antecedent of Early Classroom Participation and Achievement?" *Merrill-Palmer Quarterly* 46: 255–79.

Lam, M.S., & A. Pollard. 2006. "A Conceptual Framework for Understanding Children as Agents in the Transition from Home to Kindergarten." *Early Years: Journal of International Research & Development* 26 (2): 123–41.

Lamme, L.L., D. Fu, J. Johnson, & D. Savage. 2002. "Helping Kindergarten Writers Move Toward Independence." *Early Childhood Education Journal* 30 (2): 73–79.

Lane, K., T. Stanton-Chapman, K. Roorback Jamison, & A. Phillips. 2007. "Teacher and Parent Expectations of Preschoolers' Behavior: Social Skills Necessary for Success." *Topics in Early Childhood Special Education* 27 (2): 86–97.

Lee, V.E., & D.T. Burkam. 2002. *Inequality at the Starting Gate: Social Background Differences in Achievement as Children Begin School.* New York: Economic Policy Institute.

Leong, D.J., & E. Bodrova. 2005. "Why Children Need Play!" *Scholastic Parent & Child* 13 (1): 37.

Lewin-Benham, A. 2006. "One Teacher, 20 Preschoolers, and a Goldfish: Environmental Awareness, Emergent Curriculum, and Documentation." *Young Children* 61 (2): 28–34. www.naeyc.org/files/yc/file/200603/LewinBTJ.pdf.

Lewison, M., A.S. Flint, & K. Van Sluys. 2002. "Taking on Critical Literacy: The Journey of Newcomers and Novices." *Language Arts* 79 (5): 382–92. www.uprb.edu/profesor/mrocio/edpe3001/articulos/takingon-critical literacy.pdf.

Long, S. 2004. "Making a Place for Peer Interaction: Mexican American Kindergartners Learning Language and Literacy. In E. Gregory, S. Long, & D. Volk, 93–104.

Maccoby, E.E., & C.N. Jacklin. 1987. "Gender Segregation in Childhood." In *Advances in Child Development and Behavior, Vol. 20,* ed. E.H. Reese, 239–87. New York: Academic Press.

Mahar, M.T., S.K. Murphy, D.A. Rowe, J. Golden, A.T. Shields, & T.D. Raedeke. 2006. "Effects of a Classroom-Based Program on Physical Activity and On-Task Behavior." *Medicine & Science in Sports and Exercise* 38 (12): 286–94.

Manross, M.A. 1994. *What Children Think, Feel, and Know About the Overhand Throw.* Master's thesis. Blacksburg, VA: Virginia Tech University.

Manross, M.A. 2000. "Learning to Throw in Physical Education Class: Part 3." *Teaching Elementary Physical Education* 11 (3): 26–29.

Mantzicopoulos, P., H. Patrick, & A. Samarapungavan. 2009. The Scientific Literacy Project. www.purduescientificliteracyproject.org.

Martin, C.L., & C.A. Fabes. 2001. "The Stability and Consequences of Young Children's Same-Sex Peer Interactions." *Developmental Psychology* 37: 431–46.

Masterson, M. 2008. "The Impact of the 101s: A Guide to Positive Discipline Training on Teacher Interaction Practices, Attitudes, and Prosocial Skill Outcomes in Preschool Classrooms." PhD diss. Norfolk, VA: Old Dominion University.

McAfee, O., D.J. Leong, & E. Bodrova. 2004. *Basics of Assessment: A Primer for Early Childhood Educators.* Washington, DC: NAEYC.

McClelland, M.M., A.C. Acock, & F.J. Morrison. 2006. "The Impact of Kindergarten Learning-Related Skills on Academic Trajectories at the End of Elementary School." *Early Childhood Research Quarterly* 21 (4): 471–90.

McMillon, G.T., & P.A. Edwards. 2004. "The African American Church: A Beacon of Light on the Pathway to Literacy for African American Children." In E. Gregory, S. Long, & D. Volk, 182–94.

Medina, C., & G. Campano. 2006. "Performing Identities Through Drama and Teatro Practices in Multilingual Classrooms." *Language Arts* 83 (4): 332–41.

Mehaffie, K.E., & R.B. McCall. 2002. *Kindergarten Readiness: An Overview of Issues and Assessment.* Special report. Pittsburgh, PA: University of Pittsburgh, Office of Child Development.

Meiers, M. 2004. "Reading for Pleasure and Literacy Achievement." *Research Developments* 12. http://research.acer.edu.au/cgi/viewcontent.cgi?article=1012&context=resdev.

Miles, S.B., & D. Stipek. 2006. "Contemporaneous and Longitudinal Associations Between Social Behavior and Literacy Achievement in a Sample of Low-Income Elementary School Children." *Child Development* 77 (1): 103–17.

Miller, D., & K. Sawka-Miller. 2007. "The Third Pillar: Linking Positive Psychology and School-Wide Positive Behavior Support." *School Psychology Forum: Research in Practice* 2 (1): 26–38.

Mitchell, S., T.S. Foulger, K. Wetzel, & C. Rathkey. 2009. "The Negotiated Project Approach: Project-Based Learning Without Leaving the Standards Behind." *Early Childhood Education Journal* 36 (4): 339–46.

NAEYC. 1996. "Developmentally Appropriate Practice in Early Childhood Programs Serving Children from Birth Through Age 8." Position statement. In *Developmentally Appropriate Practice in Early Childhood Programs,* rev. ed., eds. S. Bredekamp & C. Copple, 3–30. Washington, DC: NAEYC.

NAEYC. 2005. "Screening and Assessment of Young English-Language Learners." Supplement to the NAEYC and NAECS/SDE joint position statement on Early Childhood Curriculum, Assessment, and Program Evaluation. Washington, DC: NAEYC. www.naeyc.org/files/naeyc/file/positions/ELL_SupplementLong.pdf.

NAEYC. 2011. *The Common Core State Standards: Caution and Opportunity for Early Childhood Education.* Washington, DC: NAEYC.

NAEYC & NAECS/SDE (National Association of Early Childhood Specialists in State Departments of Education). 2002. "Early Learning Standards: Creating the Conditions for Success." Joint position statement. http://www.naeyc.org/files/naeyc/file/positions/position_statement.pdf.

NAEYC & NAECS/SDE (National Association of Early Childhood Specialists in State Departments of Education). 2003. "Early Childhood Curriculum, Assessment, and Program Evaluation: Building an Effective, Accountable System in Programs for Children Birth Through Age 8." Joint position statement with expanded resources. Washington, DC: NAEYC. www.naeyc.org/files/naeyc/file/positions/CAPEexpand.pdf.

NAEYC & NAECS/SDE (National Association of Early Childhood Specialists in State Departments of Education). 2010. "Joint Statement on the Common Core Standards Initiative Related to Kindergarten Through Third Grade." http://www.naeyc.org/files/naeyc/file/policy/NAEYC-NAECS-SDE-Core-Standards-Statement.pdf.

NAEYC & NCTM (National Council of Teachers of Mathematics). 2002. "Early Childhood Mathematics: Promoting Good Beginnings." Joint position statement. Washington, DC: NAEYC. http://www.naeyc.org/files/naeyc/file/positions/psmath.pdf.

NASPE (National Association for Sport and Physical Education). 2004. *Moving into the Future: National Standards for Physical Education.* 2d ed. Reston, VA: NASPE.

NASPE (National Association for Sport and Physical Education). 2008a. "Appropriate Maximum Class Length for Elementary Physical Education." Position statement. Reston, VA: NASPE.

NASPE (National Association for Sport and Physical Education). 2008b. *Comprehensive School Physical Activity Programs.* Position statement. Reston, VA: NASPE.

NCES (National Center for Education Statistics). 1997. *The Elementary School Performance and Adjustment of Children Who Enter Kindergarten Late or Repeat Kindergarten: Findings From National Surveys* (Publication No. 98097). Washington, DC: US Dept. of Education.

NCES (National Center for Education Statistics). 2008. "All Levels of Education." Chap. 1 in *Digest of Education Statistics, 2007* (NCES 2008-022). nces.ed.gov/programs/digest/d07/ch_1.asp.

NCTM (National Council of Teachers of Mathematics). 2006. *Curriculum Focal Points for Prekindergarten Through Grade 8 Mathematics: A Quest for Coherence.* Reston, VA: NCTM.

Nelson, C.A. 2002. "Neural Development and Lifelong Plasticity." In *Handbook of Applied Developmental Science, Vol. 1,* eds. R.M. Lerner, F. Jacobs, & D. Wertlieb, 31–60. Thousand Oaks, CA: Sage.

Neuman, S.B. 2003. "From Rhetoric to Reality: The Case for High-Quality Compensatory Prekindergarten Programs." *Phi Delta Kappan* 85 (4): 286–91.

Neuman, S.B., & K. Roskos. 2012. "Helping Children Become More Knowledgeable Through Text." *The Reading Teacher* 66 (3): 207–10.

Newcombe, N.S. 2005. "What Do We Mean When We Say Modularity?" Master Lecture presented at the Biennial Meeting of the Society for Research in Child Development, April 7–10, Atlanta, GA.

NGA (National Governors Association Center for Best Practices) & CCSSO (Council of Chief State School Officers). 2010. "Common Core State Standards for English Language Arts and Literacy." www.corestandards.org/assets/CCSSI_ELA%20Standards.pdf.

NICHD–ECCRN (National Institute of Child Health & Human Development–Early Child Care Research Network). 2005. "Early Childcare and Children's Development in the Primary Grades: Follow-Up Results from the NICHD Study of Early Childcare." *American Educational Research Journal* 42 (3): 537–70.

NICHD–ECCRN (National Institute of Child Health & Human Development–Early Child Care Research Network). 2007. "Age of Entry to Kindergarten and Children's Academic Achievement and Socioemotional Development." *Early Education and Development* 18 (2): 337–68.

NIEER (National Institute for Early Education Research). 2008. *The State of Preschool 2008.* New Brunswick, NJ: Rutgers University.

Nieto, S. 1999. *The Light in Their Eyes: Creating Multicultural Learning Communities.* New York: Teachers College Press.

Nieto, S., & C. Rolón. 1997. "Preparation and Professional Development of Teachers: A Perspective From Two Latinas." In *Critical Knowledge for Diverse Teachers and Learners,* ed. J.J. Irvine, 93–128. Washington, DC: American Association of Colleges for Teacher Education.

NRC (National Research Council). 2001. *Adding It Up: Helping Children Learn mathematics.* J. Kilpatrick, J. Swafford, and B. Findell (Eds.). Center for Education, Division of Behavioral and Social Sciences and Education. Washington, DC: National Academies Press.

NRC (National Research Council). 2009. *Mathematics Learning in Early Childhood: Paths Toward Excellence and Equity.* Washington, DC: National Academies Press.

NRC (National Research Council). 2012. *A Framework for K–12 Science Education: Practices, Crosscutting Concepts, and Core Ideas.* Committee on a Conceptual Framework for New K–12 Science Education Standards, Board on Science Education, Division of Behavioral and Social Sciences and Education. Washington, DC: National Academies Press. www.nap.edu/catalog.php?record_id=13165.

NRP (National Reading Panel). 2000. *Report of the National Reading Panel: Teaching People to Read.* Washington, DC: National Institute of Child Health and Human Development.

NSCDC (National Scientific Council on the Developing Child). 2007. *The Science of Early Childhood Development: Closing the Gap Between What We Know and What We Do.* Cambridge, MA: Harvard University Press. http://developingchild.harvard.edu/index.php/resources/reports_and_working_papers/science_of_early_childhood_development/.

O'Brien, J. 2001. "Children Reading Critically: A Local History." In *Negotiating Critical Literacies in Classrooms,* eds. B. Comber & A. Simpson, 37–54. Mahwah, NJ: Erlbaum.

Owocki, G., & Y. Goodman. 2002. *Kidwatching: Documenting Children's Literacy Development.* Portsmouth, NH: Heinemann.

Pappas, C. 2006. "The Information Book Genre: Its Role in Integrated Science Literacy Research and Practice." *Reading Research Quarterly* 41 (2): 226–50.

Pappas, S., H.P. Ginsburg, & M. Jiang. 2003. "SES Differences in Young Children's Metacognition in the Context of Mathematical Problem Solving." *Cognitive Development* 18 (3): 431–50.

Patrick, H., & P. Mantzicopoulos. 2013. *Engaging Young Children With Informational Books.* Thousand Oaks, CA: Corwin Press.

Perner, J., B. Lang, & D. Kloo. 2002. "Theory of Mind and Self-Control: More Than a Common Problem of Inhibition." *Child Development* 73 (3): 752–67.

Peth-Pierce, R. 2000. *A Good Beginning: Sending America's Children to School With the Social Emotional Competence They Need to Succeed.* Child Mental Health Foundations and Agencies Network monograph. Bethesda, MD: National Institute of Mental Health, Office of Communications and Public Liaison.

Pettit, G.S. 2004. "Violent Children in Developmental Perspective." *Current Directions in Psychological Science* 13: 194–97.

Phillips, E.C., & A. Scrinzi. 2013. *Basics of Developmentally Appropriate Practice: An Introduction for Teachers of Kindergartners.* Washington, DC: NAEYC.

Piaget, J. 1930. *The Child's Conception of the World.* New York: Harcourt, Brace & World.

Piaget, J. 1932 [1965]. *The Moral Judgement of the Child.* New York: Free Press.

Piaget, J. 1951. *Play, Dreams, and Imitation in Childhood.* New York: Norton.

Piaget, J. 1952. *The Origins of Intelligence in Children.* New York: International Universities Press.

Pianta, R.C., J. Belsky, N. Vandergrift, R. Houts, & F.J. Morrison. 2008. "Classroom Effects on Children's Achievement Trajectories in Elementary School." *American Educational Research Journal* 45 (2): 365–97.

Pianta, R.C., B. Hamre, & M.W. Stuhlman. 2003. "Relationships Between Teachers and Children." In *Comprehensive Handbook of Psychology, Vol. 7: Educational Psychology,* eds. W. Reynolds & G. Miller, 199–234. Hoboken, NJ: Wiley.

Pianta, R.C., & M. Kraft-Sayre. 2003. *Successful Kindergarten Transition: Your Guide to Connecting Children, Families, and Schools.* Baltimore: Brookes.

Pianta, R.C., & M.W. Stuhlman. 2004. "Teacher-Child Relationships and Children's Success in the First Years of School." *School Psychology Review* 33 (3): 444–58.

Quillian, L., & M.E. Campbell. 2003. "Beyond Black and White: The Present and Future of Multiracial Friendship Segregation." *American Sociological Review* 68: 540–66.

RAND Reading Study Group. 2002. *Reading for Understanding: Toward an R&D program in Reading Comprehension.* Santa Monica, CA: RAND Education, Science & Technology Policy Institute.

Raver, C.C. 2002. *Emotions Matter: Making the Case for the Role of Young Children's Emotional Development for Early School Readiness.* Ann Arbor, MI: Society for Research in Child Development.

Raver, C., S. Jones, C. Li-Grining, M. Metzger, K. Champion, & L. Sardin. 2008. "Improving Preschool Classroom Processes: Preliminary Findings from a Randomized Trial Implemented in Head Start Settings." *Early Childhood Research Quarterly* 23 (1): 10–26.

Raver, C.C., & J. Knitzer. 2002. *Ready to Enter: What Research Tells Policymakers About Strategies to Promote Social and Emotional School Readiness Among Three- and Four-Year-Old Children.* New York: Columbia University, National Center for Children in Poverty.

Ray, A., B. Bowman, & J. Robbins. 2006. *Preparing Early Childhood Teachers to Successfully Educate All Children.* Foundation for Child Development Policy Report. http://fcd-us.org/resources/preparing-early-childhood-teachers-successfully-educate-all-children?destination=resources%2Fsearch%3Fpage%3D21.

Ray, K., & L. Cleveland. 2004. *About the Authors: Writing Workshop With Our Youngest Writers.* Portsmouth, NH: Heinemann.

Rhodes, M., B. Enz, & M. LaCount. 2006. "Leaps and Bounds: Preparing Parents for Kindergarten." *Young Children* 61 (1): 50–51.

Rigby, K. 2004. "Bullying in Childhood." Chap. 28 in *Blackwell Handbook of Childhood Social Development*, eds. P.K. Smith & C.H. Hart, 549–69. Malden, MA: Blackwell.

Rimm-Kaufman, S.E., K.M. La Paro, J.T. Downer, & R.C. Pianta. 2005. "The Contribution of Classroom Setting and Quality of Instruction to Children's Behavior in Kindergarten Classrooms." *Elementary School Journal* 105 (4): 377–94.

Rimm-Kaufman, S.E., R.C. Pianta, & M. Cox. 2001. "Teachers' Judgments of Problems in the Transition to School." *Early Childhood Research Quarterly* 15: 147–66.

Roberton, M.A. 1984. "Changing Motor Patterns During Childhood." In *Motor Development During Childhood and Adolescence*, ed. J.R. Thomas, 48–90. Minneapolis, MN: Burgess.

Rogers, R. 2003. *A Critical Discourse Analysis of Family Literacy Practices: Power In and Out of Print*. Mahwah, NJ: Erlbaum.

Rogoff, B. 2003. *The Cultural Nature of Human Development*. Oxford: Oxford University Press.

Routman, R. 2005. *Writing Essentials: Raising Expectations and Results While Simplifying Teaching*. Portsmouth, NH: Heinemann

Rubin, K.H., K.B. Burgess, & P.D. Hastings. 2002. "Stability and Social-Behavioral Consequences of Toddlers' Inhibited Temperament and Parenting Behaviors." *Child Development* 73 (2): 483–95.

Ryan, R.M., & E.L. Deci. 2000. "Self-Determination Theory and the Facilitation of Intrinsic Motivation, Social Development, and Well-Being." *American Psychologist* 55: 68–78.

Sahni, U. 2001. "Children Appropriating Literacy: Empowerment Pedagogy From Young Children's Perspective." In *Negotiating Critical Literacies in Classrooms*, eds. B. Comber & A. Simpson, 19–36. Mahwah, NJ: Erlbaum.

Samarapungavan, A., P. Mantzicopoulos, & H. Patrick. 2011. "What Kindergarten Students Learn in Inquiry-Based Science Classrooms." *Cognition and Instruction* 29 (4): 416–70.

Sameroff, A., & S.C. McDonough. 1994. "Educational Implications of Developmental Transitions." *Phi Delta Kappan* 76 (3): 188–93.

Sanders, S.W. 2002. *Active for Life: Developmentally Appropriate Movement Programs for Young Children*. Washington, DC: NAEYC.

Sarama, J., & D.H. Clements. 2006. "Mathematics in Kindergarten." Chap. 8 in *K Today: Teaching and Learning in the Kindergarten Year*, ed. D.F. Gullo, 85–94. Washington, DC: NAEYC.

Sarama, J., A.A. Lange, D.H. Clements, & C.B. Wolfe. 2012. "The Impacts of an Early Mathematics Curriculum on Emerging Literacy and Language." *Early Childhood Research Quarterly* 27 (3): 489–502.

Schneider, W. 2002. "Memory Development in Childhood." Chap. 11 in *Blackwell Handbook of Childhood Cognitive Development*, ed. U. Goswami, 236–56. Malden, MA: Blackwell.

Schultz, D., C.E. Izard, B.P. Ackerman, & E. Youngstrom. 2001. "Emotion Knowledge in Economically Disadvantaged Children: Self-Regulatory Antecendents and Relations to Social Difficulties and Withdrawal." *Development and Psychopathology* 13: 53–67.

Schunk, D.H. 1994. "Self-Regulation of Self-Efficacy and Attributions in Academic Settings." In *Self-Regulation of Learning and Performance: Issues and Educational Implications*, eds. D.H. Schunk & B.J. Zimmerman, 75–100. Hillsdale, NJ: Erlbaum.

Seefeldt, C. 2005. *How to Work with Standards in Early Childhood Classrooms*. New York: Teachers College Press.

Shillady, A., ed. 2013. *Spotlight on Young Children: Exploring Science*. Washington, DC: NAEYC.

Shonkoff, J.P., & D.A. Phillips, eds. 2000. *From Neurons to Neighborhoods: The Science of Early Child Development*. A report of the National Research Council. Washington, DC: National Academies Press. www.nap.edu/catalog.php?record_id=9824.

Snow, C.E., M.S. Burns, & P. Griffin. 1998. *Preventing Reading Difficulties in Young Children*. Washington, DC: National Academies Press.

Souto-Manning, M. 2009. "Negotiating Culturally Responsive Pedagogy Through Multicultural Children's Literature: Towards Critical Democratic Literacy Practices in a First Grade Classroom." *Journal of Early Childhood Literacy* 9 (1): 50–74.

Souto-Manning, M. 2010. *Freire, Teaching, and Learning: Culture Circles Across Contexts*. New York: Peter Lang.

Souto-Manning, M., & K. Swick. 2006. "Teachers' Beliefs About Parent Involvement: Rethinking Our Family Involvement Paradigm." *Early Childhood Education Journal* 34 (2): 187–93.

Sroufe, L.A. 1995. *Emotional Development: The Organization of Emotional Life in the Early Years*. Cambridge: Cambridge University Press.

Sroufe, L.A., E. Carlson, & S. Shulman. 1993. "Individuals in Relationships: Development From Infancy Through Adolescence." In *Studying Lives Through Time: Personality and Development*, eds. D.C. Funder, R.D. Parke, C. Tomlinson-Keasey, & K. Widaman, 315–42. Washington, DC: American Psychological Association.

Sternberg, R.J. 2002. "Intelligence Is Not Just Inside the Head: The Theory of Successful Intelligence." Chap. 11 in *Improving Academic Achievement*, ed. J. Aronson, 227–44. San Diego: Academic Press.

Sternberg, R.J., & E.L. Grikorenko. 2004. "Why We Need to Explore Development in Its Cultural Context." *Merrill-Palmer Quarterly* 50: 369–86.

Stipek, D. 2011. "Classroom Practices and Children's Motivation to Learn." In *The Pre-K Debates: Current Controversies and Issues*, eds. E. Zigler, W.S. Gilliam, & W.S. Barnett, 98–103. Baltimore: Brookes.

Stoddart, T., A. Pinal, M. Latzke, & D. Canaday. 2002. "Integrating Inquiry Science and Language Development for English Language Learners." *Journal of Research in Science Teaching* 39 (8): 664–87.

Strayer, J., & W. Roberts. 2004. "Children's Anger, Emotional Expressiveness, and Parenting Practices." *Social Development* 13: 229–54.

Strickland, D.S. 2002. "Bridging the Gap for African American Children." In *Love to Read: Essays in Developing and Enhancing Early Literacy Skills of African American Children*, ed. B. Bowman, 63–71. Washington, DC: National Black Child Development Institute.

Strickland, D.S. 2006. "Language and Literacy in Kindergarten." Chap. 7 in *K Today: Teaching and Learning in the Kindergarten Year*, ed. D.F. Gullo, 73–84. Washington, DC: NAEYC.

Strickland, D.S., & J.A. Schickedanz. 2004. *Learning About Print in Preschool: Working With Letters, Words, and Beginning Links With Phonemic Awareness.* Newark, DE: International Reading Association.

Tager-Flusberg, H. 2005. "Putting Words Together: Morphology and Syntax in the Preschool Years." In *The Development of Language*, 5th ed., ed. J.B. Gleason, 148–90. Boston: Allyn & Bacon.

Taylor, J.B. 2008. *My Stroke of Insight: A Brain Scientist's Personal Journey.* New York: Viking-Penguin.

Templeton, S., & D. Bear. 1992. *Development of Orthographic Knowledge and the Foundations of Literacy.* Hillsdale, NJ: Erlbaum.

Thatcher, R.W., G.R. Lyon, J. Rumsey, & J. Krasnegor. 1996. *Developmental Neuroimaging.* San Diego: Academic Press.

Thelen, E., & L.B. Smith. 1998. "Dynamic Systems Theories." In *Handbook of Child Psychology, Vol. 1: Theoretical Models of Human Development*, 5th ed., ed. R.M. Lerner, 563–634. New York: Wiley.

Thomas, W., & V. Collier. 2002. *A National Study of School Effectiveness for Language Minority Students' Long-Term Academic Achievement.* Santa Cruz, CA: Center for Research on Education, Diversity & Excellence.

Thompson, J.E., & K.K. Twibell. 2009. "Teaching Hearts and Minds in Early Childhood Classrooms: Curriculum for Social and Emotional Development." In *Handbook of Child Development and Early Education: Research to Practice*, eds. O.A. Barbarin & B.H. Wasik, 199–222. New York: Guilford.

Tiger, J.H., G.P. Hanley, & E. Hernandez. 2006. "An Evaluation of the Value of Choice With Preschool Children." *Journal of Applied Behavior Analysis* 39: 1–16.

Tomlinson, C.A., & J. McTighe. 2006. *Integrating Differentiated Instruction and Understanding by Design: Connecting Content and Kids.* Alexandria, VA: Association for Supervision and Curriculum Development.

Tomlinson, H.B. 2009. "Developmentally Appropriate Practice in the Kindergarten Year—Ages 5-6: An Overview." Chap. 6 in C. Copple & S. Bredekamp, 187–216. Washington, DC: NAEYC.

Tremblay, R.E. 2000. "The Development of Aggressive Behaviour During Childhood: What Have We Learned in the Past Century?" *International Journal of Behavioural Development* 24: 129–41.

US Census Bureau. 2013. *Language Use in the United States: 2011* (American Community Survey Reports). By C. Ryan. www.census.gov/prod/2013pubs/acs-22.pdf.

USDHHS (Department of Health and Human Services). 2008. *Child Development Services During Home Visits and Socializations in the Early Head Start Home-Based Programs Option.* http://eclkc.ohs.acf.hhs.gov/hslc/tta-system/operations/mgmt-admin/planning/planning/resour_ime_00521a1_021306.html.

USDHHS (Department of Health and Human Services) & USDA (US Dept. of Agriculture). 2005. *The Dietary Guidelines for Americans, 2005.* 6th ed. Washington, DC: USDHHS & USDA.

Vasquez, V.M. 2001. "Constructing a Critical Curriculum With Young Children." Chap. 4 in B. Comber & A. Simpson, 55–68.

Vasquez, V.M. 2004. *Negotiating Critical Literacies With Young Children.* Language, Culture, and Teaching series. Mahwah, NJ: Erlbaum.

Vasquez, V.M. 2005. "Creating Opportunities for Critical Literacy With Young Children: Using Everyday Issues and Everyday Texts." In *Literacy Moves On: Popular Culture, New Technologies, and Critical Literacy in the Elementary Classroom*, ed. J. Evans, 83–105. Portsmouth, NH: Heinemann.

Vaughn, B.E., T.N. Colvin, M.R. Azria, L. Caya, & L. Krzysik. 2001. "Dyadic Analyses of Friendship in a Sample of Preschool-Age Children Attending Head Start: Correspondence Between Measures and Implications for Social Competence." *Child Development* 72 (3): 862–78.

Vieillevoye, S., & N. Nader-Grosbois. 2008. "Self-Regulation During Pretend Play in Children with Intellectual Disability and in Normally Developing Children." *Research in Developmental Disabilities* 29 (3): 256–72.

Volk, D. 2004. "Mediating Networks for Literacy Learning: The Role of Puerto Rican Siblings." In E. Gregory, S. Long, & D. Volk, 25–39.

Vygotsky, L. 1978. *Mind in Society: The Development of Higher Psychological Processes*. Cambridge, MA: Harvard University Press.

Wellman, H.M., D. Cross, & J. Watson. 2001. "Meta-Analysis of Theory-Of-Mind Development: The Truth About False Belief." *Child Development* 72 (3): 655–84.

White, S.H. 1965. "Evidence for a Hierarchical Arrangement of Learning Processes." In *Advances in Child Development and Behavior*, eds. L.P. Lipsitt & C.C. Spiker, 187–220. New York: Academic Press.

White, S.H. 1970. "Some General Outlines of the Matrix of Developmental Changes Between Five and Seven Years." *Bulletin of the Orton Society* 20: 41–57.

Whitehurst, G.J. 1999. "The Role of Inside-Out Skills in Reading Readiness of Children From Low-Income Families." Symposium presentation at the Biennial Meeting of the Society for Research in Child Development, April 15–18, Albuquerque, NM.

Whiting, B.B., & C.P. Edwards. 1988. *Children of Different Worlds: The Formation of Social Behavior*. Cambridge, MA: Harvard University Press.

Wien, C.A., ed. 2008. *Emergent Curriculum in the Primary Classroom: Interpreting the Reggio Emilia Approach in Schools*. New York: Teachers College Press.

Wilson, H.K., R.C. Pianta, & M.W. Stuhlman. 2007. "Typical Classroom Experiences in First Grade: The Role of Classroom Climate and Functional Risk in the Development of Social Competencies." *Elementary School Journal* 108 (2): 81–96.

Wood, C. 2007. *Yardsticks: Children in the Classroom, Ages 4–14*. 3d ed. Turner Falls, MA: Northeast Foundation for Children.

Worth, K., & S. Grollman. 2003. *Worms, Shadows and Whirlpools: Science in the Early Childhood Classroom*. Portsmouth, NH: Heinemann.

Yang, O.S. 2000. "Guiding Children's Verbal Plan and Evaluation During Free Play: An Application of Vygotsky's Genetic Epistemology to the Early Childhood Classroom." *Early Childhood Education Journal* 28 (1): 3–10.

Yopp, R.H., & J.H. Yopp. 2012. "Young Children's Limited and Narrow Exposure to Informational Text." *The Reading Teacher* 65 (7): 480–90.

Zill, N., & J. West. 2001. *Entering Kindergarten: Findings from the Condition of Education, 2000*. Washington, DC: US Dept. of Education, National Center for Education Statistics.